CONFESSIONS OF A
HORNET
PILOT

CONFESSIONS OF A HORNET PILOT

FLYING THE F-18 ON EXCHANGE WITH THE US MARINE CORPS

TUG WILSON

FONTHILL

First published in Great Britain in 2025 by
Fonthill
An imprint of
Pen & Sword Books Ltd
Yorkshire – Philadelphia
www.fonthill.media

Copyright © Tug Wilson 2025

ISBN 978-1-78155-954-3

The right of Tug Wilson to be identified as
Author of this work has been asserted by him in accordance
with the Copyright, Designs and Patents Act 1988.

A CIP catalogue record for this book
is available from the British Library.

All rights reserved. No part of this book may be reproduced or
transmitted in any form or by any means, electronic or mechanical
including photocopying, recording or by any information storage and
retrieval system, without permission from the Publisher in writing.
NO AI TRAINING: Without in any way limiting the Author's and
Publisher's exclusive rights under copyright, any use of this publication
to "train" generative artificial intelligence (AI) technologies to generate
text is expressly prohibited. The Author and Publisher reserve all rights
to license uses of this work for generative AI training and development
of machine learning language models.

Printed and bound in the UK by CPI Group (UK) Ltd, Croydon, CR0 4YY

The Publisher's authorised representative in the EU for product
safety is Authorised Rep Compliance Ltd., Ground Floor,
71 Lower Baggot Street, Dublin D02 P593, Ireland.
www.arccompliance.com

For a complete list of Pen & Sword titles please contact
PEN & SWORD BOOKS LIMITED
47 Church Street, Barnsley, South Yorkshire, S70 2AS, England
E-mail: enquiries@pen-and-sword.co.uk
Website: www.pen-and-sword.co.uk

Or
PEN AND SWORD BOOKS
1950 Lawrence Rd, Havertown, PA 19083, USA
E-mail: Uspen-and-sword@casematepublishers.com

Contents

1 Somewhere Over the Pacific   7

2 California Baby!   12

3 VMFAT-101 Squadron: The Sharpshooters   25

4 VMFA (AW)-121 Squadron: The Green Knights   84

5 VMFA-134 Squadron: The Smokes   160

1
Somewhere Over the Pacific

Almost a diplomatic incident

Just as I saw the nose of the F-18 in my four o'clock come onto me, I heaved back on the stick to pull a 7.5G right-hand turn into him. His nose stayed on me, and I slammed the throttles into full burner and hauled hard back and left on the stick, this time with a boot full of left rudder for good measure. 'Let's see how he handles this,' I thought. And then my bloody left-hand engine surged with a big bang and a flame shooting out of the intake underneath my belly.

My own F-18 yawed left violently and then departed from controlled flight in a spectacular fashion, with all sorts of beeps and warnings and flashing lights going off in the cockpit. Insert any expletive you have ever heard here, because I shouted every last one of them as the jet tumbled and swayed around like a drunk dad at his daughter's wedding.

Blissfully aware of my own shortcomings as a pilot at this point, I did the only thing I could think of doing, and just let go of the stick while easing the throttles back out of burner, all the way down to flight idle. Realising that the chimp-fingered baboon in the front seat had relinquished control, the jet then righted itself all of its own accord, in time for me to watch my opponent flush out in front of me. I quickly selected my Sidewinder missile, got a good tone, and pulled the trigger, calling 'Combat 21, Fox 2. Kill. Terminate', while nursing the engines back up into the mid-power range, making sure the left-hand donk was behaving itself. It was, but I told my number 2 and his WSO (weapons system operator) that we were done for the day and were heading back to base. Bluto, my own WSO, was more than happy with that call, I can tell you.

Fizz, the number 2 pilot, sounded shocked on the radio as he acknowledged my call. He had just seen the best part of 15 tons of metal scythe through the air in front of his face with fire coming out of the wrong end, so we can cut him some slack, I reckon. Oh, and if it sounds like I seemed ultra-cool at that point, believe me, I wasn't. I was absolutely shitting myself. All the way back to Miramar, Bluto and I chatted about how lucky we had been as I reassessed my view of my 'carefree handling of engine and airframe' F-18 Hornet.

I was absolutely in love and lust with my exotic beauty, but I had obviously pissed her off somehow and she had firmly slapped me in the chops. I deserved it, though. I had been way too rough and taken her for granted. Luckily, she forgot all about it straight away, and I was as gentle as you like with her as I led my pair of fantasy rocket ships safely back onto the ground at Miramar. As we shut down on the chocks right outside the TOPGUN hangar (yes—really!), I apologised to Bluto for brutalising the trip and promised to buy him a new pair of undershorts. He was exceptionally cool about it. Bluto had previously been a FAC(A) (forward air controller airborne) in the OV-10 Bronco, calling aircraft onto ground targets during the First Gulf War over the bad lands, so he had seen worse, I guess? Not so sure he would have been as cool had we had to eject and become a very real part of a diplomatic incident.

The dark air combat cheating bastard laboratory

I wouldn't have been the first RAF exchange officer to have ejected from an aeroplane, mind you. I wouldn't even have been the first to eject from a Hornet. My predecessor's predecessor's predecessor on this particular exchange post had probably been the first F-18 Marine Corps exchange from the RAF. He had flown out of Kaneohe Bay in Hawaii—tough duty, huh? He had also departed the jet, but being much more capable than I, he had tried to recover it himself using every spin recovery action he had ever been taught on every aircraft he had ever flown. The jet hadn't responded and he had left via the ejection seat. There is something to be said for being a bit shit at what you do, I guess? Whereas he had tried using his immense handling skill (he was well known as a great pilot and an all-round great guy too) and ended up ejecting, I had just let go and got away with it. Aviation is like that sometimes.

Anyway, the debrief was interesting. The trip was supposed to be a standard sort of thing with me leading two F-18D Hornets out of Miramar, into one of the usual training areas just off the coast. We would do the trip, then land and refuel through the 'hot pits' before going off and doing it all again without getting out of the jets. At this point, I was serving on VMFA (AW)-121 Squadron which was a twin-seat F-18D front line unit. My wingman pilot, Fizz, had been on the squadron about a year before I joined, but my previous experience on the Phantom and then as a tactics and flying instructor on the Hawk at RAF Valley had catapulted me into a semi-training role on VMFA (AW)-121 (I will explain all the letters and numbers later). Fizz had been fresh out of the Navy and Marine Corps flying training system and was a slightly less than solid performer. He tended to struggle a bit when things didn't go exactly to plan—maybe a bit like me when I first started flying. The plan was to do a bit of 'canned' air combat manoeuvring (ACM), but I thought I would chuck in some unusual dynamic unbriefed stuff to see how he coped.

The first trip was a basic 1 vs 1 intercept sortie with the WSOs running the radar and talking the pilots into a bit of a visual fight. A fair few pilots on the F-18 wanted to run the radar intercept themselves as you could do everything from the front seat F-18D as if it were a single-seat A or C model. This meant that sometimes the WSOs in the back felt a little redundant. I remember some WSO students on the F-18 Replacement Air Group (RAG—our equivalent of the OCU) being told to 'sit in the back and shut up!' when flying with some of the macho alpha male bullshit pilots out there that were supposed to be instructors. Having flown the Phantom on my first tour, I was a big advocate of navigators/WSOs and figured that if I flew with a weak WSO and did it all myself, there was no way he would get any better—certainly not by just watching me guffing around the sky anyway. Bluto was one such WSO. Flying around in an OV-10 had given him a 300-knot brain, but he was now in a 700-knot aeroplane so had issues with thinking ahead while doing intercepts. These trips were as much of a work-up for him as for Fizz.

Trip one ran on rails with some good intercepts and Bluto talking my eyes onto the other jet, and we landed back at Miramar with both Bluto and Fizz's confidence nicely bolstered. On the way to the hot pits, I shut down the left-hand engine and waited for a slot to open—a bit like waiting for a pump at the petrol station. Once we were in the pits, the maintenance crew hooked us up to the pipes and we took on full tanks of gas while the right-hand engine burbled away happily at idle. It took about 20 minutes to refuel so I had a chance to do a hot debrief over the back radio frequency that Fizz and I shared. I praised him for the first trip; reminded him of the profile for the next trip; then gave him a bit of fighter pilot hype before we engaged in some dynamic visual combat.

Once we were gassed up, I started the left-hand engine and Fizz followed me out to the runway for a formation take-off and transit out over the dark blue Pacific Ocean, in a beautiful battle pair of F-18D Hornets (line abreast by about 2–3 miles). I called the base height, or simulated ground level, at 5,000 feet and kicked it all off. 'Outwards turn go!' I called and we turned away from each other by about 30 degrees. Just as we were losing sight, I called 'Inwards turn for combat, go!' and we turned in and blasted towards each other, passing left wing to left wing with about 800 knots of closing speed.

Ordinarily, I would have turned hard across his tail or pulled up into the vertical enacting some cunning and innovative gameplan I had dreamed up in the dark air combat cheating bastard laboratory in my mind, but the idea was to present Fizz with canned scenarios that he could take advantage of, to try and build his confidence. That grated the living shit out of me I can tell you, but this was about him and not me. All the time I was 'fighting', I was trying to teach Bluto what sort of service I needed from a WSO in a visual fight. He was all over it which was great to see. Fizz chose the correct moves at roughly the right times, and eventually got a kill. Job done there then. I set us up for another one, but this time, I played hard to see what he was like on the defensive. He fought hard against me, which I liked (I hated pilots who just gave up when they were seriously defensive). I then engineered a really poor mistake which he capitalised on and got us back to neutral. All good so far. That just left a guns defence exercise, and then we could finish with a full up 1 vs 1 combat split where I could fly as hard as I could and try to gun him. He would have had almost two full trips of training for his benefit by then, so it would be time to be a real fighter pilot at the end.

The guns defence or 'Guns-D' manoeuvre was a canned, fly by the numbers exercise. I would be the defender with Fizz swept back off my right wing by about a mile. On my command, he would go full burner as I broke right into him, and he would close me down into guns range. Just as he put the gunsight on me, he would call 'commence' and I would break hard into him. One of two things would happen now. If he could hack the corner, he would keep the sight on me, and I would have to overbank to 135 degrees and haul to 7.5G in full burner. He would probably have to go nose off from there and I would have successfully defeated the guns shot. That was generally how a Guns-D went. If he couldn't hack the corner in the first instance, he would need to go nose off me, level his wings and pull up into a Hi Yo-Yo move. I would then either extend away from him, or pull up to counter his yo-yo. This would probably force us into a classic rolling scissors manoeuvre. Well, it would in any other aeroplane. I'll tell you later what the batshit crazy Hornet rolling scissors looked like. I would tell you now, but this first bit is just the hook to get you to buy the book, isn't it? I need to move on and keep this fast-paced.

Ok, so now you know what a Guns-D is supposed to look like, and so did Fizz. However, I was not going to give him the standard Guns-D. I was going to mix it up and see what he did. I briefed up Bluto on what my plan was and he just said, 'OK, Tug.' He was probably just gobsmacked that his pilot was involving him in the first place. My clever plan involved a bit of deception from the outset. As Fizz closed in, I faked a hard turn back into him, but then unloaded on the stick to gain speed. He wouldn't be closing as fast as usual and I figured he would point ahead of me a lot more, taking a bigger bite of the cherry. This would increase his overtake and angle off, meaning there should be no way he could hack the turn on the 'commence' call. However, on 'commence' I would only break into him at about 4G initially, giving him the impression he could make the shot. At that point, I would hard reverse left and pull up using all the extra speed I had, and flush him outside of the turn into what was called a 'fly through', and then probably gun him. Remember that he would be expecting me to overbank and dive down to the right to defeat his shot.

Well, that all worked swimmingly to begin with. Fizz fell for the deception and took a huge bite. No way he was going to make the corner after that, but to make the whole thing work, he would need to fall for the next bit as well. He did. He kept the gunsight on, expecting me to overbank and then got the shock of his life as his supposed prey, flat-plated up and left in front of his face, breathing fire, and then slicing and cartwheeling through the ether, totally out of control.

A few seconds later, once my jet had had a word with itself, I took control again to see Fizz in front of me. As I said, I shot him with a Sidewinder—well a kill is a kill after all. They do say in times of serious peril, your life flashes before your eyes. It's a bit bloody late by then. If only F-18 ground school had flashed before my eyes prior to carrying out 'Plan Stupid' as I now looked upon it, maybe I wouldn't have tried it, and Bluto's undershorts would have been spared the washing machine, at least for another day. One thing is for sure—Mr Tug's Holy Shit Last Ditch Memorial Guns Jink manoeuvre was not adopted into the US Marine Corps F-18 tactics manual. It might have worked, but it was a bit of a one-off.

2
California Baby!

Great start to your exchange tour, Tug!

Miramar. The Pacific Ocean. TOPGUN. The F-18 Hornet. It all sounds very exotic, doesn't it? Fighter pilot heaven even? Of course, my American adventure began in true ordinary military style with a night at the Gateway Hotel at RAF Brize Norton with my wife and one-year-old daughter. Generations of RAF personnel had 'enjoyed' a night at the Gateway prior to going on deployment or overseas exercises. 'Hotel' is a loose term for the standard shitty plain accommodation in the Gateway. The RAF pretty much insisted on personnel staying there the night before flying out to wherever. I am sure in the case of people going to the Falkland Islands for six months, it was to stop them from running away beforehand.

Anyway, I soon discovered there were a couple of perks flying RAF Airways as a family, when compared to flying out on deployment as just another uniform. Firstly, we were spared the usual drama of going through security in strict alphabetical order, and again into the final departure lounge. Travelling with a one-year-old got us some semi-celebrity status, and we were allowed to board the VC-10 first and sort out the ton of baggage that comes with having a baby in tow. Front row seats, so we could have a sky cot, gave us extra legroom, and the RAF stewards and stewardesses could not have been more attentive. We were on the weekly trooper flight to Washington Dulles airport and the flight was a dream. The VC-10 cruised at 0.95 Mach so the trip went in a flash. It also helped that Holly continued her starring role of perfect child by sleeping through all of it, as soon as her head hit the cot. Holly had been born at Valley during my tour as an instructor; had slept through the night from four weeks old; and given us no trouble at all in her first year. We really should think about having another one of these sometime (careful what you wish for Tug).

Despite an easy flight, we all arrived a bit bleary-eyed and disorientated at Dulles to be met by the wing commander who was assistant air attaché at the British embassy in DC. He was a kindly (if a bit posh) grey-haired and moustachioed ex-Harrier pilot, who looked a little stunned as the Wilsons exploded into the arrivals lounge with almost a hundred bags and cases, and a whole range of baby paraphernalia. Fortunately, he had driven there in the largest estate car I had ever seen. I should say station wagon given this is a book about the States. I think it was a Cadillac and it was clad in brown wood panels. Hell's bells, it looked like he was picking us up in a wardrobe (sorry—closet!). I got Holly and my wife secured in the west wing of his car, then hopped up front to ride shotgun into town. On the way, he told us that we had arrived on the Friday before Presidents' Day (third Monday in February) so we would have an extra-long weekend in DC to see the sights. This tour was already the best deal in the RAF, and it just got better with a free mini-break in the city.

DC is a beautiful city, if you are on the right side of the tracks, and the USA's murder capital if you aren't. For a history nerd like me, it is heaven. We packed in the sights. Arlington Cemetery with JFK's grave; the White House; the spectacular Lincoln Memorial; and the heart-breaking Vietnam Memorial to name but a few. We also took in the Apollo XI command module at the Smithsonian, and then I relented on the culture and took Holly to the zoo. Each night, we retired to the Embassy Suites Hotel and still couldn't believe our luck. Surely, it was all going to come crashing down as an elaborate spoof, and I would be posted back to the living hell that was the Tornado F3?

Tuesday saw us bundling Holly's car seat into a taxi laid on by the embassy so we could go and get our induction briefs, and seemingly pick up a shed load of cash. The embassy staff were fantastic, but we were getting a bit overwhelmed by the various rules and bits of advice being thrown at us (still a bit jet-lagged as well). Fortunately, the admin personnel Sergeant noticed this—he had seen it all before I guess—and made sure we were switched on to the really important bits such as housing and furniture allowance.

On arrival in California, we would need to find a house to rent and had an allowance of $1,300 per month to do that. We would also need to furnish it, so he handed me a cheque for $32,000 and $1,000 in cash as sort of 'flash money!' I put all the paperwork and cash into a soft briefcase and then was called through to see the air attaché. This was the only briefing I had to attend alone. I figured this was going to be the under the table chat about observing the Marines and their tactics and weapons—sort of semi-spy stuff. The air attaché was a very nice chap and did none of that. In fact, over a cup of tea, all he told me was to make sure we enjoyed ourselves, and to buy a car that had at least a 3-litre engine as it would need the power to run the air conditioning while driving uphill on hot days in California. So, as no James Bond style gadgets were forthcoming, I took my leave and we headed back to the hotel by cab.

My head was spinning with all the info and the task ahead of us, and I had the usual faff of getting Holly's car seat out of the back of the taxi. We got into the lift and ascended to our floor. It was at this point, I looked at my wife and said, 'where's the briefcase?' Oh shit! We had car seat, stroller, changing bag, daughter (thanks goodness), but no briefcase. So, no paperwork, $32,000 cheque, or $1,000 cash. My face went white and I couldn't will the lift up and then down again fast enough before pleading with the hotel concierge for help. About 10 minutes later, the cab driver returned with my briefcase and I tipped him $20 before slumping down in the lift back up to our room. Great start to your exchange tour, Tug!

The following day saw us flying out of Dulles to Los Angeles, and then taking a 15-minute hop on Waldo Pepper's Flying Circus to finally land at John Wayne Airport in Orange County, and begin our new life in California baby! Once again, we exploded into the arrivals lounge with the tiny aeroplane groaning under the weight of our baggage, to be met by a smiling Alf, the guy I was replacing.

I didn't know Alf particularly well, but I knew his reputation. He was about three years ahead of me in the RAF and my career had almost mirrored his. First tour Phantom (although he had been UK whereas I had gone to Germany); tactics instructor on the Hawk (he had specialised QWI—bastard—and I had picked up a qualified flying instructor tick instead); and now F-18 exchange with the Marines. Alf was larger than life and a great guy. He was very cool and confident and had already given us a load of help prior to arriving, to try and prep us as much as possible. He had also arranged for us to go out there six months before he left so we could do a proper handover.

After hellos, shaking hands, and pats on the back, he took us to the car hire centre and we picked up a bog-standard boring-looking car that would be ours for the next two weeks. 'I'll go get my car, Tug, and I'll meet you out the front of the terminal,' he said. 'Just follow me to the hotel.' We waited outside the terminal for a couple of minutes and an old black classic Porsche 911 flashed past with Alf waving out of the window. He looked even cooler than usual. It was about a 20-minute drive to the hotel, but half way there, I saw Alf put his hazard lights on and pull over to the hard shoulder on the freeway. 'So much for the classic car,' I thought. I could see him pointing out of the window and looked up to see two F-18s roar over our heads in close formation, completing a pairs landing at El Toro, just on the other side of the road. Holy shit, they looked other-worldly.

They looked like they were from some sort of far-flung future. They looked bloody awesome is what they looked!

I had tons to do before even touching an F-18, let alone flying one. I was due to start my conversion ground school in two weeks. In that time, we would need to find a house, two cars and insure them, buy or rent a houseful of furniture, get Californian driving licences, a bank account, military ID, get flying kit sorted, sort all the utilities and phone provider, and just generally get our lives squared away before I could apply myself fully to the course.

Set the gun to rock 'n' roll!

OK, aware that this is a flying book and there hasn't been much flying so far, I wanted to whet your appetite for what is coming up with this amazing aeroplane. Bear in mind, we arrived in California on 21 February 1995, and I didn't fly in a Hornet until the 12th of June! That four-month period had a lot crammed into it, which I will tell you about later, but for now, let me tell you this little story.

I was about half way through my flying on the RAG, and my course was programmed to do Strike mission 186 (STK-186) which was low-angle strafe, so air-to-ground gunnery. I had done strafe before in the Hawk down at Pembrey Range in south Wales. The RAF had a knack of sucking the joy out of mind-blowingly exciting stuff like strafing, by making us do an academic pattern at the range requiring lots of accuracy (that's me screwed then). You fire at a large bedsheet type target that has an acoustic scorer behind it and then you get your score from the range safety officer (RSO)— usually close to zero on each pass. The Americans do things differently, thank God. We would fly out from El Toro to the R-2507 Chocolate Mountains Impact Area to do our strafing and to drop full size bombs. R-2507 is about an eighth of the size of Wales and just a big heap of desert and rocks in Southern California, near the border with Arizona. The military had dumped a load of old tanks and vehicles, aeroplanes, and SAM radar kit at various spots in the range. They had even carved out a couple of full-sized airfields, and put old jets on the runways.

You just chose what you wanted to hit, briefed up the coordinates, set up a racetrack around the target, and then just dived down onto it and blat away to your heart's content. No RSO. No score. No drama. Perfect. The Marines would also deploy FAC trainees out there to call bombs onto targets for close air support (CAS) training. Of course, there was some safety applied to this stuff. It wasn't quite the Wild West. STK-186 is supposed to be a dual check with an instructor. It is the first time firing the gun live in the jet, so it is quite an event. That day on VMFAT-101, that is Marine Fighter Attack Training Squadron 101, there weren't enough twin-stick B or D Model Hornets for all of us, so there was a bit of a conflab in ops, and I was called through for a chat.

'Hey, Tug. You've fired a gun in a jet before, haven't you?'

'Yeah.' Some mumbling.

'You've done strafe before?'

'Yeah.' More mumbling.

'Ok. You can go and do it solo then.'

'Really?'

'Er, yeah.'

I was simultaneously pleased that I wasn't going to have to do another check ride, and also shitting myself that I was going to shoot the gun for the first time whilst hurtling towards the ground at 450 knots—solo!

I had never listened to a brief more carefully, other than the night solo bombing which I had done a week before (now that is a story in itself, and coming up later—utter madness!). We walked for the jets as a formation of four with me as tail-end Charlie. As I signed for my jet, I noticed that the rounds in the gun—all 578 of them—were high-explosive! Hi-ex rounds had their own little bomb in the nose cone and would look spectacular when they hit the target. If I could hit the target of course. No guarantees there. Dear God, I was meticulous with my safety and weapons checks and having done them about fifteen times to make sure, we started up and lined up as two pairs on El Toro's twin runways. One and three were on the left runway and I lined up next to number two on the right runway. The leader called us to power up, and once the engines were stabilised, he called that he was rolling, and number two let off his brakes to roll at the same time from our runway. Five seconds later, I rolled at the same time as number three, and four sleek grey killer sharks blasted into the hazy sun-drenched sky of Southern California with the best part of two-and-a-half thousand shouty bullets between them.

Our target was a line of rusting tanks, and the leader called us into echelon and broke left over them to set up the 15-degree dive pattern in the sky. We broke at intervals, spacing out after him, and it was game on. Fly around the pattern maintaining separation on the one ahead, then dive down when it was your turn to put the pipper (aiming dot on the gunsight) onto the target and watch the clock unwind around the outside of the sight to tell you the range. When it gets to the right range, pull the trigger for less than a second, and then pull 4G to recover from the dive and climb back up into the pattern to do it all again. It actually sounds a bit matter of fact, doesn't it? Let me spice it up for you.

The Hornet's gun was the Mk-61A Vulcan 6-barrel rotary cannon—a bit like a Gatling gun. It shot 20mm shells and could carry 578 of them at a time. The gun was electrically spun up with a low rate of fire at 4,000 rounds per minute and high rate of fire at 6,000. SIX THOUSAND ROUNDS PER MINUTE!!! That's 100 every second! Come on! That is incredible. Spicy enough for you? I have to say that during my whole tour on the Hornet, I didn't meet one guy who selected low rate of fire. Oh, and they didn't call it high rate of fire. They called it 'rock 'n' roll'.

On the way to the target, I selected air-to-ground mode on the button just above the master arm switch on the left-hand side of the instrument panel, and the gun on the weapons/stores page on the left-hand DDI (digital display indicator), making sure it was set to rock 'n' roll. This brought up my pipper and the clock face in the head up display (HUD). I was in CCIP mode, so constantly computed impact point (sorry for all the stinking acronyms! If you think it's hard to follow for you, try flying the bloody jet while trying to remember what they all meant). CCIP was kind of death dot territory as the rounds would go wherever I put the pipper. There was a manual mode I seem to recall, but why the hell would you make it harder for yourself?

I rolled in and put the pipper on the tanks while making the Master Arm switch live. The clock started unwinding very quickly indeed as I dived towards the target like a vengeful lemming. I saw the IN RNG cue light up telling me I was in range, so I pulled the trigger and heard the most joyful sound as the cannon wound itself up into a frenzy with a robotic sounding VVVZZZZZZ, and it spewed about 80 explosive little bastards down range. It's always a good idea not to follow your bullets into the target, so I hauled myself up into the climb at 4G, and made the Master Arm safe. Now, the weapons instructors will always tell you not to drop a wing so you can see your own fall of shot. That is bullshit! I dropped my right wing and saw a glittery violent tap dance, as my Hi-ex rounds pummelled what was left of the tanks. Dear God, I thought I had died and gone to fighter pilot heaven. Proper strafe, that. Not for the first time with this jet, I was absolutely whooping in the cockpit. I was so in love with this aeroplane. It just kept showing me something new almost every time I flew it. I knew I was punching above my weight with her, but I hoped that once I got to the front line, she would see I was worthy of her adoration too. The next day, I got to drop proper big 1,000-pound bombs, but I will tell you about that later. I've got a bloody house to find first.

The shock of capture

Alf got us settled into the hotel and we were given a two-bedroomed suite—no regular rooms for the Wilsons these days! He dropped off a load of paperwork that we would need to fill in for our various admin stuff, such as my military ID and our driving licences etc. He said he would leave us to settle in and then swing by later to pick us up for dinner. I think that was when the realisation hit us of what lay ahead.

The weather was beautiful, even towards the end of February, so we got in our cossies and took our first dip in a California pool. We were the only ones in the pool of course. It was February, so it wasn't actually that warm for the locals, so the fact that we were swimming in the first place and our pasty white complexions had us pegged as Brits immediately. Alf lived over in Laguna Hills with his wife and three children. They were a lovely family and made us feel immediately welcome. Over a beer, Alf asked me how I felt about the exchange. I have always been completely honest, so I told him I was really excited, but also cacking myself about the ground attack side, and especially the intense close air support (CAS) that the Marine Corps was famous for. 'It's easier than doing ground attack in the Hawk, Tug,' he said, 'and you are going to love it in air combat. The radar is easy to use and interpret. Trust me, you will be fine.' It may sound odd that as a third tourist and an instructor to boot, that I needed that kind of reassurance. We all have our insecurities though, and it just made me feel better to hear Alf say that.

The next day, he picked me up and started the long and drawn out process of getting me access to El Toro and the USMC. Nobody had any paperwork, despite Alf pre-loading them, and after a few disappointed looks, he persuaded the guard house to issue a military ID card to the foreigner in the odd-looking flying suit. Next up, we went over to the ground school building at VMFAT-101, to get me registered to start a couple of weeks after. I need to explain a bit of terminology here. The 'V' meant that the squadron was a 'heavier than air' unit. That was from way back in 1920 when the US Navy also had lighter than air types (designated Z). The 'M' stood for Marines (obviously). 'FA' meant Fighter Attack, and the 'T' designated it as a training squadron. 101 were nicknamed the 'Sharpshooters' which was pretty cool, and the callsign for the squadron was 'Shooter'. Alf was serving on 314 which was the first ever Marine F-18 squadron, and they were known as the Black Knights which sounded even cooler.

Anyway, Alf got me checked in and registered for the start of ground school, but specifically asked if my security clearance had arrived so that I would have immediate access to all the secret stuff like radar and weapons. It was a civilian company that ran ground school, and the woman in charge, Tracey, assured us everything was in hand. Alf had gone through half of his ground school with no access to a lot of the material so wanted to make sure it was sorted for me. We were told it was. It wasn't, but hey—who knew? Tracey knew.

We wandered into the squadron and Alf introduced me around the bazaars. As I said, I was in a RAF flying suit and badged up with Phantoms so that was an instant connection with all the ex-Phantom drivers on the staff. If was apparent that everybody loved Alf, including the boss who was called Hammer. Alf had begun his tour as a RAG instructor on 101, but had managed to wheedle his way onto the front line, meaning that I knew from the start that I wouldn't be staying on 101 once I completed the course. Not for the first time did I think that Alf's boots were going to be hard to fill. The morning ended with a trip to 314 to meet the boss and a few of the guys. There was a chance that I would be a direct replacement for Alf on 314 so I thought it important to make a good first impression. Alf was a big and well-built guy, and so it seemed were all of the Black Knights. I was a bit of a tall slim streak of piss in those days so what the hell they thought of me I don't know.

We went straight from El Toro to the real estate agent that Alf knew and she printed off details of about twenty rental properties for us to go and check out. That would be tomorrow's job along with opening an American bank account. Another night of mellowing around the pool and we dropped into bed exhausted. We found the perfect home within a day or two and signed the contract for a move-in a week later. It was a three-bedroomed large single-storey house on a hilly street called Alarcon in the district of Mission Viejo. Big double garage; even bigger American fridge; and a beautiful outdoor area with a fire pit, that looked straight out to the mountains. The old couple who lived next door were best friends with the owners and were just lovely. They adored Holly and really looked out for us in those early days when we were still suffering from the 'shock of capture'. The best aspect of the house though? The owners had been there from the start and had secured membership access to the facilities at Lake Mission Viejo. This was a man-made lake and park area constructed during the various house builds, and was absolutely beautiful. You could hire party boats to cruise around or just swim in the warm waters of the lake, and host social events all for free. It was a godsend for my wife when I was away at work. She spent at least three days a week there with Holly.

Hi—I am Jeff

One or two major things done, so it was off to buy a car. It seemed that the Americans lumped things together, so all the car dealers were in a suburb just up from us in a place called Irvine. We were looking for a big station wagon with a 3-litre engine as our family car (see? I did listen to some of the briefings at the embassy) and found one at the first dealership for about $9,000 which was nicely inside our $10k budget. You never buy the first car you see, so we wandered around a few more car lots, being ambushed by the ultra-keen/aggressive sales guys. We were just about to head back to the very first dealer when I saw the exact same car, albeit a bit younger and in better shape. The salesman, 'Hi—I am Jeff' (it was written that way on his name tag), came over to give us chapter and verse on this amazing car of his. Having been through the spiel a few times that morning, I stopped him and just asked what the price was. He looked a little hurt that we weren't going to do the usual American sales flirting, but carried on regardless with his patter.

'Just tell me the price,' I said.

'Sure, sure. In this car, you and your wife and family could travel ...'

'Sorry. I just need the price.'

'Sure, the comfort levels are ...'

'OK stop! I need to buy a car right now. The only thing stopping me buying this one is I don't know the price. I have cash and I WANT TO BUY A CAR! How much is this one?'

'Er—$15,000.'

'Ah OK. Thanks, but it is out of my budget.'

'Well, how much do you have?'

'$10,000 only,' and we went to walk away.

'OK. OK. How about I say $13,000?'

'I only have 10.'

'Well, it looks like we are really close to a deal here. Let me say $12,500,' and he took hold of my arm. I had come across some odd folks in my life before, but this was getting like the haggling scene out of Monty Python's Life of Brian. I finally told him we were leaving to go and buy the other car when he finally blurted out, 'OK. $10,000 and it's yours!'

'Really?'

'I just need to clear it with my manager.'

We stood there a bit gobsmacked that we had just bought a car for two thirds of the asking price, when this man-mountain came out with our new best friend looking a bit sheepish behind him. Ah! The deal was off obviously.

'The car is 15, but you can have it for 12,' said the manager, 'and that's a great deal.'

'But we just shook hands on 10,' I said. There was a bit of a kerfuffle between the Hulk and 'Hi—I am Jeff' and the next thing was ...

'Ok, you can have it for 10, but you pay the licence fee.'

'How much is that?'

'$300.'

'OK. Deal,' and I shook his hand too. It wasn't worth haggling over $300 when I had just got $5,000 off the asking price. All in all, I patted myself on the back at getting one over the keen sales guys, and ticked off another major task. You know what? The car was probably only worth about $5,000 and no doubt they had a huge celebration at finally shifting it off the forecourt. Maybe 'Hi—I'm Jeff' got one over me instead?

We had contacted a furniture rental company, and they met us at the house to measure up and ask us what sort of stuff we were after. They were a husband-and-wife team who were definitely high on something when they arrived. It was an education watching them, as they raged around the house in their high octane, in your face, way. How they managed to make an accurate assessment, I don't know, but somehow, they came up with a figure of $700 per month for the whole of the three years. This would work out way cheaper for the embassy than me buying stuff with the $32,000 cheque they had given me (which I was not letting out of my sight). The $1,000 flash money went on small electricals for the house.

Genghis Khan's sister

I was feeling pretty pleased with myself that we were cracking through our tasks when it all came crashing down at the Department of Motor Vehicles. Everything you have ever heard or seen about the DMV on TV and films is wrong. It is much, much worse. We had to complete a written test on their version of the highway code before getting a driving test. That meant swotting up the night before, which I did (because I was a pilot), but my wife did not. Genghis Khan's sister was behind the counter at the DMV and was putting the fear of God into anyone who dared speak to her. We got our tests from her and went to the quiet area to fill them in as she watched over us from her machine gun nest in the guard tower. The test was multiple choice, and straight forward if you had read the rules beforehand. I finished mine and returned it to Godzilla who marked it up and, as I had passed, booked me in for a driving test the following week. My wife failed and got another test to do which she also failed. The rule was three attempts and then go back another day to try it all again. On her third try, she whispered to me to ask what one of the phrases meant, and the next thing we knew, her paper was snatched away by the clerk saying she had failed again because she was cheating. We drove back to the hotel in relative silence where my wife spent most of the night reading the California highway code before passing the test the next day.

Our driving tests were a joke. If you turned up with a pulse, you were pretty much going to pass, so it seemed like it was just a money-making exercise. The standard of driving in California was cartoon-like. However, we were then proud owners of California driving licences and those, coupled with our brand new social security numbers and military ID meant we were now on official records so could do a lot more.

As far as Muck was concerned, there was no wall

We moved into the house at the end of our first week in California, and remarkably, all of the furniture we had hired from the drug addicts turned up on the same day. It was going to take a while to settle in, so we immediately registered at the lake and started to enjoy the facilities there. We started to explore the local area, noting all the things you would normally need such as supermarkets, pharmacy, gas stations etc. If all this sounds a bit boring to you, please bear in mind we were starting everything from scratch and were still horribly jetlagged and a bit overwhelmed by the fact that we were now officially resident in California.

To get my eyes back on the prize after all this domestic stuff, Alf took me to happy hour at the El Toro officers' club (O-Club) on the Friday to show me off. This was where I met the two guys who would become my closest friends during my tour—Indy and Muck. Indy was an RAF Tornado GR1 navigator who was on exchange on a twin-seat F-18D squadron. He was by far and away the nicest guy I had ever met, and out of all the high-quality aircrew I had known in my time in the RAF, he was the very best of them. Dear God, he was wasted on the Tornado. Flying with him later down the line, his radar work and picture-building ability in the air would have rivalled any Phantom nav I had flown with. His banter was pretty good too—for a Tornado mate (I would work on that with him).

Muck was something else. He was Royal Australian Air Force and an experienced single-seat Hornet pilot. He was serving on the same F-18D squadron as Indy. It seemed that the plan was to try and keep all the exchanges on the same unit to make them easier to manage. Every eighteen months or so, each squadron would deploy to Iwakhuni in Japan for six months, or on a carrier somewhere. As exchange officers, we were not allowed to deploy at that time, so rather than manage us moving squadrons separately, they wanted to lump us all together. It seemed that once Alf left 314, I was to be sent to whatever F-18D squadron Indy and Muck were on. I had no problem flying with a WSO. I enjoyed flying solo, but when it came to fighting, it was so much better to have two people in the cockpit—mostly. I will tell you a tale or two where this wasn't the case later.

Back to Muck though. If I was being polite, I would describe him as 'down to earth'. He was also completely 'off the wall'. In fact, Muck couldn't even see the wall from where he was. As far as Muck was concerned—there was no wall. He was extremely professional around all aspects of flying and was an awesome pilot, but everywhere else he was a hand grenade, and I don't think the Marines knew what to make of him. He and Indy were serving on VMFA (AW)-242 Squadron, known as 'The Bats', and I want to share a story about them with you.

As far as I remember it, they were on their way back into El Toro with Indy doing all the radio communication. Apologies to the pair of them as the facts are a bit made up, but this was the basic sequence …

'SoCal Radar, this is Bat 31 with you flight level two zero zero.' Silence. This happened a fair bit when Air Traffic Control (ATC) heard our British accents.

'SoCal. Bat 31 level at two zero zero.'

'Bat 31, Say again' came the eventual reply from ATC.

'Yes SoCal. Bat 31 is checking in at two zero zero.' There then followed a long pause.

'Bat 31. Do you have anyone else in the aeroplane that can talk to us?' At this point, Muck came onto the airwaves in his broad Australian accent.

'G'Day mate. This is Bat 31 checking in at two hundred.' Long pause again.

'Er, Bat 31 this is SoCal. Could you put the first guy back on?'

Happy hour was banging, and you could barely move in the bar. It was full of Hornet aircrew and a lot of local girls, à la the film *An Officer and a Gentleman*. This turned out to be somewhat unusual though. Since 1991, US Navy and Marine O-Club bars were mostly deserted due to the Tailhook Scandal. The Tailhook Association was an annual gathering of naval and Marine aviators that began in 1956 in San Diego, but moved to Vegas in 1963. Over the years, the gatherings became more and more debauched, with Tailhook '91 ending up being investigated formally for all manner of sexual harassment and deviant behaviour. The inquiry went through the organisation like a dose of salts, and anyone who attended that year had their careers severely restricted. Some senior officers resigned or were encouraged to do something else outside of the military. I am not in a position to comment on the fairness or the legalities of the situation, as I was not there. All I saw was the results on the Marine Corps in terms of their bars, their banter and their sensitivity to anything that might cause offence.

At one end of the bar there was a sound system with a few flashing lights, and what appeared to be a load of drunk flying suits line dancing to a constant stream of country and western music. Alf introduced me to a load of people, all of whom I instantly forgot as I tanked up on watery American beer. He secured us a lift home at about 11pm by which time I was barely upright, but I got out of the car into a sheet of water as Southern California dumped one of its famous thunderstorms on me.

I said my goodnights and ran to the front door, where my key didn't work. I couldn't remember my address and as I had only just moved in and it was like a telephone number (something like 249645 Alarcon). I tried my key in two more doors before stumbling in to the right house absolutely soaked wet through. I had one more thing to do before ground school, and that was to buy myself a car.

I wanted a soft top and an American muscle car. It had to be a Mustang then. The classic '60s and '70s shapes were awesome, but too expensive and unreliable. There were tons of unloved '80s Mustangs around and I found one in the local automart magazine. It was white with a broad black stripe down the bonnet, a 5-litre V8 and it said 'Mustang' on the back. I went to see it and having fallen in love with it straight away, I bought it on the spot. It was a proper 4-seater so Holly's car seat fit snugly in the back and we were able to cruise around Southern California with the top down, just living the life. It was kind of cool that Indy had the exact same car, but in black. I was now ready to start ground school, but I had no idea how stinking long and tedious that was going to be.

3
VMFAT-101 Squadron: The Sharpshooters

Twelve weeks!!!

Ground school took place in a building close to the VMFAT-101 hangar and flight line. As I drove up on day one (top down in my Mustang of course!), I could see tons and tons of F-18s lined up ready for the off. I knew it would be a little while before I would fly one, but holy hell, they looked amazing! There was a mix of F-18B trainers, known as 'Tubs', and a load of single-seat A and C models known as 'Straights'. I didn't know it at the time, but there were some newer D models too. There were two big domed simulators that we would practice weapons events and intercepts in as well as an instrument trainer which had limited visuals, being set up in a night time scenario. At the lower end of the scale, there were a couple of cockpit trainers where you could practice everything from start up through to radar manipulation and basic intercepts. Even this stuff was really advanced from what I remembered of the Phantom ground school, so all looking good so far. Ah! Then we got to the meat of the academic stuff.

    I had been used to getting lectures from experts in the various systems and procedures that I would need to know to effectively operate the aircraft. Ground school at El Toro would see me sitting in a cubicle, staring at a computer screen, and clicking through slide after slide in every tech subject you could think of. Next to the computer screen was an old-style micro-fiche type of screen/box (if anyone remembers what that is?), that took a slide carousel on the top of it. You would fit the slide carousel and then insert the magnetic tape cassette and start the presentation. As each slide cycled onto the screen, a monotone voice on the headphones would rattle through a script to match the slide.

That was the idea anyway. Quite often, the slides would jam, but the voiceover would continue to run on ahead. Pausing to check what was on the picture would be fraught with the danger of jamming the whole bloody thing up. Oh, and the voice was so fast, it sounded like it was describing the terms and conditions at the end of a car commercial (25%APRsubjecttoavailabilitytermsandconditionsapplyetcetc!).

The learning was self-paced and we had twelve weeks to complete the course. Twelve weeks!!! There would be a whole host of cockpit trainers and simulators with the ground school instructors, but twelve weeks??? Come on! Day one began with formally meeting my course mates before the arrival briefings. They were all ab-initio and had graduated flying training together. Four Marines, one navy and me. They seemed a nice bunch and there was a definite mix of confident ones and under-confident guys as well. I introduced myself to all of them and they were friendly enough. I had had retreads on my Phantom OCU and had leant on them for help when I could. I was now that father figure on the course (at twenty-nine years old mind you!), but of course, I didn't know my arse from my elbow when it came to flying in the States so I would probably be leaning on them in the first instance. We had the usual hellos from the boss, who was a living legend in Marine Corps aviation, and the XO, who was US Navy and pretty arrogant from what I could tell. He had short man syndrome and an even shorter temper. Finally, we met our course commander. This was the instructor who was supposed to look after us for our duration on 101. Nice guy at first glance, but proved to be ineffectual and almost invisible throughout.

Once all that was done, we met the simulator instructors and they showed us the cockpit trainers and the sims. The domes and the instrument sim were available 24/7, so as a student you could sign one out anytime to practice your stuff. I had a couple of extras to do over and above my ab-initio course mates at this time—kit fit and swim qual. Kit fit got me sorted with American flying suits which were very cool—certainly a lot cooler than the RAF's anyway. I also picked up a set of g-pants, life preserver, and torso harness. The fittings on the ejection seat were a lot less complicated than the ones I had sat on before in the RAF. In essence, I wore the parachute harness myself rather than it being incorporated into the seat itself. There were two Koch fittings (push in buckles) for the shoulder straps, and two for the lap straps. The torso harness I wore clipped into those fittings which made strapping into the jet really easy. Obviously, just getting into the torso harness was going to be a nightmare of straps and buckles so I made sure I practiced that regularly over the twelve weeks (twelve weeks!!!). I had seen students on the Hawk max themselves out before a trip had even started by not being completely comfortable with how to put on an immersion suit and g-pants.

Once I got my US flying suits, I had name badges made up and velcroed to my chest. US name badges were different to the RAF's. They were a small rectangle of black leather with the wings embossed on them along with name, rank and callsign. I had a set of these, but mine also had Royal Air Force on them along with my nickname of MR TUG! I also wore a pair of RAF wings above my name badge. I was very proud of my wings (still am) and wanted them displayed.

Is it frog?

Finally, I was fitted for a flying helmet. The RAF spent a small fortune on the best and most robust flying helmets in the world. The USMC? Not so much. My flying lid was a somewhat flimsy fibreglass/plastic thing that had a cheap set of headphones sewn in and a dark visor that could slip off if the elastic holding it onto the helmet was too slack. It had a Velcro cover that you just put in your pocket when you went flying. To complete the system, there was a huge full-face rubber oxygen mask with the microphone inside it. It clicked into metal housings on each cheek of the helmet and took some getting used to as it went right under your chin and almost onto your throat. You will have seen in movies like *Top Gun* how the pilots would sometimes fly with their masks hanging down? I never did that once. Ejecting like that would probably see you lose your helmet or getting smashed in the face by the mask. Also, it supplied you with oxygen and I didn't want to mess around with that. It was just a case of getting used to this new and unusual kit.

And so, to swim qual. As far as I could tell, all of the Marines hated swim qual. There were lots of elements to it including swimming (no shit) in your flying suit; use of the life preserver; drown-proofing where you floated face down for what seemed like hours to preserve energy (only taking your face out of the water to take a breath); breathing underwater through the oxygen mask; and finally, the dunker. This simulated you crashing into the sea in a helicopter on the way to/from the carrier. We sat in a mock-up cockpit of a CH-46 Sea Knight that was suspended over a huge diving pool. They then 'crashed' us into the sea and the dunker would sink or rotate and sink and we had to get out without drowning. We did it about six times I think and then did it blindfolded to simulate night time. People dreaded the dunker, but to me it was a bit of a day out, almost like a theme park.

Once I was kitted up and not drowned, I set about trawling my way through the tech presentations. Subjects like hydraulics, electrics and to a certain extent, engines (except when they talk about afterburner) are tedious at best, but when you study them through computer-aided instruction (CAI) they are soul destroying. Each subject took me through the knowledge download and then ended with a pass/fail multiple choice exam. If you answered the question correctly, the screen would go green, and red if you got it wrong. However, you then got another go so it wasn't like it was really testing you. One of the hydraulics questions would look like this:

What is the hydraulic pressure at the undercarriage down lock valve? Is it:
   a) 230 bar
   b) 270 bar
   c) 280 bar
   d) A frog

Obviously not d, so select c. Screen goes red so try again. Select b and the screen goes green. Congratulations, you have passed this question. Not far from the truth—really!

After hours of going through tech and learning a few checklists, I decided to have a little look at the more advanced stuff like the radar, RWR and weapons. The displays on the DDIs looked a little complicated, but the data on the various screens seemed to be presented in an easily digestible fashion. The buttons round the outside of the DDIs opened up multi-layers of screens, so navigating around them would take a bit of practice. Nearly all of the functions on the screens could be carried out by using the cursor which was controlled by a computer mouse like switch on the right-hand throttle under your index finger. This was the most important part of the HOTAS system (hands on throttle and stick), but was one of only about sixty functions.

Probably a good time to tell you about the jet huh? Where the hell do I start with the Hornet? I reckon that McDonnell-Douglas got the kid who was on work experience in the design office, and put him in a room with all the crayons and some magic mushrooms and said to him, 'Draw the craziest aeroplane you can come up with, kid.' And he did. Somehow along the way, that picture ended up on the desk of the board who were no doubt still shitfaced from the office Christmas party the night before, and they said, 'Yeah—let's build that then.'

'Really? It looks a bit batshit.'

'If we all agree, we can go home early.'

'Gets my vote, Boss.'

It looked like nothing else out there. The straights were compact, maybe a little stubby, but they looked like Bruce Lee—all muscle and nothing wasted. Beautifully sculpted lines around the rounded intakes flowing back to the smoothest of twin jet pipes. The smooth, almost feminine looks were offset by the ugly pitbull undercarriage and double nosewheels. This was a carrier jet remember, so it had to live with the sheer brutality of flying off the boat. It's topline was like nothing I had ever seen before. Just aft of the radome and slightly below the front window were three largish holes. The middle one was where the bullets came out of the Gatling gun/cannon/death-breathing-chaos-machine (call it what you will, but fucking awesome comes to mind), which was phallically positioned right between your legs in front of the instrument panel. The two holes outside of that ejected the exhaust gas from the rounds and let in cooling air. Beautiful bubble canopy that opened up and back (important for later) giving an excellent view all around, even between the tails if you were shit at air combat and spent all your time looking behind you. The front of the wings had a slight sweep to them, but were dead straight at the back and had both leading and trailing edge flaps as well as ailerons. Now here is the clever bit. People used to call this a 'soft wing' system. If I wanted to manoeuvre the aircraft, I would move the stick and in a conventional aircraft, a bit of aileron for left and right and a bit of stabilator for up and down would move. If I move the stick in the Hornet, the jet will decide which control surfaces to move for the quickest and best effect. That will include quite a bit of rudder too. The Hornet had those amazing twin tails that angled out by 20 degrees. They looked like nothing on earth, but were an integral part of the flying solution. I generally found that it was best not to look at what bits were moving outside, as that would just frighten me. The airbrake, or speedbrake for those of us used to flying McDonnell-Douglas aircraft, was a bloody huge slab of metal that hinged upwards between the tail fins and looked AWESOME!

The oddest-looking bits were the LEX (leading edge extensions) which were fill-ins from just below where the pilot's knees would be, back to the leading edge of the wing just above the engine intakes. Obviously, something to do with stability and manoeuvrability, but do you know what? The left-hand LEX HAD A LADDER FIXED IN IT!!! Ha! Your own personal ladder that dropped down so you could coolly climb up into that amazing cockpit. Let's do the cockpit later though. I want to talk about the bits that go whooooosh and bang.

You can probably guess that I was a fan?

There were two hard points on each wing, and there was also the centreline station. Add to that a couple of recessed hard points on the outside of the intake that could take a missile, or laser or FLIR pod. And to top it all off, you can stick a Sidewinder missile on each of the wingtip rails! This jet could carry just about anything. It was its own personal bringer of doom. Air-to-air fit could include Sparrow or Sidewinder which I had flown with before, and the newer AMRAAM missile. Yes, I know that is tautology like PIN number, but I am on a roll here, I am so excited. AMRAAM was a bad old bastard of a weapon, but it was in my holster now! Air-to-ground? Take your pick from 500, 1,000 and 2,000-pound dumb bombs or laser guided; Maverick missiles; Walleye flying bomb; Rockeye cluster munitions (yes, illegal now); napalm (definitely illegal now); Harpoon missile; HARM SAM killers; and don't forget that gun!

That amazing gun that we could use for air-to-air too. I reckon McDonnell-Douglas could have given me a job in sales you know? I seriously, completely, and totally bloody loved that jet, and I hadn't even flown it by then! The cockpit was nothing short of orgasmic. I had only flown old aeroplanes before. The Phantom was about 102 years old and the cockpit was designed by Fred Flintstone. They were all dirty and stinking of oil, and as soon as you sat in one, you felt like you needed a wash. These Hornets were younger than me, by some distance and the cockpits looked like operating theatres. I felt like I should have had a wash before getting in them, so I didn't sully them. It was spacious, as far as a fast jet could be, and full of futuristic stuff. I had never used a HUD (head up display) before so that was a novelty. Below that was a keyboard called the up front controller (UFC). Basically, it was a keyboard where we did all of our manual data entry such as waypoints, IFFs, radio frequencies etc, that all related to what you had selected on your DDIs. Those DDIs could show you the radar picture (a classic B-scope display or an azimuth/elevation display) as well as an air-to-ground radar picture. There was also a flight controls page that detailed the status of the four flight control computers, as well as a stores page, RWR, fuel and engines and a few other bits way too boring to mention. All of these pages had multi-layers of data selectable using the buttons around the outside. The middle DDI was the moving map display. Never had one of them before either so it was like Christmas Day for me.

You can probably tell from the last few paragraphs that I was a fan? It was more than that though. I was actually in awe of it to start with and I couldn't believe my unbelievable luck that I was the chosen one getting to fly it. Hopefully in twelve bloody weeks. OK, let me really blow your mind now and talk about the HOTAS. The stick top had about ten moveable controls/switches on it. Some of them had different functions depending on whether you were in bombing mode (boring) or fighter pilot awesome mode. They also had different functions on the ground. From just the stick, I could trim the aeroplane, disconnect the autopilot, steer on the ground, select missiles and fire them, drop bombs or shoot rockets, and generally feel like an aviation God while doing it.

The throttles (in addition to making the engines noisy) allowed me to talk on the radios, use the speedbrakes, deploy chaff and flare, engage autothrottle, do some weapons and sensors shit, and control the radar elevation scan. Finally, as if that wasn't enough, the right throttle had the cursor controller which I have already mentioned. My left index finger would become the most dextrous digit on my body as I would use the cursor on the displays, and up in the HUD. I will come back to the weapons selector and the air combat radar mode selector (called the castle switch) later when I start doing air combat on the course. For now, it is back to the mundane.

You mean thank you Tracey?

I plonked myself down in my cubicle and opened up a couple of sessions to review before my first cockpit trainer with one of the sim instructors. Once I was happy that I knew my stuff and my checks, I thought I would get ahead of the game and swot up on the radar, only to find that I was blocked from opening up the lessons. A quick rattle through the ground school programme showed that I was blocked out of all the weapons, radar, RWR and ECM stuff—the whole ish. I went to see Tracey who told me my security clearance had not come through.

'Remember when you said a few weeks ago that it had definitely arrived, Tracey?'

'No.'

'I was here with Alf and you assured us everything would be OK.'

'No, I didn't. And anyway, you should have told me you were blocked the day you started here.'

'I wasn't blocked then.'

'Yes, you were. You are not allowed to see SECRET NOFORN material.'

'Already been through it Tracey, so you might as well let me back in.'

Her face went a bit pale as I am sure there were some contractual issues with letting foreigners see sensitive stuff. Anyway, she was adamant, so I had to go and see Bay—my course commander. As I was only just starting the transition phase of the RAG, it wasn't imperative that I was into the radar and weapons stuff yet, so he obviously didn't see it as a priority. I could detail all of this in painful chronological order, but suffice it to say, I asked Bay tons of times to help sort it—he didn't. I went to see the XO who got very angry about it and said he would sort it—he didn't either. And Tracey assured me she would chase up my clearance with the DoD (Department of Defense)—guess what? She didn't. So, I went through most of the RAG with no access to the critical information I would need in order to operate the Hornet as a weapons platform.

My clearance finally arrived seven months after my arrival in California. I was three weeks away from finishing my RAG course and going to the front line. Tracey flounced into the ground school crew room as I was waiting for a simulator ride and announced it to me.

'Ok,' I said flatly.

'You mean thank you, Tracey?' she replied. For once I couldn't think of a darn thing to say, and just went back to reading the hard copy weapons manual I had signed out of the secret document cabinet that I didn't have access to read—apparently.

The tedium of ground school allowed me to get to know my course mates and also a few of the flying instructors who came over to give the odd lecture. As an RAF exchange pilot, I was a bit of an oddity so a few guys really wanted to chat, which was great. I got into the history and psyche of the Marine Corps and instantly fell in love with it. Their patriotism and camaraderie for their brothers and sisters in arms really chimed with me and my experiences on RAF fighter squadrons. What was even better was that I kept being told, 'As far as we are concerned, you're a Marine now, Tug.' I hadn't been through any of their training programme; I wasn't a US citizen; but the fact that I was wearing their colours and was willing to stand shoulder to shoulder with them for three years meant they would walk over broken glass for me. Well, that is the impression I got and I lapped it up.

I was hanging out in the crew room one day when this short guy in a flying suit walked in and said 'Hi.' I didn't know him from Adam, but I recognised a shitload of rank and stood to attention and said, 'Hello, Sir.' He was a major general.

'You must be on exchange huh? RAF?'

'Yes, Sir. Tug Wilson. Nice to meet you,' I said and held out my hand.

'Pleased to meet you Tug. Charlie Bolden. I used to fly A6s and am just here converting to the Hornet. How are we treating you?'

'All good, Sir. Couldn't be better.'

'OK, hope to see you again sometime, Tug. Good luck.' He dropped a hefty document on the table and left. Seemed a really nice guy, especially for a 2-star. I had a quick glance at the document he had left and saw there was a picture of the Space Shuttle on the front. Turns out it was a full flight plan for a Shuttle mission. I opened it up and there in black and white it said:

Mission Commander—Charles F. Bolden Junior.

Holy shit!!! I just met an actual living breathing astronaut! Bearing in mind I was an Apollo programme space history nerd, I can't tell you how excited I was. And he was the most unassuming man you could ever meet. Charlie, as I now knew him—scratch that—Major General Bolden, Sir, flew on four Shuttle missions and would go on to become NASA Administrator. He was the first African-American to do so. Oh, and he was also a Vietnam veteran, so when he said he flew Intruders, it was a little more than that. What a man, and so modest! I would have been walking around with all sorts of space badges on my flying suit and probably a t-shirt saying 'Oy! I'm a bloody astronaut you know?'

OJ and MJ

It was finally time for me to start flying the simulator. I had done a few cockpit trainers where I was taught all the checks from pre-start through to shut down, and also how to manipulate the controls and displays. It was time to put it all together and see if I could actually remember how to fly. I jumped in the instrument trainer which had three huge screens in front of me and sealed me off when the canopy closed. Starting jets up is too boring to talk about here, but trust me when I say there was a lot of manual data entry using the UFC for waypoints etc. It would have been easy for me to use my right index finger to type all the latitude and longitudes into the UFC, but I wouldn't be able to do that easily in the air, what with having to fly the aeroplane with that hand—you know? Pilot shit. We were taught to slap our left hand onto the left side of the UFC and type using our left thumb. Over time, I would be able to input data without looking at the keyboard as my thumb would 'know' where each button was. Crikey, with my dextrous index finger and then my rampant thumb, I could probably make it as a concert pianist. Or a porn star.

So, after a month of balls-aching computer lectures, I took to the runway and powered down it in my F-18 Hornet, sort of. I had always hated going to the sim. Miserable old bastard instructors who beasted you while you sat in the black box, sweating and crying. This was a dream though. I know it was only an instrument trainer and it was configured for night visuals, but I hadn't flown in nearly three months so just wanted to get my hands on something vaguely aeroplane like. Even though it was mostly procedural stuff and instrument approaches, it was amazing to be pole-ing a Hornet around. Actually, the learning curve for me was a bit steep as I had to learn about new airspace regulations as well as adapt to talking differently on the radio. The Americans speak the same language as us, yes? Not quite. We are two countries separated by a common language and there were some specific idiosyncrasies on terminology and the like that I would need to get used to. The F-18 seemed pretty easy to fly, even for an average player like me, and after fifteen sims in all, I was ready to get my teeth into the transition phase of flying. It should only have been eight sims, but I signed out the box a few times myself for personal practice, and Alf gave up a half day of his weekend to come and watch one to make sure I was up to speed. The pre-first flight sim, FAM 8 was in my logbook four times as it had a currency on it and it kept lapsing as the squadron schedulers forgot to fly me in time!

We are almost there folks—my first trip. I just want to mention a couple of events that were going on in the States before we get to that. If you just want to read about flying, then skim this bit. We arrived in California about a month after the OJ Simpson trial started. It absolutely dominated the news and TV schedules for almost the whole of 1995 and was a TV drama played out for real. The other event was that Michael Jordan, the greatest basketball player of all time, came out of retirement. The highest paid sportsman in the world, the living legend of basketball, was back. This was too big a story not to follow and I immediately got into the NBA and followed Jordan and the Bulls. Waste of time telling you that? You will see why this was so important later in the book.

I suppose you want to talk about flying then? First trips in new aeroplanes are always tricky so I had pleaded with the ops guys to put me in a back seat sometime, just as a passenger. If nothing else, even if I didn't get my hand on the stick, I could at least hear the language on the radio, orientate myself a bit in the airspace, and get used to wearing the flying kit for real. I finally got my wish on 12 June 1995 as I climbed up the ladder and sat in the back seat of a pairs low altitude training (LAT) sortie for one of the students on our senior course in the other jet. I tried to follow the start-up procedure, but shit just happens in an aircraft when you are not controlling the sequence. I concentrated on watching what the ground crew were up to, as this is never included in ground school. The canopy came down and we taxied out into a waiting bay for the last chance checks. This is a US thing and no doubt comes from carrier ops where independent checking of kit is essential before being flung down the deck by the catapult. We had to show our hands while people were under the jet so they would be confident we wouldn't move any surfaces and donk them. Onto the runway and we blasted off towards the coast before picking up the routing for R-2507.

And so began the most brilliant two-and-a-half-year ride of my life

On the way, my pilot who was called Milk, was good enough to show me all of the weapons checks and just generally chatted to me until we hit the range. He then went full on single-seat mode and concentrated on the trip alone. I had no problem with that as he had briefed me beforehand that would happen. The RAF practically lived at low-level so I was uber-confident down there (Cold War Germany mentality). The US air forces were not low-level specialists so LAT sorties were run on numbers and procedures to minimise risk. I say minimise risk. We were down at 100 feet at times and also doing outrageous 3-dimensional jinks that had us pointing at the ground, fairly low at 450 knots.

Milk had to fly his own jet, but also closely monitor his student in the other one, hence he had little capacity to talk to me. I sat there and soaked up being thrashed around at high G in the hot baking Arizona/SoCal sunshine. I was pleased that I was following what was going on; was able to interpret what the displays were telling me; and also that I didn't feel sick after three months of not flying. I do wonder if they deliberately gave me a LAT trip to see if the low-level RAF guru was going to throw his ring up. That would have stopped me whining about going flying now, wouldn't it?

The gas was used up scorchingly quickly on a trip like this and only an hour after getting airborne, we landed back at El Toro, off the first approach. I didn't get a great look at the circuit, but there didn't seem to be many surprises, and Milk chatted me through the HUD landing symbology. I had used it in the sim and to be honest, it was a dream. Speaking of which, I now had the F-18, BUNO 163771 in my logbook showing that I had flown for one whole hour in an F-18 Hornet. Even if I failed the RAG and made a crippling embarrassment of myself and my air force, they would never be able to take that away from me.

Two days later, having completed and passed sim FAM 8 for the fourth time, I climbed into the front seat of a twin-sticker to start my raging hot love affair with the prettiest jet on the planet. This would be my first kiss and I was floating on air. Would she like me? Would I be good enough for her? Only one way to find out, I guess. Buckle up, Tug, take the plunge, and ask her out. And so began the most brilliant two-and-a-half year ride of my life.

My instructor on this first ride was a guy called Timbo. He was born in the UK so the schedulers thought he would have some empathy with me, being British and all. The fact that he moved to the States when he was five years old, identified completely as an American, and couldn't remember anything about his early childhood in the Motherland, was neither here nor there. He was pleasant enough and could see how excited I was to go flying, in the brief.

I was still getting used to the flying kit so we walked a little early for the jet, and there it was! A beautiful twin-seat B model, just sitting there on the sun scorched pan waiting for me. Timbo took me round the external checks and I touched as much of the jet as I could (for some reason, I had always run my hand down both sides of the radome like it was a horse—an old habit from the Phantom). I checked the safety pins and locks were removed from the undercarriage and hook—hell's bells, there was a lot of heavy metal on those bits—and finally, it was time for me to climb in the front. Being a Brit, I was a bit of a novelty, so the ground crew wanted to chat. As much as I wanted to be sociable, I was concentrating more on not screwing up strapping into the ejection seat, and doing all my checklists properly. Start-up went pretty much as advertised and the HUD and displays fired up into life. The displays looked a little raw compared to the cockpit trainer displays, and this would be even more apparent when the radar would be painting real targets, rather than the synthetic ones in the trainers. Although we were out on the pan and not in a shelter, the noise from the engines was beautifully brutal. US flying helmets had a much cheaper comms suite then RAF helmets and the ear pieces did little to cut down the outside noise. Who cared though? It looked bloody cool on my head, and I was sitting in a Hornet!

I called ATC for taxi and true to form, they ignored me, so I called again and I think I got clearance to go (couldn't quite understand them) so I engaged NWS and slowly nosed out onto the taxiway that took me out to final checks. As we left our slot, the maintainer stood to attention and saluted. I just waved back at him and he gave me a slightly bemused look and off we went. I pulled us into final checks and put the parking brake on. Hands out of the cockpit so the guys could check underneath without me clonking them on the head with the stabilator or flaps. Following another salute, wave, bemused look combo, I was heading for one of El Toro's four runways.

I stumbled my way through the pre-take off checks, bringing the canopy down which plunged us into relative silence and a much more pleasant air-conditioned temperature, and called on the radio for our clearance. Timbo was nice and relaxed even though he realised he was having to teach me a lot more basic stuff than he would to any of the US students on the course. Basically, I was unfamiliar with just about everything from a procedural point of view. However, my naïve Forrest Gump style approach appealed to his better nature and simultaneously allowed me to be a bit shit. All flying in the States required a flight plan so rather than just getting airborne, like in the UK and blasting off into low-level, this took a bit more coordination. To prevent us having to file a flight plan for every single trip, there were some standard out and back plans called stereo routes to the standard training areas. I had programmed the routes into the nav kit using my left thumb on the UFC during start up, and there it was, all on the moving map on my centre DDI. We got our clearance and I switched to the Tower frequency to call for take-off.

There was still a niggling doubt that I was actually dreaming this and was about to wake up, or that it was an elaborate hoax, but despite that, I found myself lined up on the runway ready to go. I powered up holding the jet on the brakes and then let them off and we lurched up like a sprinter off the blocks. This was to be a dry power take-off only on the first trip. I guess the idea was not to max us out with the speed of the afterburner, but dear God I was tempted to slam those throttles through the gate into full rocket mode when I hit the dry power stop. Anyway, it seemed fast enough as the jet sped down the runway, and all too soon she gracefully eased airborne like a silent movie actress slipping off a chaise longue. Gear up, flaps up and the HUD automatically changed to navigation symbology and I was away. A quick couple of calls to ATC (which I had to repeat of course) and we were heading out over the mountains (and our house) to get to the play area just off the Pacific coast.

Call the ball, Tug ... Huh?

OK, some of you are going to be a bit disappointed with this bit. I must be kidding right? This is the Hornet! How the hell can you be disappointed? Well, I must be honest with you and say that I remember very little about that trip. I remember getting airborne and definitely the circuits, which I will tell you about in a bit, but all the stuff in the middle? No recollection at all I'm afraid. I could make some shit up if you like, but that wouldn't fit with the whole honest confessions style of my books. We probably did a fair amount of general handling, looking at performance and angle of attack. Fairly sure we went supersonic too. The Hornet had no trouble getting through the Mach, but was a bit limited on top speed, especially when compared to a F-16 or F-14D. Oh, and we definitely did a bit of nav kit and radar manipulation.

I was hands on the whole time while Timbo talked me through some stuff, and then it was back to El Toro for some circuits. I flew a radar approach with ATC for recovery into a precision approach radar (PAR—a classic talkdown) which gave me plenty of time to look at the landing symbology in the HUD. Of course, I had used it in the simulator, but things are different in the air. Firstly, the jet is bouncing around in the wind and the HUD looked a bit like it was on elastic as it reacted to the bounces. Secondly, you have the light to contend with so it might not be so easy to see unless you turn the brightness up full which detracts from the picture of the world behind the symbology. Finally, you lose half your brain when you climb into the aeroplane for real, so what seemed relatively easy in the sim, turns into a stinking nightmare in the cockpit.

The HUD had a compass reading at the top which obviously moved when you turned the aeroplane, an airspeed box below it to the left and an identical box on the right, level with it, that displayed the altitude. The angle of climb and descent ladder filled the middle of the HUD top to bottom. These lines were in 5-degree increments with the angle of climb lines being solid and the angle of descent ones being hatched. There was an aeroplane symbol in the middle which looked like a little circle with wings and a tail fin. This might seem a bit noddy telling you this, but remember that I had never used a HUD so even the simplest of things put a smile on my face. The whole ladder tilted left and right with the angle of bank. That was the basic HUD symbology you got on every display, be it for nav, attack or take-off and landing. However, when you put the landing gear down, a magical thing happened. An extra little bit of symbology appeared next to the aeroplane symbol, called the E-bar. Whoever invented the E-bar is one of the greatest heroes in aviation history in my eyes. This tiny little thing allowed me to land the aircraft safely at the right speed with minimal drama.

There is a saying that anyone can land an aircraft—it is the angle and speed of arrival where all the skill is. The Hornet HUD made landing easy. And that is coming from someone who has had their fair share of 'precarious' landings—OK, let's call them ugly! So, to land the Hornet then, you put the aircraft symbol on the end of the runway you want to land on, and cross check with the ladder that you are 3 degrees nose down. If it is 5 degrees nose down then you are too steep, so dive down a bit until the end of the runway is right there on the ladder at 3 degrees, and then bring the aircraft symbol up to the runway again. That sorts the up/down stuff. All this time, you are doing the left/right thing as well. The E-bar is a capital E just to the left of the aircraft symbol. If the middle sticky-out bit of the E is directly next to the aircraft symbol's wing, then you are at the correct angle of attack and therefore the correct speed, for landing—so long as you are 3 degrees nose down. If you are at the bottom of the E-bar, you are too fast (too little angle of attack). Therefore, the top of the E-bar is a bad place to be as it means you are too slow and with too much angle of attack. That equals danger! Keep decelerating from there and the E-bar goes way above the aircraft symbol and we get into Flick, Stall, Spin, Crash, Burn, Die territory.

Now, I either made that sound too simple for the pilots out there reading this, or grossly overcomplicated for the non-pilots. Trust me—it was easy. All you had to do was put the aeroplane symbol on the end of the runway and then move the throttles to put the E-bar where you wanted it. There was an even easier way to picture it for real. The throttles control the E-bar (a bit more to it than that, but let's go with that, OK?). If I am too fast, the E-bar will be above my aeroplane symbol, so I would want to reach up with my hand and pull it back down towards me. Therefore, I pull the throttles back towards me. Too slow and I would want to push the E-bar back up to the aeroplane symbol. Now I push the throttles up. For a pilot of limited talent and technique, procedures like that are a godsend.

Enough explanation. I managed a grease-smooth landing off the instrument approach. Not bad for my first landing in the jet, and I powered up to take us up into the visual circuit. Timbo took control to demo the first one, and a couple of things became apparent. Firstly, he left the landing gear down throughout. I guessed this was a habit from being around the carrier. In the RAF, we would retract the gear after each roller (touch and go in American parlance) and then put it back down again on the downwind leg of the circuit. It suited me to leave it down—one less thing to screw up before landing. Secondly, it seemed Timbo was flying the whole thing like an instrument pattern. Again, it was probably a boat thing, but I was used to doing spacing downwind and tipping into finals, completely visually by looking out of the window.

I think they turn finals on the boat as soon as they are abeam the landing end of the ship. This takes into account the fact that the boat is moving away from you as you turn finals, and it makes the separation for you. At an airfield, which isn't steaming into wind at 30 knots, you go beyond the abeam point, and tip into finals usually as the swept wing tip goes over the threshold of the runway. Timbo was getting abeam and then counting so many seconds before turning finals, to simulate the boat moving away from him. I was looking out of the window to spot whatever visual cue I could find. Both techniques work. I just had to adapt mine for the Hornet, and Timbo was good enough to let me do my thing so long as I didn't crash and kill us. Once we were lined up with the runway, Timbo said in cockpit, 'Ball half low' or some such banter. I had no idea what he was talking about so just concentrated on the HUD to soak up the technique for getting us down. Holy crap, he clonked us into the ground hard and then powered up to get us airborne again so he could hand control to me for a go.

The Hornet was a dream to fly in the circuit, all dirtied up with gear and flaps so I made a passable attempt first go. I used my visual cue to tip into finals and called 'Shooter 42 finals gear down.' As I rolled out on finals, the runway was 3 degrees nose down with the little aeroplane on it and the E-bar slowly descending towards the correct AoA. A little power when it got there to hold it and a small check back on the stick before landing as I pulled the throttles to idle should see us grease it on nicely. It was at this point, Timbo decided to confuse me.

'Call the ball, Tug,' he said.

'Huh?' I asked, confused—and a bit busy trying to land the jet.

'Call the ball.'

'Erm ... THE BALL!?' I shouted.

'Huh?' Timbo's turn to be confused. He kept quiet until I landed and as we got airborne again, he took control to figure out what was going on.

Just to explain here, 'The Ball' refers to the meatball light in the middle of the Fresnel lens. This was a British invention that had been incorporated into an optical landing system (OLS) to help pilots land on aircraft carriers. The ball was a vertical series of lenses which gave out different colours depending on your angle of approach. There was a horizontal line of green lights either side and the ideal approach had an amber meatball lined up in the middle of the greens. If you were too high, the ball would be above the greens. Too low and the ball was low and turned red in colour. It was all stabilised to the movement of the boat so gave you a constant picture on a pitching deck.

Now, I had heard all about this, and even seen it in the movie, *Top Gun*, but I didn't know that every Navy and Marine Corps airfield had an OLS just to the left of the runway. They even painted a fake carrier deck on the runway so pilots could practice carrier landings before going out to qualify on the boat itself. Of course, I was so busy trying to land the damn aeroplane without crashing to notice any of this at El Toro. Timbo flew the next circuit so I could just look out of the window and have a look at the meatball. I only picked out the OLS at the last minute and couldn't really see the lights to save my life, as Timbo smashed us into the runway again. Surely, we could be a bit gentler with this beautiful jet, even though the undercarriage was built like a brick restroom (note the American vernacular? I was really getting into it now!). Anyway, it was my go again and the same thing happened. I couldn't see the ball so I just got on and landed anyway with a nice smooth arrival. 'Sorry mate, I just can't see it,' I said. We only had gas for one more circuit, and so Timbo told me to just do what I was happy with and so I did. My last landing was definitely one we could walk away from, and only 80 minutes after take-off, my first date was over and done with. I like to think that not crunching her into the ground each time on landing meant that my pretty little Hornet was going to give me a second date. And do you know what? I couldn't wait.

I looked just like Tom Cruise

I taxied into our parking slot and realigned the nav kit to our final position before shutting down. Timbo was happy in the debrief, and after consulting with the XO and boss, it was decided that as there were no plans to send me to the boat during my tour, we could kiss off the ball and just crack on and land the jet normally. As it was one less thing to deal with during circuits, I was happy.

Oh dear. How many of you bought this book thinking I was going to reveal what it was like flying from the carrier? Sorry folks. At the time of my arrival, there was a Status of Forces Agreement in place which prevented UK nationals from deploying into US-only areas of tension/conflict that the UK were not involved in. Given that a carrier battle group could be deployed at very short notice, having me or Alf or Indy on board would be an embarrassment and a logistical problem at best, and a diplomatic nightmare at worst. Therefore, it was not deemed worthwhile putting us through the four-week boat work-up when we couldn't deploy on it anyway. I had mixed feelings about it. On the one hand, I was gutted. My one chance to fly off the carrier was gone before I started. On the other hand, though? Did I really want to spend four weeks of my life cooped up on board, sharing a tiny double-bunked room with another sweaty stinking pilot that I barely knew and doing bloody circuits all day? Added to that, an operational tour on the boat lasted six months so I am pretty sure that would have gone down like a shit sandwich with my wife. Don't worry though. I had an absolute ball even without the boat stuff, so there are plenty of stories to fill this book.

It was after the weekend before I would get my second date with my alluring new object of desire. In the meantime, we were still discovering new experiences and taking a big bite out of Americana. We were making the most of the lake, and had found a traditional diner called Ruby's Diner which would become a regular weekend brunch haunt, especially when we had visitors to stay. That weekend also saw me attend my first baseball game.

On my previous tour as an instructor at RAF Valley, we had an ex-F-16 USAF exchange officer called Sharpe who somehow had arranged an official tour for some of us to the United States about a year before. One of the things he wanted to do was take us to a ballgame in New York—a Yankees game, no less. Unfortunately, our trip coincided with a players' strike so the game was off. Sharpe had been posted to Edwards Air Force Base, north of LA, and phoned me to say his course of test pilots were doing an outing to see the California Angels play the Yankees in Anaheim. The stadium was only about 45 minutes' drive for me so he asked me to go along. It was an amazing experience to see the ballpark and the game. Sharpe introduced me to his course buddies and it seemed I had more kudos due to my Phantom tour rather than my solitary Hornet trip. That game started a life-long passion for baseball within me, and I craved going to the ballpark. It sounds clichéd, but the game did go right down to the end of the ninth inning, with the Angels just beating out the Yankees—not all games would be that exciting.

Speaking of exciting, my second date came around on the Monday. More of the same with lots of circuits. Even by this stage, I was finding the circuits and landings fairly easy. Sorry if that sounds arrogant, but I really had won the lottery with this jet. I had two trips the following day with hugely contrasting personalities. My first hop (as the Marines called them) was with a young captain called Pancho. I think he was of Mexican descent and was a very nice guy. The second hop was with JD who was neither Mexican, nor nice. I would often see Pancho over in ground school topping up his knowledge by reading through some of the lessons—very professional for an instructor. He was a dream to fly with. A very good nurturing style of instruction that put me instantly at ease. Bear in mind here, this was only the third time I had flown in the US, so he helped me no end, and I didn't hate a single one of the ten circuits he made me do.

JD was miserable as sin, and a very angry young man. He was on my back instantly for not changing radio frequencies soon enough, or not understanding all of the calls, or not being American, or God only knows what. Anyway, I knuckled down to it and after six more circuits, he figured out I was unlikely to crash my Hornet into the centre of LA, and after the debrief, he wrote me up as fit to fly solo. On 22 June 1995, after a final check ride in the simulator, I walked out on my own to a pan full of dogfighting spaceships, and climbed into 164053 for my first solo. I looked just like Tom Cruise did in *Top Gun* in my torso harness and g-pants, carrying my helmet and kneeboard. That is if Tom Cruise was a gangly, pasty-white Brit who was shitting himself—which he wasn't.

Another aside here. I had bought a kneeboard from the local pilot supply shop. There were pockets in my g-pants where I kept maps and books with airfield approaches in. However, there was so much other guff I needed to carry that I needed somewhere central and organised to keep it all. Enter the 9-G kneeboard. Muck had recommended it to me and it was brilliant. It tied around my left thigh, secured with an elasticated band and clip that expanded as my g-pants inflated. I was able to store all sorts of stuff in it such as training area information, bombing patterns, intercept and combat rules as well as waypoint and frequency cards. It was like a bit of my brain dumped all in one place. During ground school, my course mates had bantered me for being a bit of a dinosaur when they caught me preparing and drawing a local area map. Their argument was that the Hornet was supposed to be the first so called 'paperless cockpit'. Maps were on the display and all the check lists were stored digitally in the DDIs too. All well and good until you have a total electrics failure in the jet. My local area map had all of the diversions marked on it with contact frequencies and airfield details, and I always carried my flight reference cards with me. It may have been force of habit, but as I prepared my map, I was subconsciously lifting off data to help me build a picture in my mind of the surrounding 100 miles or so—invaluable information for someone like me who needed a lot of prep to succeed.

The Gouge

Anyway, I was strapped into my jet (a B model as there were no straights available), kneepad secured on my left thigh, so I thought it was time to start up and go. Salute, wave, huh (?) and again in final checks, and I was on the runway ready to go and wreak havoc in US airspace on behalf of Her Majesty the Queen. No cocking around this time—it was straight into full burner and flaming hell, the jet rocketed down the runway like a … well, like a jet fighter in full bloody afterburner! No kidding, I yelped with glee and blasted off into the ether. Gear up, flaps up, cancel burner, and navigate my way out over the ocean, trying all the time not to sound like a dickhead on the radio. And then, in the play area, I switched to a silent frequency so it was just me and my latest squeeze with nothing and nobody to interrupt our liaison.

What followed was the most amazing hour of pure flying I had ever done. I couldn't stop looking in the mirrors. Firstly, to look at those sexy canted tail fins, and secondly to see how awesomely cool I looked! I explored the envelope into some high AoA manoeuvring and then gunned the burners in a straight line to shatter the Mach. Supersonic solo in the best dogfighting jet in the world. Another brilliant experience. Another story to tell. I got all of the adrenaline out of my system ready for recovery and some circuits. I only got five of them in before the fuel ran out and I had to land. Shocking that I was disappointed I couldn't do more circuits, but there we are. That's how much fun the Hornet was. I absolutely adored it already and was desperate for the next hop.

Shit! There now followed a whole bloody month on the ground. The ab-initio guys on my course did some close and tactical formation flying, but it was decided that I didn't need any of that and could just pick it up on the intercept trips in the next phase. The planning board behind the ops desk had all our names on it and each trip laid out for a tick and a date when we had completed them. My line had a load of sorties with red crosses through them meaning I didn't need to do them. Hmmm—that might come in handy in the future—trust me.

In preparation for the next phase of the course, which was called All Weather Intercept or AWI for short, I had a load of radar and weapons lessons to go through, all of which I was not allowed to look at. That left my knowledge a little sparse when it came to doing the intercept sims before flying. These were done in the intercept trainers mostly, which were full cockpits that you could fly around and a 'working' radar that the instructors could generate targets on, for us to intercept. All of the sim instructors were ex-Phantom or Hornet, or both, and were mostly very good guys. I got the one knobhead for my first intercept sim, didn't I? Rivet had initially been a Phantom RIO (radar intercept officer—

navigator in simple terms) who had converted to pilot and flown Hornets. He was a thorny bastard at the best of times and given that I hadn't flown for two weeks and was still blocked from ground school, he caught me on a very bad day. There were a number of questions we had to find answers to before the brief, and I prepped by asking Alf, Indy, and Muck where I needed to. However, there were only so many times I could lean on them, and it was probably time for a reckoning with ground school.

Rivet was his usual prickly self and he asked me the radar and weapons questions, which I could only answer with, 'I don't know.' Before I could finish with, 'I'm not allowed to see the lessons', he absolutely lost it with me and started a full-on bollocking before saying he was failing the sim before we even started. I let him rant a bit, and when he said, 'What makes you think you can turn up here, not do the work, and not know your fucking stuff?' I let him have it. Ordinarily, I would have climbed the greasy rage pole with him and let loose, but I was actually steely calm (Jesus—I must be maturing, huh?).

'Nothing, mate,' I calmly replied.

'What the fuck does that mean?!' he shouted.

'The reason I have come here having not done the work, and not knowing my fucking stuff is because the fucking Marines Corps, and by extension you, will not let me look at the fucking stuff in the first place. If you would like to take it up with the XO, boss, defence secretary, or the president, on my behalf, then be my fucking guest, Rivet.' That's probably torn it, I figured, but by that stage I didn't care. Rivet asked me what was going on and I gave him chapter and verse about my clearances.

'Right—let's go in the trainer then.' He then proceeded to teach me everything I needed to know from scratch, all off the record. He doubled the length of the trainer to give me extra tuition, and from then on, I was the pet project of all the sim guys, but especially Rivet. They all went above and beyond for me, and everything I knew about the radar and weapons and how to do intercepts, by the time I got back into the cockpit, was completely down to them—and mostly to Rivet.

Now, we may have only been 45 minutes from Angel Stadium, but we were also only 45 minutes from Disneyland. During my month on the ground, we planned a family trip to take in Disneyland, Universal Studios in LA and ending with a night on the Queen Mary in Long Beach. Disneyland was magical—no other word for it. I remember being a kid growing up in North Yorkshire and seeing Disney specials on TV, dreaming an impossible dream of going there one day, knowing deep down that it would never happen. And here I was watching my daughter cuddling Goofy and riding in a teacup. Like I said—magical. Universal was a little less child-friendly, especially when I decided to avoid the jam on the freeway and take Santa Monica Boulevard instead. I had heard of it in a song so figured it would be a nice drive. It was, for a bit, near the beach. Then it went through downtown LA and we ended up driving through the Badlands. It probably wasn't the proper Badlands, but it bloody well felt like it. Anyway, we survived gangland LA and drove through the docks that afternoon for a nice night on the Queen Mary. It was in a bit of a shit hole, but was lovely on board. There was a big round aircraft hangar on the water next to it, that used to house Howard Hughes's huge Spruce Goose aircraft, but that had been moved to Oregon and the 15-hour drive just wasn't worth it.

As OJ Simpson got deeper in the shit during his trial, the Wilsons held a 3rd of July party in the garden to celebrate the last day of British rule. It was a bit of banter that was well received and we invited all the families from Holly's playgroup, Alf and Muck's families, Indy, and the neighbours. I also invited the guys on my course, but none of them turned up. Alf told me that this was not unusual for the Marines to ignore social invites. I would see this quite a bit in my time in the States and could never quite get my head around it. They were a strong brother and sisterhood when in uniform, but it was rare to do something with them out of uniform. We put on lots of British food and I had a Union Jack on a flagpole next to the Stars and Stripes. Our neighbours (who were lovely, by the way), had bought us the Stars and Stripes as there was some kind of law stating that if you fly any kind of flag, you must have the Stars and Stripes up as well.

My month in terra-firma confinement was finally over and I was about to get some continuity at last. To date, it seemed like my exchange tour had consisted of trips to Disneyland (we went there a lot as military discount halved the price of admission); seeing the sights of Southern California; lazing in the sunshine in the garden; oh, and a bit of flying or simulator on the RAG. I mean, I should have been going through the lessons in ground school, but as I couldn't access the ones I needed for the rest of the course, it was pointless hanging around twiddling my thumbs. When Tracey was away, I would go and ask the ops clerk if I could sign out the secret weapons manuals. He had no idea I was blocked out of seeing them so happily let me have them. I reckon I could have probably gone to the local stationery shop and got them copied for myself without anyone knowing. I tried hanging out in the ready room (crew room) over on 101, to just chat with the instructors, but it wasn't that kind of atmosphere. There was a definite split among the instructors with about half of them being great guys who wanted to chat, and the rest being a little offish, almost like they didn't know how to treat me. Out of that group, there were two complete arseholes, and I flew my next trip with one of them.

Smiler had flown his first tour on a twin-seat F-18D squadron as he was deemed a little dull and maybe not up to the single-seat job. There was a rumour that he had been short-toured to get him off the squadron, as everyone disliked him. The RAG was an easier job than the front line, so he had been posted there and had only just qualified as a basic instructor (not allowed to do the more complicated aspects of the course). He had a bit of a chip on his shoulder about the single-seat thing and was one of those guys that the students didn't want to fly with. I knew none of this, but it was 'the gouge'.

The gouge was all the stuff that you needed to know, but wasn't officially taught. When starting a course in the States, you would immediately go to your senior course and say 'gimme the gouge.' I got most of my initial gouge from Alf and Indy, but had to lean on my course buddies for a lot more. Somehow, I missed the gouge on Smiler. It was an ironic callsign as he was a miserable son of a bitch. The odd thing was, I wasn't programmed to fly that trip with him. I was down to do the first radar intercept trip the day before with a guy called Weld. He was the antithesis of Smiler and a brilliant instructor. Weld got his callsign during the first Gulf war. A package of F-18s were going into Iraq on a bombing mission and Weld was embedded with them as a HARM shooter. The High-Speed Anti-Radiation Missile was a SAM killer. If a SAM fired up its radar, the HARM seeker head would see it, and if you pulled the trigger, it would shoot off the rail at high speed (no shit!) and ride the radar wave right to the target and blow it up. On the way out of the target area, the package had been lit up by SAMs and had manoeuvred hard this way and that, pulling lots of G to defend against them. After all of these break turns and defences, the leader of the package looked out to see the HARM shooter still welded to his wing with HARMs screaming off the rails to kill the SAMs. That might not be the exact story, but it is close enough.

Back to the plot. We were to launch as a 3-ship with the leader being the target, and numbers 2 and 3 being the fighters. Once we got to the play area, number 2 would go to one end and the other two jets would go to the other. As number 3 held in an orbit, 1 and 2 would race towards each other to conduct an intercept for number 2. Once that was done, the leader would turn around and go straight into the next intercept against number 3 as number 2 repositioned to the edge of the area and waited. It meant that the leader bounced between us, and we got plenty of intercepts done—enough for both fighters to prove their prowess and pass the trip. It was a clever use of assets, as with only two aircraft, you would have to bat and ball the role of fighter, and if one of the students was struggling, you might not get enough good intercepts done to get a pass.

As we walked out to the jet, Weld was asking me how I was enjoying the States and what I thought of the Marine Corps etc. It was just so mellow with him and I couldn't wait to get airborne. I loved him even more when he said, 'Look, Tug. I know you know how to do an intercept so how about we do a couple of academic ones and then just have a bit of fun yeah?'

'Perfect Weld. Thanks.' And for the first time, the jet broke on start-up. There was a spare aircraft for us, but we would need to shut down, run across the pan (in the searing heat mind you), and get started up in quick time so as not to keep the other jets in our formation waiting. As I checked in with Weld on the intercom, he said, 'Just start her up Tug, and I will do all the waypoints for you.' What a great guy. He knew I would be on the back foot so just took all the pressure off me. Would you believe it? The spare had a hydraulic leak and so we had to cancel out and the other two jets went off without us.

Assuming I can find the bloody target in the first place

I was ready to go again the next day with Smiler, and no doubt you will think I am spinning a line, but we had to run for the spare again—exactly the same scenario as with Weld. This time, as I was hurriedly starting up and trying to strap in, I asked Smiler if he could put the waypoints in for me, and I got this response:

'Fuck off, you can do them yourself! What do you think I am? A fucking WSO?' I'll cut him some slack and say he had a point if I was going to a single-seat squadron, but everyone knew I was going twin-seat. And it was only trip 6 for me in the F-18 and the United States for God's sake, so a bit of help might have been nice, as we were keeping the other jets waiting again. Weld he was not—obviously. I stayed calm-ish and forced myself to slow down so I didn't make any stupid mistakes through rushing. Once I was happy, I called that we were ready to the leader and taxied out in sequence behind 1 and 2. Everyone knew by now that the odd looking British guy used to wave to the ground crew rather than salute, but either Smiler hadn't got the gouge about me, or was spoiling for a fight after I asked him to help with the waypoints, but I noticed him hanging out of his cockpit trying to see what I was doing as we taxied out of final checks.

The flight itself went well. He was supposed to demonstrate the first intercept to me, but didn't, so it was in at the deep end. No big deal, as the radar display and controls were a dream to use. Before each intercept, I would go through the pre-intercept checklist which consisted of setting the correct range scale on the radar; selecting Sparrow missile and making sure it was tuned; selecting range while search (RWS) mode on the radar, and also checking the fuel. In the past on the Phantom, you had to lock the radar onto the target to see what range it was from you. The APG-65 Hornet radar gave you the range and a whole host of other information while it was still in search mode. This meant you had more situational awareness on all the other targets while you were intercepting the one you were interested in.

At the 'fight's on!' call, I would snap towards the bandit and use the wheel on the throttles under the middle finger on my left hand, to motor the radar scanner up and down to search the airspace in front of me. As soon as the APG-65 saw the target, it would put a box on the display (with no top on it) and a little tail coming out of it. That tail was called the aspect vector and it was a gift from the Gods as it made doing intercepts incredibly easy compared to what I had done before.

Intercepts for me, on the Hawk in particular, consisted of back-plotting the range and bearing of the target from my nose and using the compass to work out their heading using mental arithmetic and geometry. We got the range and bearing from a ground intercept controller (GCI) and this was known as Bravo control. On the Phantom, my navigator would find the target on the radar, possibly using GCI for information, and then would study the movement of the blip on the scope for about 5 miles before announcing their heading, height, and speed to me in the front. I still have no idea how they did it while hunched over the scope and being thrashed around by a chimp like me—they really were supermen. I would also back things up in my head using range and bearing, and my skill at mental maths. Once I got contact in the Hornet though, the radar told me everything I needed to know instantly. Right—let me try and teach you intercepts in the Hornet then!

First things first is the display or scope. This was a classic B-scope so square shaped. Imagine a cheese wedge coming out of the nose of the jet—that is the shape the radar beam looks in, from 60 degrees left of the nose to 60 right. I can narrow the scan down to as little as 10 degrees to concentrate on one small area, but will probably leave it in a wide scan until I get contact on a target and then narrow the scan around it. If I narrow the scan down, I can actually move it off centre by using the cursor controller. I move the scanner up and down using the whirly-wheel I have mentioned already. Right, now take the point of the cheese wedge at your nose and 'pull' it out to both sides to give you a straight line that makes the flat bottom of the square B-scope. If I had a cheese wedge display, it would be more intuitive, but it would be difficult to see things close in as the wedge narrowed towards me. The B-scope skewed how the targets behaved on the display, but gave you a better picture close in. Assuming I can find the bloody target in the first place, I will see a box with a tail coming out of it. If the tail is pointing straight down vertically, it means the target is looking straight down his nose at me. Therefore, if he is on my radar centreline at the same time, he is pointing straight at me, and we are on a collision. If the aspect vector is pointing left of the vertical out of the bottom of the target, he is looking out of his left window at me. We then judge how many degrees that aspect vector is away from the vertical. If it is out of the left side of the box, he is a

90 left. The bottom left-hand corner of the box is a 45, and we eyeball it from there.

What I need to do is influence the intercept to turn him into a 20 left or right. Twenty aspect gives the radar missile such as Sparrow or AMRAAM a little bit of lateral movement in the sky which aids its tracking. It also gives a lot of closure head on which those missiles love, as there is lots of kinetic energy involved meaning it hits the target harder, and it has a lot more range due to that closure. If there are any weapons instructors reading that last bit and shaking their heads at the way I have simplified it, I have a message for them. Despite you delivering all those immensely boring weapons lectures and patting yourselves on the back at a job well done, most of us regular normal mortal pilots don't actually give a shit about the science of it. The rockets go whoooosh; they crash into stuff; and go bang—job done!

So how do I turn my target into a 20 left? It's all geometry of course, but rather than work it all out using maths, I can just fly the picture I see on the scope using the wonderful gift of collision. Let's say my target comes on the scope with a 30-left aspect. If I turn my aircraft to put that target at 30 right on the scope, I will have put them on a collision course. If I hold that heading, he will stay on collision and due to the anomaly of the expanded base of the B-scope, he will come all the way down the scope on the 30-degree line until we collide (assuming we are at the same height). He doesn't have to come to the middle of the bottom of the scope to hit me, because all of the bottom of a B-scope is me. Confused yet? B-scope theory is a whole hour or two of lecture so it is not surprising if you are. Are you happy to accept that some clever shit happens on a B-scope? Great—let's crack on. By the way, most of my radar technical knowledge on say PRFs, jamming, sensitivity etc. consists of 'clever shit happening'. I want to be able to use it, not build the bloody thing!

OK, I can shoot at a target that has a 30-left aspect, but it isn't the ideal shot, so I need to 'heat up' the intercept to turn him into a 20. The way I do this is by turning left to force him onto the right-hand side of the scope. As he gets closer to me, his aspect vector will move towards vertically down as I am beating him to the collision. In reality, he has to look closer to his nose to see me as it progresses. When his aspect vector has rotated to bang on a 20, I come back to the right to move him to 20 right on the scope (which puts him back on a collision) and hey presto! I have a 20 left aspect which will hold at 20 left while he is on collision at 20 right on the scope. Left and right are interchangeable here, and if I have to change a 10-aspect to a 20, I have to 'cool off' the intercept by smashing him to the opposite side of the scope compared to his aspect vector. Phew! Sounds complicated I know, but trust me, this was dead easy.

As we rage towards each other, I don't stare at the radar but flick my eyes through it and process the picture as I look in the HUD and outside the aircraft. I have put my cursor on the target and then inserted (pushed the cursor in, like clicking a mouse) to designate him as my priority target. This puts him under the trigger for an AMRAAM, but also gives me his heading, height, and speed at the bottom of the B-scope. I can shoot an AMRAAM from search mode on the radar (I will have to explain that later in a bit more detail), but for the Sparrow, I need to put the cursor on him and push again to lock him up. There were other ways of locking, but that will do for now. Either way, priority, or lock, I will get a square shape up in the HUD called the Target Designator box (TD box) that shows me where the target is visually. Obviously, at 30 miles away, I won't be able to see him, but it was a big help to get tally on an aeroplane from about 15 miles in.

The missiles and the radar computers do some more of that clever shit to tell me when I am in range to take the shot, and I get some symbology in the HUD and on the scope to help me get the best shot, and to give the missile the best chance. I would get a steering dot and an allowable steering error (ASE) circle (see QWIs? I do know some stuff!). Put the dot in the circle and when you see the 'IN LAR' caption flash in the HUD, pull the trigger and off she goes. I will talk about AMRAAM later, but with Sparrow, once I have taken the shot, I break out away from the target and put him right on the edge of the scope, then reverse the turn and nibble away at it keeping him on the edge as I convert to his stern. Switch to Sidewinder, get the tone and pull the trigger again to take that shot.

The break out is called the F-pole manoeuvre, and allows us to support the Sparrow through to impact whilst not getting too close to the target. It also generates some space for us to be able to turn in behind him and shoot him again. Right, the whole thing I have just described is called an attack reattack or ARA and this is what I am doing on the trip with Smiler.

The word asshole was invented just for him

Yes, back to Smiler. If it seems like I have said a lot about intercepts and not what happened on the actual trip, then it is because I got absolutely nothing out of Smiler. Even when we were holding and waiting for our turn, he wouldn't engage with me. Aside from that, he gave me no help, advice, encouragement or even criticism as I did ARA after ARA. I might have well have been solo. And this guy was an instructor? Maybe he was out of his depth? Maybe I was just awesome? (unlikely, I know). Maybe he was dead? Whatever it was, it rubbed me up the wrong way. Unfortunately, this turned out to be my longest Hornet ride so far at 1 hour 45.

On the way back to El Toro, I couldn't stop myself from poking the bear. I was in close formation with the other jets and needed to switch over my TACAN radio aids navigation kit to the Oceanside beacon. I knew the frequency was 100x (I remember it to this day because of what happened) so dialled it up. Smiler wasn't paying attention, and then I asked if he could dig the frequency out for me as I was a bit busy in close formation. Well, that did it. He raged about how I should know it or find it for myself etc. etc. much as he had about the waypoints on start-up. 'Already got it, mate,' I said, which obviously puzzled him. We broke into the circuit and I eased my beauty back onto the deck. The debrief was going to be interesting.

For some reason, we didn't bother with a formation debrief which was a bit odd. It was the first time I had flown in formation on the Hornet, so I was expecting a bit of critique, or at least an acknowledgement that three jets had flown in close proximity to each other, but no. It was straight into a one-on-one with the USMC's ray of sunshine. He opened up with a bollocking about me treating him like a WSO. Who did I think I was etc? Then a further bollocking about me not saluting the ground crew and how disrespectful it was to those Marines. I let him bluster for a bit more, but when he asked me why I didn't salute, I just calmly said, 'Queen's Regulations state I am not permitted to salute without a hat on.' His face went purple.

'You had a cover on!' The Americans called any headwear, including a flying helmet, a cover.

'A cover isn't a hat, Smiler.'

'Yes, it is!'

'Not according to QRs, mate. I'm happy to get a set sent out by the embassy if you like?' OK, I was being a bit of a dick, but I had seen below-average bullying instructors when I was a student, years before. Now that I was an experienced pilot and an instructor myself, and way more experienced than Smiler, I thought I would nip it in the bud. He was a bit nonplussed, and after only 10 minutes, he said we were done, and he went to leave.

'Hold on,' I said, 'are you going to debrief the intercepts?'

'Fuck that. It's 1730 and I am going home.'

Unbelievable. I stood up.

'We are not done here—sit down, as I've got a debrief for you.' I thought he was going to explode, but he meekly sat down and I tore into him about his performance as an instructor.

'We just flew for almost 2 hours together, during which you offered me nothing in terms of instruction, help, critique, or encouragement. I did five intercepts during the trip, none of which you can be bothered to debrief—not my geometry, radar handling, comms, weaponeering, nothing. In fact, we have debriefed for only 10 minutes and you used all that time to bollock me for treating you like a WSO when I asked you for help and you obviously have a bug up your ass about the saluting thing.'

I was on a roll then. I took him through my aborted trip with Weld and the fact that as an instructor, he should be able to recognise when to step in and help—if nothing else, to not hold the rest of the formation up. If all he could focus on after an intercept sortie was saluting the ground crew, then he either had his priorities wrong, or just wasn't up to the job of teaching and debriefing properly. I went on …

'And the Marines you said I was disrespecting? Those would be the same Marines you completely ignored while we were crewing in, would they? The Marines I was chatting to all the time? Here's the deal, mate. You are by far and away the worst instructor I have ever seen in any air force. I know this will never happen as you are just not good enough, but I would love you to get an exchange tour to a foreign air force, and then come up against an instructor like you on trip six. Weld is an instructor, Smiler. You are just an asshole, so if you could now just fuck off and leave me to debrief my own film, I would appreciate it. Now, we are done here.'

I turned away and slotted my video into the player so that I could run through my intercepts. By the time I had cued up the first one, Smiler had left me to myself. I am pretty sure the word 'asshole' was invented just for him.

I had two hops the following Monday, both of which were with great guys. I needed to bury the ghost of Smiler and also needed to get my head completely into flying. That might sound like an odd comment, but I had spent a lot of time over the weekend on my RAF ISS (individual study school) work. ISS was a service writing correspondence course that you had to do if you wanted to be promoted to squadron leader. Flaming hell, it was a tedious balls ache of a thing, but I had an ambition to return to the RAF as a flight commander on a fighter squadron so needed to get promoted. It was almost unheard of to return from exchange as a flight lieutenant and you just needed to have passed ISS part one to go in front of the promotion board, so long as you fit all the other criteria as well (which I did). Everything had to be hand written in the correct format for the document in question, and the range of different types of correspondence was mind-boggling. They each had different sizes of indents for paragraphs and headings, and it took hours to write one or two of these letters for each assignment. Having spent ages getting it right, or so I thought, I would post them off to the Admin Blunties who ran the school, and then weeks later, I would get them back in the post covered in red pen with 'must do better' or some such shit written on them. What I would have given to fly one of these knobs in the back of my Hornet, and then say 'must do better' to them as they puked their ring up. Ah bollocks—think of the promotion, Tug.

My next instructor put a smile on my face immediately. We were going off to fly a low-level navigation route. This was absolutely my bag as I had done loads of this on my Phantom tour in Germany, and also teaching it on the Hawk. In fact, low-level flying had been one of the only in-person lectures we had on ground school. It was given by a US Navy instructor called Beamer. He started by saying that overall, he had flown about 100 hours at low-level. He then asked me how many hours I had down there.

'Well, we don't log it as such Beamer, but at a guess I would say about a thousand?' His face creased into a huge grin and he asked me if I would help give the brief! At the end of his bit, I stood up and gave a few hints on general low-level flying and how to navigate down there. Of course, we would be using the kit and the moving map, but the basic techniques would still need to be used. Anyway, I had heard that quite a few of the instructors had requested to fly my low-level trips (no pressure on me then!) and Two Dogs must have won me in the lottery. He was brilliant in the brief, telling me we were just going to go out and have a bit of fun. Now, most of the callsigns I had heard, I either knew the story behind why the guys had them, or could work them out.

Callsigns were an American thing designed to help take the rank out of the cockpit, and in the USMC, they were either derogatory or just banter. I could not work out Two Dogs, so asked him on the way to the jet. With a big smile he said, 'Oh. I am part American Indian, Tug.' I stopped dead in my tracks and burst out laughing.

'You know the joke then, Tug?' he said, laughing also.

'That is just brilliant!' For those who don't know the old joke he was referring to, here it is:

In days of old, when a child was born into an American Indian tribe, the mother would walk out of the tent and name the child after the first thing she saw, So, White Cloud; Running Horse; Two Dogs Fucking.

After I stopped crying with laughter, we crewed in and had a very pleasant time flying a low-level route up to Palm Springs and the Death Valley area. The navigation was easy using the kit, and the route was a set piece which we flew in glorious weather—somewhat different from punting around in the gloom and the clag of the UK. All low-level routes in the US were pre-planned so it was just a case of printing off a copy of the right map from the planning system and you were good to go. Plug in the waypoints to the nav kit including Time on Targets or ToTs, and just blast airborne. I hated planning maps, but felt a bit uncomfortable doing it this way. Yes, the hatred never went away, but actually physically planning the map helped me to build awareness and study the route whilst I drew it, so I knew it was a good thing to do. Anyway, the kit worked perfectly, and my own back-up nav techniques weren't too dulled off by this stage, so all in all it was a very pleasant trip.

In the afternoon, I finally got to fly an intercept trip of high to low ARAs with Weld. He was as good in the air as he was on the ground and gave me all sorts of tips throughout the sortie. He then debriefed my intercepts properly, drawing them up on the board from the notes we had both made in the air, before putting the tape in to verify what he had just debriefed. This was the normal fighter pilot sequence of events. Even though the Hornet had a video recording facility, proper fighter crews make notes after every intercept, then try to reconstruct them in diagram form on the whiteboard in the debrief. We do the same with air combat fights too. Once we have it all drawn up, we then put the tape in to check radar handling, comm and weapons shots. The Hornet had a full-sized VHS style video recorder behind the seat in a straight, and in a recess behind the cockpits on the left-hand side of the jet in a tub. It would record all of the comm and either the HUD or the B-scope. Towards the end of the intercept, I would have to switch the recording up to the HUD just before it turned into a visual fight.

It was a delight to watch an accomplished fighter pilot and instructor do his thing properly and actually teach me. This was only my second intercept trip, but I had done seven intercept trainers by then so was handy on the radar for these simple academic events. Weld tightened up my radar handling with some subtle changes and declared me more than fit to have a go at it solo. I had another trip the following day back at low-level, but this time using the air-to-ground radar for nav and targeting. After that, it was back on the ground for a week. My next trip was going to be a full-on snogging session with Miss Hornet 1995—I just didn't know it right then.

Remember I told you there were two arsehole instructors? We did the joy of Smiler earlier, and now we come up against Sneak. Sneak had everything going for him. Single-seat Hornet pilot; very capable; perfect muscular build; handsome; wraparound teeth. The only thing that was missing? A personality. He acted so superior and most of the other instructors seemed to avoid him. No way he would demean himself and talk to any of the students. Thankfully, I never had to fly with him, but I did come across him that weekend in a restaurant. My wife and I decided it was time for us to have a night out without Holly, so we booked the babysitter that Alf's family used and headed to a local Italian restaurant. When I say local, what I mean to say is it was just down the road, so we walked to it. We were petrified of leaving Holly the first time so didn't want to drive across town. As we arrived at the restaurant, our table wasn't ready so we headed to the bar. Unfortunately, Sneak was there with his wife and it was one of those awkward moments where he didn't want to see me and vice-versa. I held out my hand for him to shake and introduced him to my wife. Nothing was forthcoming until his wife saw us and asked who we were.

'Er, this is Tug. He is just one of the students', I heard him say. Sod that! He wasn't getting away with calling me just a student. I reached past him to shake her hand and said, 'Actually, I am the RAF exchange pilot.' It turned out that she was US Navy herself, and she asked what I had flown. When I said the Phantom, she got very excited as her father had been a USMC Phantom pilot in Vietnam. While my wife and I spoke to her, Sneak was a bit isolated and we made no effort to make things easier for him. Thankfully, our tables were ready shortly afterwards. No way Sneak was going to get an invite to our next 3rd of July party.

Come and live here Tug—you know you want to

Actually, it would turn out that nobody at El Toro would get an invite, as it was announced that we would be moving to Miramar after the RAG. Miramar! TOPGUN! Living in San Diego? You must be kidding me? It would mean going through the whole rigmarole of finding another house, but who cares? San Diego! Around this point, it was time for Alf and his family to depart for the UK. He had a final massive BBQ at his house in Laguna Hills and that was that. He had been promoted to squadron leader and was heading back to fly the Tornado F3. So, it was time for me to step up and take his place. If only I could get the bloody RAG finished. I had been in the US six months and was less than half way through my course! I needed to take some action here. The other thing about Alf leaving was that it brought it home to me how quickly this tour was going to go. One minute he was flying the greatest dogfighting aeroplane in the world (I might have mentioned that already). An exotic belly dancer of a jet, and the next, he was going to be sitting in an F3—the spindly wheezy kid who was shit on school sports day. I had better enjoy my love affair while I could. My next trip was the stuff of dreams for a fighter pilot. I walked out to my jet to find it was a straight. My first ever trip in a real single-seat aircraft. I had flown solo may times, but always with another empty seat behind me or next to me. This was the real thing, man!

Bloody hell it looked amazing. I lovingly ran my hand along the radome, as was my habit, and then marvelled at the fact there was a ton of room behind my seat where the video recorder was. There was always talk of Hornet pilots securing their golf clubs in there whenever they went 'on the road' (flying off for the weekend somewhere). This was a regular occurrence in the US, where squadrons would send jets on the road to do sorties over the weekend. You could basically plan to go anywhere you fancied in the country, so long as you banged in three trips a day. This was a bit like the Ranger trips we used to do on the Phantom. Take a couple of jets away in Europe for the weekend. The difference with us was, we got to our destination on a Friday, put the jets to bed, got shitfaced, and didn't see the jets again until Monday morning when we flew back, hungover. Most of my course mates had been on the road already, picking up the formation and intercept trips that had been crossed out on my programme. As the course progressed, it appeared that a lot more red crosses were turning up on my line. That's because I was so frustrated with my slow progress, that I had crossed a load of boxes out myself one night when everyone had gone home, to hurry things along. How the hell I got away with it, I will never know, but thank God that I did. There is a good chance I would still be there if I hadn't.

Back to my beautiful jet. Having stroked it like some creepy old man, it was down to business and out for a pairs formation take off. I had done one of these dual before and off we went with me acting like an excited schoolboy as two frankly awesome straights pierced the El Toro morning. All of my euphoria at being in a straight for the first time vanished as I concentrated on getting the intercepts sorted. They were a combination of all altitudes and once again, the radar picture was so easy to interpret, they went like a dream. Bear in mind they were only 1 vs 1 intercepts and it would be a different thing altogether with more than one target, but we all have to start somewhere.

My best friend Mitch, who I had met on day one of our air force careers ten years previously, and had gone through the whole of flying training with, was coming to stay with us for the weekend. He had brought his girlfriend out to the West Coast for a touring holiday and was making good on the promise he made to come out and see us. Mitch had made that promise after I had flown with him on my last Hawk trip as an instructor at RAF Valley. Before we could meet and reminisce though, I had one more trip to knock off. Bloody night flying. This would be my first night trip in the F-18 and it was supposed to be a 2-hour extravaganza all over Southern California and into Nevada. As I have always said, I had a love/hate relationship with night flying. When it was good (clear nights) it was very, very good, but when it was bad (most nights in the UK) it was horrid. Fortunately, I was flying with an instructor who hated flying in the back at night, so we hatched a plan that rather than doing the 2-hour bore-ex, we would do a practice diversion down the coast to Miramar, for some night circuits to 'familiarise me with the station I was moving to.' Great plan, and after several instrument approaches and circuits, we plonked it back down at El Toro after only an hour and went home. Now that's the way to do night flying. I have to say though, that night was crystal clear and it was gobsmacking to see the almost radioactive glow of all the lights up in Los Angeles; the relatively dark area all down through Orange County and the USMC Camp Pendleton training area; and finally, the bright lights of San Diego beckoning me. 'Come and live here, Tug—you know you want to.'

I was going bloody bombing!

That was it for the week, and so we got ready for Mitch's visit. He and his girlfriend Maggie were the first of many of our friends and family to take advantage of us living in California, and we loved having visitors come out to see us and stay. They had driven to us directly from a couple of nights in the Yosemite Valley. It sounded spectacular and we made a plan to go there ourselves while we were on the posting. Mitch's girlfriend then told him to 'tell the story.' Apparently, they were later than planned when they got to Yosemite so Mitch had been driving like a maniac to get to the top of a specific road climb. Maggie had been berating him for rallying up the narrow dangerous hill and was in a bit of a mood with him and had stopped talking to him. They got to the top of the hill and Mitch got Maggie to get out and look at the sunset with him. Still in a bad mood, she reluctantly agreed that it looked amazing, but not enough to fully forgive him for almost killing them. Then he went down on one knee, held out an engagement ring, and proposed to her!

That was Mitch all over. An eye for the occasion; a true romantic; and always doing things better than me! Can't fully recall how I proposed, but I'm sure it involved lots of alcohol. Speaking of which, we cracked some fizz and celebrated with the betrothed. We made the most of the weekend with them as I knew that the following week was bringing with it the abject horror of the strike phase which meant I was going bloody bombing. OK, I knew I was flying a multi-role aeroplane, but at heart, I was a traditional fighter pilot. Intercepts and air combat were my bag. Bombing was for pilots who couldn't hit a moving target. Shove something big on the ground for them to aim at and let them fling iron at it all day. Bomber pilots—easily pleased, the lot of them.

The Strike phase would begin with pure academic bombing over at the air-to-ground range at El Centro. How to describe El Centro? Hmmm. It is in California, but I am sure that any self-respecting Californian will try and palm you off by telling you it is in Arizona. It is an embarrassing shit hole of a place, or at least it was in the 1990s. It might be a beautifully regenerated paradise these days, but if I was a betting man, I would guess that it is probably still the piles on the arsehole of the universe. Not a fan—can you tell? There was a naval air facility there, but you would do anything to avoid landing there just in case the jet broke and you got stuck. The range was about 10 miles north-ish as far as I remember, and my first trip there would see me dropping 26-pound practice bombs on the bombing circle, or somewhere near it, knowing me.

There was a big square box (maybe an ISO container, although it could have been a tank for all I know) in the middle, and then a series of concentric circles radiating out from it. I had been allowed to look at the ground school for the procedures at the range, and for what was called the 'Course Rules' for NAF El Centro (stuff that we would put in an airfield Flying Order Book in the RAF). This meant I knew how to join and depart and generally conduct myself in the area, but I wasn't allowed to see any of the weapons symbology. As usual, the sim instructors were brilliant with me, and taught me all I needed to know to set up the weapons on the stores page and interpret and use the HUD symbology. There was an extra element to bombing though, and that was the Z-diagrams (rhymed with tea rather than head—Americans huh?). These were all in the manuals and detailed things like dive angle, release height, minimum height etc. for the dive procedure. There was a Z-diagram for every weapon and every type of delivery. The Z-diagram was briefed up as part of the sortie brief, which made the fact that I was not officially allowed to see them even more laughable.

We were heading off as a 3-ship with us as number 2. As with all academic bombing, we set up a circuit around the target with a long run in to perform a 15-degree dive pattern straight ahead onto the target. All well and good, but this first trip would see us carrying out a manual run and then finish off with runs using Continuously Computed Impact Point (CCIP). I can barely remember the manual run thank God. I had done manual bombing in the Hawk, and in my case, my technique was close your eyes, hold your nose, and fling the bomb somewhere in the general direction. The score could be a direct hit (DH) or it could land in another county altogether. The joy of bombing.

CCIP used a bit of kit, and when you selected it a vertical-ish bomb fall line would appear in the HUD. Prior to this, I had to select CCIP on the stores page on the left DDI and then select A-G and Master Arm to live (a button and a switch to the left of that DDI). Crossing the vertical fall line was a small horizontal line called the release cue. Once I dived towards the target, the release cue would move down the fall line and then turn into a cross at the bottom of that line. You would then run the cross (correcting for left and right) up through the target and then 'pickle' the bomb off as the cross went through the target, using the bomb release button on the top of the stick. You then get another DH or it flies into … sorry, already done that.

My CCIP stuff was ok and certainly more accurate than any bomb I had ever dropped in the Hawk. You had to take into account crosswind on the run-in; try and pickle the bomb when your wings were level; and look at the target to pickle rather than the cross. It's a peripheral vision thing apparently. We are quicker at processing peripheral vision, so if you concentrate on the cross, by the time you process that it is on the target, it is too late and you pickle long. Shit—I hate bombing.

Do you mean cheat, Chuck?

The Marines all shouted 'Shack!' on the radio if they got a DH and there was a healthy amount of rivalry between everyone when it came to scores. All in all, despite it being El Centro and bombing in general, I had an almost pleasant time of it. Once again, the Americans had injected some fun into something the RAF made you miserable while doing. The day after, I flew my next Strike mission with a guy called Chuck. He was awesome. Built like a big thing where people go to defecate, he had a mile-wide smile constantly plastered on his face. He told me he had been trying to get programmed with me for ages and was keen to go on the road with me. Had I been staying on the RAG as an instructor, I could see that Chuck would have been an excellent squadron mate. We were also on the same page. He saw himself as a fighter pilot who sometimes needed to drop bombs. My kind of guy.

This trip would see us using the automatics in the system. The first attack, I would use the auto-designation system. Same set up as before, but instead of using CCIP, I would push on the castle switch on the stick top, and it would put a dot in the middle of the aircraft symbol in the HUD. Put the dot on the target and hit the pickle button. That dropped a diamond around the dot on the target and gave a fall line and release cue. Hold the pickle button down and when the release cue got to the aircraft symbol, the bomb got released. By the way, if you are bored with all the bomb symbology explanations above, I feel your pain, OK? Remember that I am still in the academic phase here. Later on in the book when I am dropping all sorts of stuff, I will just say 'the bomb went off', or something like that. Even I am losing the will to live right now.

Now, once I have designated the target and have the diamond in the HUD, I can refine that designation using my cursor controller. That updates the fall line and the release cue to increase the accuracy of the bomb. As a bit of competition within the formation, the leader has briefed that there would be no refining on the first run to see who got the best bomb from the first designation. Chuck re-briefed me afterwards.

'Tell you what, Tug. How about you just refine the designation anyway so we win the best bomb competition.'

'Do you mean cheat, Chuck?' I asked.

'Yep!'

Like I said—my kind of guy. Of course, we won best bomb, but somehow our video tape 'didn't seem to record', and we got away with it. I was starting to get a bit of continuity with two trips coming up the next day. I was the kind of pilot that needed continuity to help consolidate all of the learning, and drive it into my brain. The stop-start nature of the RAG was not ideal, but by this stage of my career, I should have been able to handle it. Not flying allowed all of the imposter syndrome doubts to surface, with me constantly wondering if I would be able to do it when I finally got back into the air.

Two Dogs took me back to the range and we bombed using the full designation slew function which Chuck and I had cheated with on the last trip. Each time I moved the diamond with my left index finger, the bombing solution was updated and the bomb fell off as the release cue reached the aeroplane symbol. A 4G pull had us recovering from 15- and 30-degree dives before we levelled off downwind in the pattern for another go. My scores were getting better and I was in real danger of actually enjoying this bombing lark. We couldn't have that though. A few nights later would see the Marine Corps ripping all of the joy out of bombing and replace it with a pant-shittingly scary horror story of a trip—night dive bombing.

To prepare me for that abomination, my pleasant 'mates' trip with Two Dogs was followed by a solo trip of night formation flying. I hadn't done any of the official formation trips in the programme (not ones I had crossed off myself—before you ask), so had picked up the techniques and positions ad hoc on my intercept trips. Close formation is the same in any aircraft. Move forwards, then up, then in to position, followed by tiny inputs on stick and throttle to anticipate the leader's turns and vertical movements. Yeah? How about bounce up and down on the wing while thrashing the controls all over the cockpit and trying to saw the throttles through the console. And while you do that, remember to hyperventilate, sweat, and generally shit yourself. And the first time you do it at night? Do it bloody solo, Tug.

Beamer hadn't drawn the short straw

At least we got airborne in the daylight and logged 30 minutes before it got proper dark. The pairs' take off was nice and smooth, but to formate and manoeuvre with a jet that still took my breath away just to look at it, well ... Sometimes I look back on things and wish I could have just relaxed, looked out of the window, and absorbed how totally flippin' brilliant it was flying these futuristic machines. Unfortunately, I was never that good to be able to do that! As it got darker and darker, I dug in and concentrated on being as smooth as I could with my jet, hoping that she would appreciate how hard I was trying to make this a pleasant experience for the both of us. When I say pleasant, what I mean is not horrendously alarming. We carried out a couple of pairs approaches and then split for individual instrument approaches to land. As happy as I was to get my sorry ass back on the ground, I knew that the next hop was even closer.

That weekend, we rented a big party boat at the lake and had Muck and his family and Indy over. The boat was loaded with booze and food and we cruised around the lake for a couple of hours. We cruised around the lake a lot as it happened, because it wasn't very big at all so 2 hours was a long time. Despite that, it was sunny and relaxed, and we marvelled at the millionaires' row of houses up on the quiet side of the lake. Once we were done with the boat, we disembarked and saw the evening out swimming in the lake and having the inevitable BBQ. I had got to know Indy and Muck a fair bit by then and we were already forming a strong bond between us. They had just heard that they were going to be posted to VMFA (AW)-121 Squadron at Miramar when 242 deployed abroad. That meant I would be joining 121 also. Another thing I learned that day was how good a swimmer Indy was. He scythed through the water like a greased dolphin, and when I asked where he had learned to swim like that, he casually announced that he had been in the GB junior team or some such and used to train with Sharon Davies and the Olympic squad! He was so modest that I knew he wouldn't have mentioned it if I hadn't asked. Me? I would have had a t-shirt with 'Oy! I swim for Britain, you know', to go with my astronaut t-shirt.

OK, let's get it over with—night bombing. How does this sound for a stupid plan? Take four Hornets and put one instructor in the lead with three solo students. Launch them at night and make them fly in close formation to the range. Then set up a screaming Jesus 30-degree dive pattern and bomb onto the target which was only illuminated by a mouse with a head torch (not far from the truth) with only a faint crucifix of cheap lights around it to show you the attack direction line. Separation from the other three jets is done purely on a bit of timing, radio calls, and the odd flash of anti-collision lights. The fact that I thought it was mad wasn't the worst thing in all of that. No, it was the fact that the instructor leading us was absolutely shitting himself in the brief that really got me worried.

Beamer hadn't drawn the short straw. All the straws had gone by the time he drew and so he was stuck with us. We were all a bit bemused as he stumbled his way through the brief and told us how 'fucking dangerous' the hop was at least four or five times. I could only wonder what the ab-initio guys were thinking at that point. It didn't help that Beamer was 'dipping' throughout the brief to help calm his nerves. Dipping was the foulest most disgusting habit I had ever seen. Basically, it was chewing tobacco, although rather than chomp through a big chunk of sticky brown shit, the guys would carry a small tin of shredded/powdered tobacco and take a big pinch and wedge it between the front of their bottom gum and the lip. You would see them walking around with a lump at the front of their mouths as if they had stuck their tongue in there. OK, so far, no drama. However, the tobacco would help to produce a ton of saliva which had to be disposed of. Too disgusting to swallow so why not spit it out? Where you may ask? How about into a clear plastic bottle so that everyone can see your horrible brown spit with flecks of tobacco floating in it? Hell's bells, it is making me wretch just writing about it. A lot of the Marines I met dipped. Beamer was going for it big style in the brief and had almost filled a half-litre bottle by the end of it. Maybe he was hoping to keel over from tobacco poisoning before having to fly the trip from hell?

The mouse with the head torch had fucked off for the night

There was no last-minute reprieve, and the four of us trudged out to the jets like condemned men. I was number four again. I think they thought that being a bit more experienced, I should be able to play catch up a little better when it came to joining in close formation at night. We took off at 10 second intervals from both runways and I marvelled as number 3 rolled and his burners lit up the world around me. There is a temptation to look directly at the burners of the guy in front of you, they are so seductive, but that destroys your night vision for about 30 seconds. I shielded my eyes and watched 3 roll. Ten seconds later, a distinctly worried British exchange officer slammed the throttles through to the very loudest setting, and blasted airborne into the dark, the unknown, and the downright dangerous.

I picked up the guys ahead of me on radar and used it to close in smartly. Fast enough to get us all together as one unit, but not too fast that I didn't get eyes on all three of them as I joined. We transited to El Centro again in a loose finger four formation with 2 and 3 on each of the leader's wings, and me outside number 3. In the daytime, El Centro looked like a nuclear wasteland in the desert. At night? No idea. I couldn't see a stinking thing. Beamer checked us in with the range and after a bit of manoeuvring, he called us into echelon starboard (it might have been echelon right in those days in the US, but I love saying port and starboard, so let's go with that). Number 3 and I moved across outside 2 and we tightened up into echelon. 'Not too close though!' Beamer had briefed. It might have been a little loose, but I was number 4 so was on the end of the whip of any movements by the others. Did I mention all of this is happening at night? In the pitch bloody black?

Beamer called that he was breaking downwind and we followed at suitable intervals to make the spacing work. As I broke and climbed downwind, I was vaguely aware of Beamer calling, 'in hot,' as he was in the dive for his first run. By the time I turned onto attack heading, the pattern was formed and I looked out for the lead-in lights of the crucifix. Well, the RSO was obviously in energy saving mode as it appeared he hadn't turned the lights up to full. So, while trying to find the target, do my weapons switches, listen to the radio, call 'in hot,' sight the symbology onto the target and get the bomb off, I can guess you can picture what an absolute shit storm it was?

I eventually got an idea of the crucifix, but as far as I could tell, the mouse with the head torch had fucked off for the night and I was bombing an arbitrary black area vaguely in between a large badly lit crucifix of lights. The bombs had flash charges in them so the RSO could score them. He needn't have bothered. Hurtling towards the ground at 400 knots in a 30-degree dive put paid to any thoughts of accuracy or discipline, or anything other than just not crashing into the wasteland. After my second run, I had the capacity to look out of the window when I was downwind to see the other guys' bombs flash randomly in the big black void, and sometimes nowhere near it. I finally slung my last bomb off somewhere or other and we regrouped as a formation for the transit back to El Toro. Beamer wasn't going to push his luck so he split us off one by one into the instrument pattern, and a PAR talkdown saw me land safely having survived the craziest trip I had ever flown in my life.

Beamer was a different man in the debrief. He was positively euphoric at all of us having cheated death. The last thing he wanted to do was debrief any of our films, so I have no idea if my bombing technique was any good or not. I had no desire to prolong the agony either so I put the top down on my Mustang and drove home with the balmy night air blowing in my face, wondering if the last 3 hours of my life had really happened. Unfortunately, they had, and I will be forever scarred by the experience. However, the poor bastard who flew with me on the next trip is still in therapy last I heard.

Those Assholes!

The next three hops were right up my street. Low altitude training or LAT for short. These flights included very low flying and manoeuvring, as well as three-dimensional patterns to simulate SAM defensive moves. As I have already said, we practically lived at low-level in the RAF, and I had taught a lot of low flying myself. The instructors on the RAG expected me to be good at it, so there was a bit of pressure on, but I was really looking forward to doing something I was extremely comfortable with. Chips, my instructor, was a relatively young US Navy guy and he immediately told me that he had only just qualified as a LAT instructor, and I was to be his first student. He was very precise in the brief, if a little nervous, and we whooshed off to R-2507 to do our thing. LAT is conducted on the numbers, very strictly. By that I mean there were procedural hoops to jump through for every one of the dynamic manoeuvres we carried out, starting with how to descend into low-level. From memory, I think the rule was that whatever altitude you were at, you could only descend with one percent of nose down. For example, passing 3,000 feet, your maximum dive angle would be 30 degrees. As you pass 2,000 feet though, you have to make a positive adjustment up to 20 nose down and so on. Each time you passed through a gate like that, you had to say it out loud in the cockpit. 'Passing 3,000 for 1,000, 30 nose down', or some banter like that.

Initially, it seemed a bit noddy to me, but I have to say that from a safety point of view, it definitely worked. First job was to descend to 100 feet. Wow! I had lived at 250 feet in an aeroplane, but 100 feet was ballsy given that the Americans did very little low-level. I have to confess that I had flown at 100 feet or below quite a lot during my Phantom detachments to the Falkland Islands (all of it horribly illegal), so I knew what it looked like. Bloody low, if you were wondering? We always used to joke about mud-moving squadrons having to do a long work-up of operational low flying (OLF) to get down to 100 feet, whereas you did it in one trip in the Falklands!

I did all the correct mouth music to Chips and finally settled us down at 100 feet. We were in the desert so didn't really get any impression of stuff whizzing past us, but I did notice Chips breathing a bit faster. OK, once we were down there, it was time for some turns and this is where it all started to go wrong. Chips asked for a 4G turn to the right rolling out heading west. I had to repeat the instruction to him, then he said, 'Go!' and I put the jet on its side, and squeezed to 4G. For any newcomers to fast-jet aviation, this is how we turn the jet at 420 knots—by pulling it around the corner. At that speed, just a bit of right stick is not going to have a huge effect. Once you get the jet on its side and pull, it rages around the corner. As soon as I pull, I look out of the top of the canopy to see where we are going, and Chips lost it. 'I have control!' he shouted and he took the stick, levelled the wings, and pulled up to 1,000 feet. 'Terminate!' he shouted. I figured there was something wrong with the jet, but he just gave me control again and told me to step down to 100 feet. I asked him what was wrong, but the poor guy was just hyperventilating. We went through the same procedure and once again, he took control from me and pulled up. I had no idea what the hell was going on.

'Is everything OK, Chips?' I asked.

'What are you doing with your head?'

'How do you mean?'

'Where are you looking?'

'Out the top of the canopy mate, to see where we are going?'

More hyperventilating. He then calmed down enough to tell me that he needed me to only look in a scan from the top of the HUD sight glass up to the canopy arch while doing the turns, so we didn't crash into the ground.

'Sorry Chips, but by the time we process that, we have already been there.' I pointed out of the top of the canopy. 'That is where we are going and we need to clear that airspace before we go into it.'

'Just do what I said, OK?'

We try another turn with me just looking at the scan he briefed, but this time, I pulled up.

'Sorry Chips, but I can't physically do it. It's too uncomfortable and frankly, dangerous.'

This put us at an impasse, but I managed to convince him to let me try my own thing, and if he wasn't happy with how I was doing, we could knock it all off and head home.

So, with Chips using up heartbeats like you read about, I settled down and blasted around at 100 feet like I was born for it. My head was on a swivel. Out the top of the canopy, scan the HUD, top of the canopy, scan the HUD, and so on. Chips relaxed a little to only mildly alarmed as he saw that I knew what I was doing (a first for me) and after an hour of fun for me and horror for him, I put us on the ground at Yuma for the first time. LAT used the gas very quickly so the first hop was split into two with a land away at Yuma in Arizona. Yuma was close to R-2507 and had the AV8B based there. This was the Marine version of the Harrier. Funny thing with the AV8B—in the RAF, we used to send our very best students to the Harrier as it was very intense to fly and operate. The best students in the Marine Corps were sent to the Hornet with the also-rans going to the AV8B. Little wonder that the safety record on the AV8A (the B's predecessor) was shocking.

Enough of that though. After clearing the runway at Yuma, I popped the canopy up to taxi in and the 110-degree fire slapped me in the face. God help us, it was hot there! However, working on the old fighter pilot attitude of 'always taxi with the canopy up (because you can)', I braved the heat and trundled along the taxiway doing my after-landing checks. The canopy rails in the F-18 angled slightly downwards from rear to front, and it was cool to rest your forearms on them as you taxied in. Foolishly, I had rolled the sleeves up on my flying suit as soon as I had popped the canopy, and in the short time it had been open, the metal canopy rails had heated up to hotplate temperature. Thinking I looked like Joe Cool in front of all the below-average Harrier mates, I rested my arms on the rails and then yelped like a stuck pig as my forearms burnt on the hotplates. I am sure Chips would have bantered me had he been paying attention, but it was almost like he had retreated into a happy place.

He looked a little ashen when we crewed out and said he had to go and telephone the squadron to get some advice. Crikey, it looked like I was going to fail the trip over what I saw as a fundamental basic of low-level flying. Not sure where this was going to leave me as there was no way I could train myself out of a black-and-white safety issue such as that. Chips had a different look on his face when he came back from his call. 'Those assholes!' he said. I looked a bit puzzled. 'They knew what was going to happen. That's why they put me up with you!' By all accounts, the experienced LAT instructors had paired Chips with me in order to put the frighteners on him for his first LAT trip. The upshot was that they told him to just hold on for the ride on the second trip, and he would be OK with me. The second trip included all of the three-dimensional stuff seeing me pull up, bank hard left or right (whichever he called for), and then stepping back down to 100 feet in the prescribed manner. Chips held his breath as my head flashed around the cockpit, but was good enough to keep quiet and not scream. I can only imagine how relieved he was to get back on deck at El Toro. I was humming in both senses of the word. Totally exhilarated with the flying, but stinking like the Devil's crotch after two sweaty trips and an hour on the ground in the Yuma furnace.

A few of the instructors were howling with laughter when they saw the look of pure fury on Chips's face, and I was included in the banter. They all asked me how scared he was and then all wanted to do my next LAT trips. For the first time on this tour, I felt as though I had made my mark and impressed a few people. With any luck, I would be able to do the same thing on the air combat sorties. Got to finish the bloody bombing phase first though.

The bloody bombing phase got bloody brilliant from then on. In just one week, I did the strafe trip I wrote about earlier; dropped a couple of inert 1,000-pound bombs (no bang); low pop-up attacks at 15-degree dive angle; hi-pops in full burner to 45-degree dive; pairs section pops; and a couple of LAT hops. Seven trips in five days and every single one of them, solo. I was in heaven. Not only were the trips amazing in themselves, the fact that I was trusted to do them on my own on the first go, was just awesome. Pop attacks had us running in at low-level and then canting off to the right of the run-in heading by 30 degrees (might have been 45—I forget) before pitching up and then rolling into a wingover left to set up a 15-degree dive attack. Quick designation and refine, and off went the bomb. 4G recovery, then let back down to low-level and back into the pattern. These trips were relentless with no time to relax—I was lapping it up. The hi-pop had us banging it into burner and climbing up to about 12,000 feet to turn into a 45-degree dive. The steeper the dive angle, the more accurate the bomb. Ballistics (no need to be like that) apparently.

The Holy Shit Stuka Trip!

Dropping the thousand pounders was something else. They were released from the pylons with explosive bolts, and the jet shuddered a bit when they went. Big bombs landed pretty much where you aimed them. Ballistics again, and even though they were inert with no explosives, they made a bit of a nuisance of themselves when they hit the ground. Do you know what? I almost feel like I should tell you the strafing story again, it was such a gobsmacking trip, but I finished the week with the solo LAT which was no more than a 1 hour 20 minute dream of Tug's low-level extravaganza benefit concert. While I thrashed around on my own, I was shadowed and watched by an instructor in another jet, calling out the manoeuvres on the radio to me. It was the best week of flying I think I ever had, and every single bit of it was ground attack. I think my new love was trying to tempt me with forbidden fruit. A couple more days should see off this temporary infatuation I had with my bomb-laden beauty, and then we would hit the heights of unadulterated ecstasy together in the air combat arena.

We had started to scope out areas around Miramar to live. La Jolla and Del Mar were way too expensive, and areas like Mira Mesa, which were close to the air base were a bit run down and too damn hot in summer, being inland. Indy was going to be moving to Mission Beach about 20 minutes south of Miramar and much closer to San Diego, so we narrowed our search down in that area. I would have a couple of weeks after the end of the RAG to move down there before I started on 121 so we tried to get ahead of the game a little bit. Meanwhile, the Lake had put on a series of open-air concerts, and that weekend we went to see Tom Jones of all people. I doubt Tom had even heard of Mission Viejo, but there he was nonetheless, banging out the classics while women threw their knickers onto the stage. The average age of the women doing the throwing was a fair bit older than in Tom's heyday, so some of the knickers were on the large side. We were definitely going to miss the luxury and ease of the Lake, but if we could swap it for the beach, then that was no bad deal. San Diego was one of the most desirable cities in the US to live and would be completely different to the huge commuter style development of Mission Viejo. We would also be permanent members of a front-line squadron as opposed to me being 'just a student' (thank you, Sneak) which would change our social dynamic too.

As dreams of beach living filled our heads, I had the utter delight of the air defence and air combat phases on the horizon in the best dogfighter of the lot. I just had to clear the ultimate test of air-to-ground expertise—close air support—the bread and butter of the Marine Corps. I had two CAS trips on the RAG and I wasn't looking forward to either of them. I'm not sure if there was a dual trip with an instructor in the syllabus, but if there was, I must have crossed it out by accident. Maybe 101 assumed I had done it before, being a low-level God (I wish!), but I was staring at two solo hops, so in at the deep end again. There were two other bombing missions to complete before I got to CAS. First up was radar bombing which I did with Rocky. If you could picture the classic Marine, it would be Rocky. High and tight haircut, square head, compact muscle man, extremely confident. He was a good instructor and took me through the air-to-ground features of the radar. We would run in to the target and highlight it with the radar. Once we had contact, we would select Expand 1 which magnified the picture on the screen allowing us to refine the designation more accurately. There was an Expand 2 function which magnified even further, but as far as I recall, this painted a synthetic picture of the target rather than the raw radar. I might be wrong on that, but take it from me, I only did radar bombing twice during my whole tour, and used Expand 1 and 2 purely to try and paint my car in the car park at Miramar when I was bored on recovery. Any Tornado bomber pilots reading this will wail in frustration that all of that neat Gucci kit was wasted on me. What can I say? You are absolutely right.

Having flung my radar designated bombs all over the circle at El Centro, it was time to try high-altitude bombing with a 60-degree dive angle. I like to call this the 'Holy Shit Stuka' trip! This one should have been a whole lot of fun as it included steep angle strafe as well. Unfortunately, the XO was leading us and he had a major bug up his ass in the brief for some reason. He was less than impressed that I didn't have all the answers to his questions, but after once again pointing out that I wasn't allowed to read anything due to my security status (the very status he had promised to sort out in a week about twenty weeks prior), he seemed to get even more annoyed that he had to teach the British moron from scratch. He was also on the backs of my course mates, so much so that we were all frowning at each other, wondering what the hell was going on. So, we dutifully followed NATO's angriest man out to the flight line and crewed in. As I popped my video tape into the recorder, I had no idea what a problem it was going to cause me later. Transit to R-2507 went smoothly, and the XO called us into echelon and broke over the tank column he had selected in the brief to be our target.

It can be a total shit show

The 60-degree dive was the ride of my life, and it was so exhilarating that my bomb sighting went to shit and I slung my first bomb into Mexico it seemed. It looked like a 4G pull wasn't going to crack it so I squeezed a lot harder on the stick, losing much more speed than planned which then screwed up my pattern and spacing from everyone else. I fought hard to get back on parameters and my next bomb could probably be described as 'in the vicinity'. The last two worked as advertised and then bang—we were straight into the strafe runs. High-angle strafe. How the hell do I describe how orgasmic that was? There are no words, folks. Even today, I can't come up with anything that will come close to describing it. Once again, my beautiful Hornet had shown me that fantasy was now my reality, and all I had to do was hold on for the ride.

As I crewed out from the ride of my life, I tried to remove my video tape, to find that the door on the recorder was jammed. The ground crew tried to help, but it was stuck good and proper. I figured it was only a small problem meaning I would have no film in the debrief (thank God, given my first two runs), but alas no. The recorder was unbolted from the aircraft and I had to accompany it to the maintenance shed so it could be dismantled and the tape removed. I wasn't allowed to let it out of my sight as the tapes were secret and we had to sign them out from ops. I sent word to the XO that I would be delayed for the debrief, but had no idea it would take a full 50 minutes to get the damn tape out. Unfortunately, when it came out, the tape was destroyed, so I wrapped it up and wandered back to the squadron. This was going to be interesting. I walked into the debrief holding what looked like a badly wrapped birthday present, and sat down with the XO glaring at me.

'Sorry about that, Sir. The tape jammed.' It was stating the bleedin' obvious given that I was holding about 30 feet of magnetic ribbon, and I am sure that my two course mates were happy that the heat was off them for a short while. That didn't last long though as Mister Angry snatched their tapes from them and proceeded to systematically destroy them with the precision of a blunt instrument. Every dive attack had a ton of mistakes in his eyes, and my two colleagues were machine-gunned with criticism—none of it constructive.

From what I could tell, my first two attacks would have sent him into apoplexy, so I scrunched the ribbons of my tape in my hands when he wasn't looking, just to make sure it was beyond salvageable. He finally ran out of steam, and with a final bit of advice along the lines of 'You were all shit!' or something like that, he stomped out in that almost farcical way that short angry people do. The guys were a bit stunned, but cracked a smile when they saw me still holding the mess of tape, and finally, we all burst out laughing at the reaming out we had got. Nice to see that aircrew are the same the world over—a bit of banter is such a good coping mechanism when things go a bit awry.

The day came when I had to immerse myself in the Marine Corps way and try my hand at CAS. There was a fair amount of pre-planning to be done. I took a map and plotted out all of the holding points known as control points (CPs) and the initial points (IPs) that would lead us to the targets, and I studied it religiously the night before. The general sequence was that you would launch out of El Toro to R-2507 which was becoming pretty standard. The instructor in the lead aircraft would split the two students off to different CPs where we would set up a racetrack pattern to hold awaiting our instructions. He would then act as a FACA (forward air controller airborne) and call us in on targets. He did this using the 9-line. The 9-line was the standard way in CAS of directing assets onto targets and consisted of nine lines of information (no shit!) passed in the same order every time.

It started with the IP and then a heading from the IP and whether it was a left or right offset for the attack heading; distance from the IP to the target; target elevation; target description and then most importantly, the location of the target. We would input that as a grid reference or a lat/long. After that, line 7 told you what sort of mark would be on the target. This could be white phosphorous smoke known as 'Willey-Pete' which was fired from rockets on the jet or mortars on the ground. The mark could also be laser for laser-guided bombs or infra-red. The 9-line finished with position of friendly forces (extremely important) and the egress heading after the attack. As add-ons, you could get a time on target or a time to target with a time hack. The procedure was to write the data down on a pre-prepared kneepad; transfer the numbers into the nav kit; build the route and add the timing to it. Sounds a bit complicated huh? Bear in mind, I am also trying to fly the bloody jet at low-level all the time I am doing this admin stuff, and the clock is ticking. To be honest, it is all a bit fraught. To be brutally honest? It can be a total shit show!

On start up, I was meticulous in entering the waypoint data of the CPs and IPs. The first run was pre-planned, so I built the route for it and would only need to add the TOT. Thank goodness, as it was busy as hell just doing that. We were dropping the 26-pound practice bombs and had enough for three runs. The TOTs were generous, giving me lots of time to get sorted. The second CAS event was to be a bit more intense. Rocky was the FACA and sent me my first 9-line. Plenty of time for the TOT on run 1, but as it turned out, I would need every flaming second of it. I went to build the route to the IP and plug in the lat/long of the target, when my UFC flashed, and most of my waypoints dumped, leaving me with a screen full of zeroes! 'Shit!' I shouted in cockpit and frantically searched for my IP. No joy at all as it seemed the nav kit had given up the ghost. I must have pissed off Lady Hornet somehow on this trip and she had slapped me in the face.

I quickly put the lat/long and elevation of the target in; looked at my map and handwritten 9-line; did a quick bit of mental arithmetic; and set off in the rough direction of the IP. Quick as I could, I shoved in the TOT while blasting towards my best guess of where the IP was (I used a rough heading from the map using my route study from the night before). I didn't have time to put the IP in the kit, as I was pretty much over it by then (I think) so off on heading and at what felt like the right moment, I cut off right and popped up to overbank left into a 15-degree dive. Rocky had flown over the target just before me and dropped his practice bomb to make a puff of sand that he could talk me onto. I called 'In hot!' and he cleared me to drop. I moved my designation from the pre-planned lat/long to where his bomb had gone, and just prayed as I held the pickle button down. As soon as my two bombs went, I pulled out of the dive and egressed to the next CP (maybe). 'Shack!' shouted Rocky, proving that it is always better to be lucky than to be good. What a mess!

As I got to the next CP, I finally took a breath and cleared the sweat from my face. All of the time I should have been recovering at the CP and relaxing a bit, I spent manically typing in the waypoints. My left thumb was dancing like a worm on speed as I forced the points in. The next two runs were OK, but I still have bloody nightmares about that first one. I was finished with bombing now so it was back to being a fighter pilot until the end of the course. It was going to be another eleven days before that happened though, so I had booked some leave to coincide with my parents coming out to stay with us.

Even now it brings a tear to my eye

I owe everything to my parents. My dad was from Kent and had been an armourer in the RAF and served for twenty-two years in places like Singapore and Malta where the RAF's reach matched Britain's old colonial responsibilities. My mum was a North Yorkshire girl, born and bred. They married young and lived the adventure that service life offered in the '50s and '60s. Children brought a new perspective and they turned their focus onto instilling the right values into my brother and me, encouraging us to work hard at school. Dad gave up his career in the RAF to give us a more settled life so we could concentrate on our schooling rather than being moved every three years. We moved into a council house in Mum's old town of Thirsk and Dad commuted to Binbrook in Lincolnshire for his last tour, meaning we saw him only every other weekend during that time. He had his first heart attack shortly after leaving the RAF, and that dictated the rest of his life, punctuated with illness and further heart attacks. The knock-on effect was that he was out of work for significant periods. The stress must have been enormous and my mum must have been beside herself trying to make ends meet (she was Yorkshire though, so tough inside, and just got on and coped). Despite all of this, my brother and I were blissfully unaware at our ages that anything was wrong. As I got older, I watched them putting money away each week into a tin for rent and utilities, and started to understand what they were having to do to live with two growing boys.

Despite not being able to afford the finer things in life, they gave us something much more precious—their time and their attention. They would spend hours on end playing board games with us and that became a tradition in our family that I continued with my own. Nearly all of the kids on our estate left school at 15 to get jobs, but my parents insisted on us staying until after A-levels to give ourselves the best opportunity and choices. They sacrificed everything that they could, to do that for us, and I will be eternally grateful and forever in their debt. I am sure some of you will think that I am over-egging it. Another 'council house kid done good' story, 'blah blah blah'. I don't care what people think about this aspect of my life. It shaped me into the man I am today. It gave me values that I still hold true. It is who I am. I owe my parents everything.

They arrived completely knackered and bewildered at LAX at about the time my bloody nav kit was dumping my waypoints into oblivion. By the time I got back home after the debrief, they were already there. My wife and Holly had met them at the airport in LA as it was way too difficult to get them connected down to John Wayne. Dad was not in the best shape and I think it was a minor miracle that he was able to make the journey. I think the last time they had flown had been when they returned from posting with us in Malta back in 1968, so almost a thirty-year gap. They spent three weeks with us and it was magical. Some days they just sat in the back soaking up the sun, with Mum constantly employed playing with Holly. I am sure it did them both the power of good. Dad seemed to have a new lease of life and I was determined to show them as much as I could. This was the holiday of a lifetime for them and probably the last time they would manage it.

I took them to Disneyland with Holly, which was probably just a cheap way of getting somebody else to ride in the teacups with her (I was sick of those bloody teacups by then), but I also made a point of taking Dad to a baseball game. I was an old hand at it having been to one whole game before. Angels stadium is now one of the oldest ballparks in the US, and was a great slice of Americana to show off to Dad. I bought us ball caps and told the lady in the ticket office this was my dad's first game and he had come all the way from England to see it (nobody in the US knew what the UK was so always asked 'Hey are you from England?' when they heard the accent). She gave us discounted tickets behind home plate about half way up the stand. Dad was a quiet man, but I had never seen him so animated while the game was on. Sitting there in his ball cap, eating an Angel Dog, and jabbering away with me about the game. He even stood up and sang 'Take me out to the ball game' during the seventh inning stretch (the official break between the seventh innings). Even now, as I write this, it brings a tear to my eye. It was truly magical. He would only last five more years after that.

And what of my mum? She maximised her time with Holly, swimming with her in the lake, and even in the surf at San Clemente; playing the same old games over and over again in the way that toddlers do; soaking up the sun while Holly slept; and just generally living the Californian life. They flew back after their three-week break, not knowing when they would see Holly again, and apparently slept for about a fortnight, they were so shattered. They had had the time of their lives. I could only hope that when I told them that I was only in California because of them, that they believed me.

I returned to work on 101 completely refreshed and eager to get the last lap done. Following a couple of sims, I would get three more intercept trips building on the basic radar ARAs I had previously done, and then nine air combat 1 vs 1 hops before putting it all together for the fighter-weapons phase at the end of the course. My last 1 vs 1 and the two fighter-weapons trips would be against the F-5 aggressor squadron VMFAT-401 based at Yuma. The aggressor squadron was manned by Marine Corps reservists who were F-4, A-4 and F-18 guys previously. They were very experienced, knew their stuff, and could fly the F-5 like you read about. They were a hard fight. I get ahead of myself. I need to get my intercept head back on. Three trips saw me progress from 1 vs 2 through 2 vs 1 and finally 2 vs 2 intercepts. I was now using the AMRAAM and all of my trips were in the newer F-18C or D models. The As and Bs could not carry AMRAAM at that time so it was only the best jets for Tug now until the end of the course. 121 Squadron also had some of the newest F-18Ds out there so I really was going to be spoilt.

The 1 vs 2 introduced me to AMRAAM against multiple targets. Up to now, I had simulated firing AIM-7 Sparrow missiles at one target at a time in single target track (radar lock). We had to support Sparrow all the way to impact by locking up the target, providing a constant wave of radar energy that would reflect off the target and into the seeker head of the missile. This was called a semi-active missile. AMRAAM was an active missile in that it had its own radar and could intercept and destroy its target with much less support from me. I could fire my AMRAAM, and when it was a certain range from the target (depending on altitude, speed, amount of manoeuvring required—all very secret stuff I wasn't allowed to see), it would go 'see ya,' and bugger off to do its own thing. When it got to that point, I would call 'pitbull' over the radio, and by that stage, the target would need to turn itself inside out to defeat the missile—or teleport somewhere else entirely. Pitbull was the codeword that the missile had gone medium PRF active in its own radar. PRF is pulse repetition frequency and is proper radar shit so let's just leave it at that, hey?

If you shot AMRAAM inside that range, it would come off the rail already active and you could just turn around and run away—proper fire and forget. When AMRAAM was selected, a big circle appeared in the HUD. If anyone flew inside that circle, you could actually shoot AMRAAM visually and its radar would go into a search pattern and track the first thing it saw—that could be a friendly too if you weren't careful (remember that for much later in the book!). That was why lots of people called it the 'air shark'. It was a nasty cold-hearted killer that would eat whatever was in front of it. Mostly, we would employ AMRAAM using our F-18 radar. The main search mode was called Range While Search (RWS). RWS was good for scanning a wide area of airspace, usually up to 80 nautical miles to get initial contact. Once it was painting targets, we would select the group we were interested in and narrow the scan pattern around it before switching to Track While Scan (TWS). TWS provided a much better update rate, helped by the fact that we were concentrating all our energy into one specific area. The TWS set would then load up the targets in order of priority. The one it deemed the greatest threat, or the best shot for us, or something like that, became the L&S target (launch and steering). Basically, he was under the trigger.

The HUD circle now had markers on it showing me the max range of the missile (RMax), the min range (guess what? RMin) and somewhere in-between was the range where, ordinarily, the target cannot escape if we shoot, known as no escape (Rne). Once the target marker got inside RMax, the word 'SHOOT' appeared in the HUD. When it got within Rne, the 'SHOOT' cue would flash. If I didn't like the L&S target that TWS gave me, I could step over to the next one using the nosewheel steering button just below the trigger on the stick top. With multiple targets, I would shoot, step, shoot, step, shoot, step, shoot, rippling rocket mayhem across the sky.

The uncontrollably violent, hooligan offspring of my love affair

OK, re-reading the last few paragraphs, even I am sick of the technical stuff. There was much more going on, but I will drip feed it to you through the stories later on. In essence, the radar did a lot of stuff for you, but you still had a lot of finger drama to do to get the missiles off. Once they were off and went pitbull, you could either turn around and run away bravely, or press in and clean up what was left of the carnage your air sharks had caused. Being a fighter pilot in an aeroplane that acted like a contortionist when it was turning, I was always desperate to get to the merge and have a punch up. The 1 vs 2 trip was designed to get us manipulating the TWS and getting the shoot, step, shoot stuff organised, as well as interpreting all of the symbology. The basics of doing an academic intercept were still required, but this time I would see two targets on the B-scope. By analysing their position on the scope, I could determine what formation they were in. This could be line abreast, known as azimuth, or line astern, known as range. Or maybe there would be a mix of both, swept left or right. Their formation would determine which side I would offset to in order to give my AMRAAMs the best shots and also to enter the visual fight with some advantage.

I was leading some of the missions now so manipulating the formation for the best outcome of the sortie, managing the airspace and fuel, and doing all the comm to ATC. Air Traffic had got used to me by now and even SoCal Radar was chatting to me like we were old buddies, which made things a whole lot easier. We were out in the training areas off the coast, so I would take a height split from the targets either up into the sun, or maybe low so I could highlight them against high cloud to help get tally for the merge. The better my radar handling got, the more aggressive I could be with the intercept in terms of height splits and manoeuvring. It all came to me reasonably quickly which was nice. Well, it should have done really given my previous experience. However, it was great to feel on top of things for once. The radar was awesome, and the AMRAAM was like the uncontrollably violent, hooligan offspring of my love affair with the Miss World of the fighter community. Even doing the 2 vs 1 trip with Smiler couldn't spoil my whirlwind romance with this jet. He was pleasingly silent throughout, as I led my wingman through some clean-cut intercepts into coordinated pairs combat manoeuvring in order to shoot the bandit. I then had a couple of goes as the wingman. Smiler was supposed to be teaching me the rudiments of pairs intercepts (or section intercepts as the Americans called them), and the canned dance in the sky of free and engaged tactics, but I had flown it for three years and taught it for another three. He was nothing but a passenger as I swept into the fight from on high as the wingman, or engineered the perfect (well, near enough) entry to the merge as the leader. I was absolutely loving it—every second.

The radar found the target no problem. We would have one jet searching in the high block, and the other looking low. We coordinated over the radio and melded the radars into the same height block once we had sanitised the airspace for other bandits. We both took pre-merge shots with our AMRAAMs and timed them out, before preparing to enter the fight with the leader going head-to-head to make the bandit predictable (he had to pass nose to nose with the leader otherwise the leader could turn on him and shoot him easily) and the wingman hooking in with lots of advantage. A shot from the wingman meant the bandit was now tied up with him, while the leader separated out from the fight to then reposition out of plane (high or low) for the re-entry. He then came back into the fight, unseen by the bandit, called his wingman out, took the shot, and then ran out in perfect battle formation with his wingman, all the time checking each other's six o'clock.

Phew! Are you lost yet? Confused? I had been at it for years so could see the patterns forming in the air and make sense of them. All I had to do was add in the American comm, the switches on the radar, and the weapons knowledge the sim instructors taught me (for the avoidance of doubt and possible future legal action—no they didn't! I made that shit up for dramatic effect) and wrap it all up in my ultimate fantasy machine. Fighter pilot heaven? Yep—already said that. The 2 vs 2 was another step up meaning we had to 'sort' the formation for shots, so we didn't both target the same aeroplane. There was a contract for sorting briefed up beforehand depending on the formation of the bandits. It might be side/lead/high which meant our formation would target whichever bandit was on our side first. Let me explain that. If we are running in line abreast, and I am the leader on the left, I would target the left most bandit on the radar and my wingman would take the one on the right, so long as they presented in azimuth. If they presented in range, the leader takes the leader (i.e. closest on the radar scope). If they are split in height, the leader would take the highest one. If they were swept, I would look at the formation and call the sort on the radio depending on what I saw.

Leave your trousers off as more porn is on the way

Allied with this is the type of intercept I will run for our pair/section. It may be a single-side offset where both of us stay on one side of the bandits, or I might call for a bracket where we separate out as individuals, one either side of the bandit's formation, in a pincer movement. You can see there is a lot to think about, so in the pre-planning stages, we build a timeline for the intercept. This is predicated on what weapons we have, what the threat aeroplanes and weapons are, and what altitude block we are in (low, medium, or high). The timeline would dictate when to sanitise your height block; when to meld both radars into the bandit's block; when to sort by; and when to shoot. Although at first glance, it seems a bit inflexible, it was a good starting point to instil radar and intercept discipline, and I was a big fan of it. So, the 2 vs 2 went off without a hitch and my reward was to move into the air combat phase—at last!

By this time, we were gearing up for the move to San Diego and had found a nice house in Ocean Beach that would suit us for the next two-and-a-bit years. The main road running through OB was called Sunset Cliffs Boulevard—oh come on! We were going to be living about four blocks from the beach halfway up a hill that gave us an amazing view of the ocean, blocked only by the odd palm tree lining the street. 4536 Del Mar Avenue, Ocean Beach, CA 92107 was going to be our address! We would drop down to San Diego each weekend just to get our bearings and found that we were less than 10 minutes from Sea World and only about fifteen from the world-famous San Diego Zoo. Both places would be amazing for Holly. It put us much further from Disneyland of course, but by that time, I think even Holly was pig sick of that bloody mouse.

Now, if you want to dim the lights, put on some soul music, and get in the mood, let me tell you about the air combat phase on the RAG. This is proper aviation pornography, folks. You probably think I am overdoing this, but let me assure you, I am not. So, my first trip in the orgasmatron (watch Barbarella for that reference) was BFM 140 (Basic Fighter Manoeuvres) which I flew with an instructor called Joker. He was easily the happiest Marine I had met so far and told me he was looking forward to seeing what a Phantom guy thought about the F-18's combat moves. His joy was infectious even after 2,000 hours on the Hornet. I couldn't wait to fly with him. BFM 140 was a 1 vs 0 so nobody to fight against—just go up there and try to pull the wings off the thing without crashing. The F-18 was everything I had ever dreamed about in a fighter. We explored the almost unreal manoeuvring envelope it had, with Joker even out-whooping me at one point. There was obviously some academic stuff to teach me such as how much height I would need to roll over and pull through without hitting the ground, and how quickly the jet accelerated. That turned out to be not as good as an F-15 and nowhere near as good as an F-16. Did I give a shit though? Nope.

Joker took me through the unparalleled gobsmacking beauty of the Hornet's outer reaches of the handling envelope next. It was unlimited in angle of attack, even with a centreline fuel tank on and still handled as much as 35 AoA in other fits. Jesus! We were limited to much less than that in the Phantom so this was like being in a spaceship. I know I should have paid attention as we passed various AoA milestones, but I do remember that at one point we heard 'rainfall' on the windscreen which came on at the same AoA each time. This was due to the noise of the airflow over the canopy, or something like that. We got down to 100 knots at one point, and I envied Joker every stinking minute of the 2,000 Hornet hours in his logbook. We had a look at the onset of G and pulled into a screaming Jesus diving spiral to sustain 7.5G. This was the most G I had pulled and I crunched over in the cockpit forcing out an imaginary poo as I grunted to keep the blood up in my head. I was so amped up though; it was no problem. Hard work nonetheless, and although I wanted to stay up there all day and take on anyone who thought they were hard enough, the fun juice ran out and we had to make our way back to El Toro.

Well, if that was how good it was not fighting somebody, then bring on the bad guys! Joker was excellent in the debrief and heaped on the praise. He told me it was the best 1 vs 0 he had ever seen. True or not, it gave me a great boost and I was chuffed to bits that I hadn't made a fool of myself on the one bit I was looking forward to most of all. I'm telling you now—if you ever need a fighter pilot who is ace at fighting against himself, then I'm your man! I had made a point of not marking off any of the BFM trips myself as I wanted to get as much hands-on violent flying as I could. I moved swiftly through the offensive perch work on the next trip. Sport of Kings that one. All of it behind another jet, taking tons of shots and getting used to the air combat modes of the radar. OK let's take a break from the porn and do a bit of tech. Leave your trousers off, as more porn is on the way after that.

The ACM modes of the radar were just unreal. The sensor control switch at the top of the stick looked like a small flower head with four petals separating out of it. Romantic and gentle description of a switch that helped me to rain death on my adversary, but you get the picture? In normal day-to-day flying, this switch designated which DDI had priority, and put the cursor on it, which I moved with my porn star left index finger (sorry—no more porn just now). If I pushed aft, it was the centre DDI and similar for left and right. If the priority was already on the right DDI and I pushed right again, magic started to happen. The radar would go into Auto-Acquisition mode (AACQ) and it would lock the first thing it saw. If I was highlighting a target on the scope, it would lock that one.

Now, if I pushed forwards on the switch, I entered the air combat modes of the radar. Forwards put me in Boresight mode (BST). A 3.3-degree circle would appear in the HUD and if I saw an aeroplane and put it in the circle, the radar would lock it and whooooosh!!!! I could shoot them down—

assuming I knew they were hostile. The F-18 was so manoeuvrable that I would end up using BST a lot, as most fights would end up with me pointing at the bandit, rather than them being behind me. I know that may sound arrogant, but believe me when I tell you how awesome this jet was in ACM. Pull aft on the switch, and we went into Vertical Acquisition mode (VACQ). The radar would then go into a batshit crazy search pattern only a few degrees either side of the nose, but from minus 13 degrees to plus 46 degrees quickly. Anything out to 5 miles got locked in that scan pattern. This was a godsend for close-in fights when the bandit was out the top of the canopy. Wide Acq (WACQ) mode came up if I rocked left on the switch. This put a little rectangle up in the HUD which I could slew around using my cursor controller. It would lock the first thing it saw in the rectangle out to 10 miles. This was great once you exited a fight and wanted to clear your path, and was more selective than AACQ, which matched the range scale on your radar so you could be searching a massive amount of airspace rather than just 10 miles.

Finally, if you selected the gun on the weapons switch by rocking backwards, you entered Gun Acquisition mode (GACQ) which put up a 20-degree circle in the HUD and searched basically the HUD field of view out to 5 miles. The ACM modes took a bit of getting used to and it was a bit of a finger drama the first few times. Each intercept or ACM trip, we would have to carry out a full radar and weapons check on the way to the play area to make sure it was all working. I won't bore you with all the details in full as I know you are skimming this bit to get to the porn, but it entailed checking all the ACM modes as well as the symbology of the weapons in the HUD and the growls/tones of the Sidewinders. The offensive BFM trip went really well, but then it was time for the absolute misery that is defensive BFM. Chuck took me up for that one and almost made it pleasant. Lots of looking over my shoulder at 7.5G and trying to stop the bandit shooting me down by simulating banging out chaff and flares. And then we finished with the Guns-D with me out the front (unfortunately). Just as the bandit came nose on to take the shot, I broke hard to 7.5G into him. The first time, he stayed nose on, so I overbanked to 135 degrees and screamed down to the floor with my eyes flicking between the altimeter and the bandit. As soon as the shot was defeated, we terminated the exercise, and my prize for not dying was to do another one. This time, he came nose off and I pulled up to counter him and we ended up in a rolling scissors—sort of. I had been in lots of rolling scissors fights in my life, but nothing like this in the Hornet. Usually, it looks like two aircraft barrelling around each other in big vertical loops, each desperately trying to get in behind the other one. The F-18 had a go at doing it traditionally, and then obviously thought that was boring, so pulled up into horrifically steep and slow speed climbs, and then pretty much swapped ends to come back down again into the bandit's 6 o'clock. Holy shit! This was the stuff of fantasy. At some point, you should flush the bandit out the front and then just increase the AoA (to bloody unlimited levels!!!) and set up 'the tree'. You seem to be climbing without moving forwards and he is below you getting flushed out in front and with no options but to wait for the inevitable.

OK, trousers definitely off for this bit as I explain to you what the inevitable is. Eventually, I will have climbed away from him to make enough separation between us for a gun shot. Imagine you are sitting in the cockpit with your nose really high, and under you by about 1,000 feet is the bandit. In any other aeroplane, I would have to roll inverted and pull down into his six to get the gunsight on him. Now the physics of that mean 1,000 feet is nowhere near enough height to do that and pull out of your dive to get the gunsight on. Trust me when I say you would whistle through his tail giving away all the advantage you had of flushing him out the front in the first place. This isn't any other aeroplane though. This is the mad professor's wet dream jet. This is what you do in the F-18:

First, select the gun. Now simultaneously slam the throttles from full burner back to idle while violently shoving the stick forwards towards the instrument panel. Every other aeroplane in the world at that time would surge its engines and probably go flick, stall, spin, crash, burn, die. The Hornet though? That just pivots the nose around the wing axis so it nods down quickly, and as soon as the nose rotates through the horizon, you wrench the stick hard back into your guts and slam those throttles back to full burner and miraculously, you don't flick, stall, spin, crash, burn, die! You are pointing directly at the bandit's six, the radar locks automatically because you selected the gun, and you put the pipper on the bandit's canopy. Squeeze the trigger while calmly calling 'Shooter 31, guns kill. Terminate.' Then pinch yourself and wonder if that really happened.

Man! Those engines!

OK, trousers back on—that's the pornography covered for now. It is almost impossible to describe how spectacular the Hornet was in air combat, even to my mates who had flown other aeroplanes. The best I can come up with for them is that it was like flying a Hawk on serious mind-bending drugs. And then thinking, 'I haven't had enough drugs yet, so I'll have some more.' Crazy. Out of this world. I had two more dual hops and two solos on this phase and for once, they came thick and fast. It was full on air combat for me as the instructors wound up the fights seeing what they could throw at me and how I would react. I know I have said before that I was in heaven, but now it felt like I was in the upstairs VIP bit of heaven—you know the bit where the bouncer angels check if you have the right sandals on? My jet did everything I asked of it in the fights. My next dual was with an older guy called Cluffy. Really nice guy and I remember that we got into some close fights where he encouraged me to use AMRAAM a lot more rather than go for a gun shot. One fight ended up with the bandit right out the top of the canopy heading back towards our tail. I pulled hard and selected VACQ and it damn well got a lock (I love this radar!) and Cluffy shouted 'Shoot!' so I squeezed off an imaginary AMRAAM. Not a chance it would have hacked the corner, but there was the flashing SHOOT cue in the HUD. We put the tape in during the debrief and everyone agreed it was a valid kill. I knew AMRAAM was good at range, but had no idea what a nasty little bastard it was at close quarters. Cluffy would regret that little bit of advice he gave me the next day when he flew against me on my first ACM solo.

Half way through the trip he told me he was going to fight full up so try his best against me. We only had one long fight where all we got were snap gun shots against each other (not enough tracking to call a kill). I was running out of gas so either had to get a kill or engineer a bug out back to base. Trying to outrun an AMRAAM was going to be tricky and would need the perfect bug out. As it was training and not real, I sacrificed all my energy in a mad, pull as hard as you can move, and loosed off an AMRAAM. I then fell out of the sky and only just recovered in time to stay above the hard deck. Cluffy had called terminate after my shot and we headed home. Our smiles were a mile wide walking back in and all I could do was thank him for the best time. My smile was even wider in the debrief as we went through our mega-fight step by step. Finally, we had a look at my dodgy AMRAAM shot which turned out to be far from dodgy, and Cluffy said, 'you should have claimed the kill, Tug. Nice one.' My last two trips on the phase were the following day, and I couldn't wait for them. Afterwards, it wasn't until that evening when we settled for the weekend that my body told me how knackered it was and pretty much refused to function properly for most of the Saturday. 7.5G sustained, and lots of it, had taken its toll. There will be some F-16 guys out there calling me a pussy and saying 9G is where the men fly etc. I couldn't imagine what sustaining 9G would feel like, and don't really want to know if truth be told. That must be why all F-16 guys are short and look like their faces have melted.

All I could do that weekend was drag my sorry arse to the lake for our last couple of outings there. In about a week's time, we would be living in Ocean Beach and taking Holy in the surf. The drug addicts were happy for us to take our rented furniture down to San Diego with us, which was a relief not having to go through finding another firm. I imagine that the British embassy paying them $700 per month every month sweetened the deal. There is of course a good chance that they had completely forgotten where we lived and who we were, so wouldn't have got the furniture back anyway. Three more trips would see me finish the RAG at last, and what a brilliant set of trips they would be. The fighter weapons phase took all of our knowledge and skills from the intercept, formation, and air combat rides and wrapped them up in a load of fights against the F-5. The F-5 was a tough little jet to fight against. Yes, it was old, but it was small (so hard to see), sleek and very quick. As I said before, it was also flown by some of the most experienced fighter pilots in the Marine Corps. The first trip was a 1 vs 1 to show us how to use the advantages of the Hornet against the advantages of the F-5. It was a pure rate fighter so accurate speed control on their side, to get around the circle of the fight quicker than its opponent. It could add speed really quickly when not pulling G.

It isn't fair to say the Americans flew air combat on the numbers, but the idea was to fly a 'yardstick Hornet' at the merge. That was to arrive in the visual fight with the best turning speed and rate around the circle. We taught a bit of that on the Phantom and the Hawk, but mostly we tried to get people to look out of the window and fly the picture they saw. You still had to handle the jet properly, but this more flexible approach to the fight gave us more options if things didn't run on rails (which they rarely did). That's what I thought anyway, and it was a good excuse for my lack of accurate speed control and handling, I guess. I fought like a bastard against that F-5, but blimey, it was tough. It was like trying to swat a dragonfly. You can't fight what you can't see, so I sacrificed a bit of manoeuvrability to make sure I could keep my eyes on him. This extended the fights a bit, but we eventually got the kills. Just some balance here—we should have won the fights as we were in a Hornet. I don't want you to think I am setting myself up as an air combat God here. I was handy after years of doing it, and I had been given an absolute gift with this aeroplane. We had to finish the trip with a bloody Guns-D which was as unpleasant as always, and after a quick splash and dash at El Centro, we were back on the deck at El Toro.

So, after seven long months on the RAG, I finally got to fly my last two trips. They could not have gone better. Firstly, I was flying solo for both of them. Secondly, I was in a straight F-18C with the more powerful General Electric engines in it. Finally, my leader was Chuck. The plan was for us to fly out to R-2507 and conduct a full 2 vs 1 intercept to air combat trip; land at El Centro for a full debrief and refuel; launch into a 2 vs 2 for my last trip and then blast back to El Toro to land and congratulate me on passing the course. We briefed up both trips at El Toro and then I raged airborne for the final time out of Orange County in what I can only describe as a runaway horse with its arse on fire. It was slippery as hell, I can tell you, and the poor F-5 didn't stand a chance against us. I had a go at being the leader and the wingman on the intercepts. We took plenty of shots pre-merge for practice, but the only shots that counted were in the visual dog fight. One of the intercepts we ran an eyeball/shooter profile where the F-5 was declared as an unknown so we couldn't shoot at range. The eyeball would go close aboard the F-5 at the merge and declare it hostile visually, and the shooter would hook in to take the first shot. We had a quick debrief on the ground at El Centro afterwards and just before walking for the jets, Chuck asked me if I wanted to lead the whole shebang for the 2 vs 2.

'If you trust me Chuck, then why not?'

'Awesome! Let's go kick some ass, Tug!'

And kick ass is just what we did. Leading puts some extra responsibility on you, but I should have been able to handle it. 2 vs 2 is a bread-and-butter trip on the fighter front line, and I had already led some simple trips on the RAG, so it was time to crack on. Get this trip right, and I would pass the course and be a bona-fide F-18 Hornet pilot, ready for the front line. I only remember one bit about that hop. We had merged with both F-5s and Chuck had hooked in and shot one almost immediately. I had ditched a load of speed to nose point my guy, but didn't have enough energy to snap my nose and get the shot straight away. We were in a looping manoeuvre with the F-5 extending away from me. Keeping the pull on wasn't going to help, so I violently unloaded on the stick to zero G. This took all of the drag off the jet and helped it to accelerate. I only pushed momentarily, but those bloody engines in full burner added almost a hundred knots to my speed in a heartbeat. I snapped the nose up with the radar in VACQ, got a lock, and my pretend AMRAAM scorched off to claim yet another victim who really shouldn't have bothered turning up in the first place.

Even Chuck couldn't believe it when he saw my tape.

'Man! Those engines!' was all he could say, and with a shake of my hand, the RAG was done for me. Seven months to do just 55 hours. Forty-five trips in all with only twenty-five being with an instructor. I flew with nineteen different instructors in those twenty-five trips so consistency was a bit of an issue. However, it did mean that if I got an instructor I didn't like or rate (I'm looking at you, Smiler!) then at least I knew there was a good chance I wouldn't have to fly with them again. On the flip side, I am damn sure Chips was happy never to even see me again let alone fly with me, after the trauma of those LAT trips. So, as the rest of my course finished the fighter weapons phase and then went on to carrier qualification, the Wilsons packed up and drove down to San Diego, where we would bed into our American adventure proper. After two weeks off, I drove my soft-top Mustang through the main gate of Miramar, where my gorgeous F-18D lounged on the line, waiting for me to continue our passionate affair.

4
VMFA (AW)-121 Squadron: The Green Knights

Ooh Rah, Sir!

Just arriving at a Marine Corps base was an experience every morning. I would regularly play 'guess the greeting'. Stopping at the main gate, I would have my passes checked by the guards on duty, and I would always say, 'Good morning, Private. How are you today?' in my best British officer accent. I would then receive one of three greetings:

'Ooh Rah, Sir!' was greeting number one, and the most popular.

'It's another great day in the Corps, Sir!' would be number two.

Most bizarre though was greeting number three. The guard would salute and bark at you. The US Marines were nicknamed 'Devil Dogs' by the German soldiers who fought them in Bellau Wood in 1918. The name stuck and was an important part of Marine Corps history. The bark seemed to come from deep down in the back of the throat and came out sounding like 'awrgh!'

I loved the USMC's traditions and stories. Their motto of 'Semper Fidelis' said it all really. 'Always Faithful.' Not just faithful, but always faithful. That is an important distinction for a Marine and is probably one of the reasons why they alone were trusted to guard the US Embassies around the world. Quite often you would hear Marines saying 'Semper Fi' to each other, just as a matter of course. Their brother and sisterhood was something to behold and left a lasting impression on me. Having received a resounding 'Ooh Rah!' on my first go through the gate at Miramar, I dropped straight into the guardroom to get a car pass, and then headed to the flight line. Indy and Muck had joined VMFA-121 a few weeks before me as I was finishing up the RAG, and

Indy had told me to head for the TOPGUN hangar when I got there. I knew the TOPGUN school was based at Miramar, but I still got a shock seeing it painted on the side of the hangar in big letters as I parked up. Another pass check at the entrance to the flight line, and I asked the barking sentry where 121 was and he pointed right at the TOPGUN hangar. No way?! Yes way!

As I walked across the pan, I was gobsmacked to see row upon row of single-seat Hornets from 314 Squadron (featured in the film *Independence Day*), 323 and 232 Squadrons, and two units of twin-seat F-18D models of 121 and 225 Squadrons. 242 Squadron, which Indy and Muck had served on at El Toro, had deployed to Iwakuni for six months, leaving 121 to pick up the foreign strays. Oh ... and there were also two lines of F-14D Tomcats on the pan. They would be the last squadron of Navy jets to move out of Miramar as it became fully USMC. They looked huge, but I had no concept of the size until I entered the TOPGUN hangar. TOPGUN had an F-14 which they used as an aggressor aircraft and had painted it up in a blue Soviet colour scheme. Dear God it was beautiful! Menacing as hell, but beautiful nonetheless. It was bigger than huge up close. The jet pipes were almost as big as London Underground tunnels, but the wingspan? That was just freakishly large for a fighter. This thing basically set up residence at one end of the hangar like a surly dragon, just daring you to walk past it.

Ten minutes later, I had finished walking past it, and climbed the stairs up to the 121 spaces. It's a big thing joining a fighter squadron, and it felt even bigger doing it as a Brit in the States. I would always make a beeline for the boss's office and ask permission to join his squadron. I thought it was a polite thing to do and, so far, it had endeared me to my bosses (well initially at least!). I was a stranger in a strange land here though so had no bearings whatsoever. As soon as I got on the 121 corridor, I bumped into a couple of aircrew who saw my wings and said, 'Hey! You must be Tug. Welcome to the Green Knights.' That was a good sign. They both shook my hand and I asked them where the boss's office was.

'Oh, you mean Killer?' Ah—not such a good sign then. I forgot that everyone used callsigns, even for the boss. They took me up the corridor to his office, chatting all the way, and announced me to Killer. Killer was a lieutenant colonel (wing commander equivalent) and was a WSO.

'Tug, welcome. Great to see you!' said Killer and he sat me down and called through the XO. The XO who was also a lieutenant colonel and second-in-command was called Junk, and I actually knew of him. He had been on exchange himself at RAF Leuchars on the Phantom years before I had flown it, and he had almost legendary status in the RAF. He was a

New Yorker and spoke in the classic nasally tone that all New Yorkers seem to have. Almost every other sentence he said, started with 'Nyaa.' I took an instant liking to both of them. An added bonus was that Killer was not mad. I had worked for some mad bosses previously so that was a nice surprise.

They asked what my background was and my kudos took a leap forward when I mentioned the Phantom. It doesn't matter which air force you are from; the Phantom is a world-wide brotherhood. Killer had been a Phantom WSO on his first couple of tours. When I then said I had been a tactics instructor and then QFI at Valley, Junk got very animated and started telling Killer about the high-quality training we delivered at tactical weapons training. Not sure I deserved quite the level of praise he was throwing at me, but the upshot was that he recommended to Killer that they get me through the air combat work-up sharpish so that they could designate me as an ACTI (air combat training instructor) and get me teaching it! I hadn't even flown on the squadron at that point. That changed almost immediately when Killer said they would get me on the schedule that afternoon.

I would be put together with Indy and Muck, and the three of us would be working directly for the ops officer, Hoover. Hoover was a major and the nicest of guys. Ex-Phantom WSO again and just a good gentle soul. If he was nonplussed at having another foreigner in the office, he certainly didn't show it, and after much handshaking and backslapping from Hoover and his rag tag bunch of Commonwealth expats, I started to get settled in. I stowed my kit with the flight equipment crew and Indy showed me around the squadron, introducing me to my new squadron mates as we went. It was all very pleasant, exciting, but also disorientating. However, 121 had a good vibe as far as I could tell. A couple of doors down from ops was the ready room. This was a bit like a crew room, but also doubled as the main briefing room. It was set up like it was on board a carrier, so all the seats faced forwards and were a bit like airline seats. The seats at the front were for the execs and had covers over the head pads in squadron colours, with their title written on the back. It looked pretty cool, but I found it wasn't really conducive to the crew room atmosphere I had been used to in the RAF.

The squadron badge was very cool also. Black background with a green knight chess piece on it. The knight had a bright red eye giving it a sinister look. Each Marine Corps squadron had its own callsign, and ours was 'Combat'—awesome! Finally, our motto was 'Have gun. Will travel.' This was from an old TV series about a gun for hire in the Wild West and was just perfect for a fighter squadron.

Sorry Calvin, that was awful

It was in at the deep end for my first trip at the front line. I was number 4 of a 4-ship going off to do a 2 vs 2. I was fully expecting to do a dual handling check ride with an instructor pilot as my first trip, as that is what would happen on joining a RAF squadron, but obviously not here. Junk was leading it and I was flying with Hoover. Junk used the brief to introduce me to the other guys and also to show me how things were done on 121. I was shitting myself a bit with it being my first go and being exposed to seven other aviators on the squadron all at once, but I had to break my duck somehow. What better WSO to fly with than Hoover though? He was relaxed the whole time, walking me through the procedures for kitting up and signing the jet out. The ground crew were already used to Muck so my little idiosyncrasies went unnoticed, or were tolerated, compared to his own peculiar brand of madness. Start-up was easy as Hoover took on the nav kit for me, and we taxied out as four sleek grey war machines, ready to take on the world.

Junk had briefed the take-off as a 'herd' go. This meant that we lined up as pairs on each of the twin runways, and once we powered up, Junk called 'rolling,' and we did two pairs formation take-offs at the same time. I stuck to the wing of number 3 and was pleased that my formation take-off went well. Four jets blasting airborne, all of them in burner, must have sounded brutal back on deck. In the cockpit though, all was smooth and quiet as we pressed out over the Pacific. It was a dream flying with a proper back-seater again. Hoover did all of the nav and radar stuff, handing the radar off to me so that I could do the weapons checks. I handed it back with a simple 'your radar' call in the cockpit. The whole crew thing came back to me instantly and Hoover and I worked together like we had been crewed for years. I seemed to do OK in the intercepts. We swapped fighter and target roles, and with Hoover running the radar, I was able to concentrate fully on flying in tactical formation, building the intercept picture in my mind and getting the visual entry into the fight sorted. A bit of visual manoeuvring and missile shots rounded it all off nicely. I had been doing it all myself on the RAG, so even though this was only my second ever 2 vs 2 in the F-18, I was able to read and interpret what was on the scope.

The last intercept came around, and as we were preparing for it, I thought I should have a try at running the radar myself.

'Do you mind if I have a go on the radar this time, Sir?' I asked. Because Hoover was a major and therefore a squadron leader equivalent, I was still in the habit of calling senior officers 'Sir', even in the cockpit.

'What was that, Tug?' he asked with an almost incredulous tone in his voice. I thought I had broken some sort of F-18D protocol or something, asking for the radar.

'Sorry, Sir. I was wondering if it was OK if I had a go at the next intercept.'

'Ha! Tug—that is so lovely how you asked that! Most guys just shout MY RADAR and take it off me. Thank you for being so polite and asking. Of course you can have a go. It's your aeroplane anyway!' I could almost picture his broad smile under his oxygen mask. I better not screw it up then and spoil the moment.

It all worked as advertised, and finally Junk brought us home to Miramar. For once, the weather was a bit punk with haze and a low sun destroying the visibility, and it was impossible to see the airfield as we ran in. Junk took us through the overhead of the airfield and split us off for individual talkdowns with Air Traffic Control. All Hoover could say in the debrief was about how polite I had been in the cockpit. It obviously made an impression on him, because he said it three times! He was a great guy and a wonderful human being, and I would absolutely love flying with him and working for him. I'm not sure that being known as the politest fighter pilot in the States fitted the impression I was trying to cultivate, but I would take it for now.

The deep end continued with my next trip being a 4-ship bombing mission at the range doing section pops and hi-pops, but trip 3 was the deeper than deep end. Night tanking. No dual check at night. No dual check on the tanker. This would be my first ever go at air-to-air refuelling in the F-18 and it would be in the dark with two other jets around me. More madness. All the other guys in the formation would be on night vision goggles (NVG), including my own WSO who was called Calvin. I hadn't done the NVG course so would be the only one doing old fashioned night flying. Pepper was the training officer on the squadron and was leading the trip. He was a rat-like character who dipped almost constantly, including in the briefing. The tanker was a Marine Corps C-130. I had tanked before from a C-130 in a Phantom plenty of times in the Falkland Islands, so at least one little thing would be familiar. We lined up as a 3-ship on the same runway, and this time took a 30-second stream to go and join with the tanker. Once airborne, I got 1 and 2 on the radar in search and then saw the tanker a few miles ahead of them on the scope. I hung back a little to let 1 and 2 join and plug in, and then eased the throttles up to join on the right wing of the tanker. When I say I eased the throttles up, what I must have done was slam them to full dry power. Rather than lock up the tanker and get the VISIDENT symbology in the HUD to carry out a controlled join, I figured I could just do it in search mode using the speed readout and watching the overtake. Of course, I ballsed it up completely and sailed past the tanker with about 50 knots of overtake and the throttle hard back at idle with the speed brakes out.

'Oh bollocks!' I shouted. 'Sorry Calvin, that was awful.'

He sat there chuckling. 'I could see that was going to happen, Tug,' he laughed.

'Great! Thanks for telling me now. Ten seconds ago might have helped!' I bantered back. Suitably embarrassed, I then set up for the slowest join on the tanker in aviation history, and after hanging out on the wing, waiting for a free hose, I popped the refuelling probe out and dropped in behind.

The probe in the Phantom ended up somewhere above my head on the right-hand side, and I relied on my navigator to talk me into the basket. The Hornet continued to delight me, by putting the probe out just to the right of the radome in my normal line of sight. Now, I have had variable success with air-to-air refuelling in my time (read my first book, and the one after this!), but even I could walk this probe into the basket with no drama. However, I asked Calvin for some commentary to get me in the first time. Having screwed up the join already, my confidence wasn't all that high, so I was happy for the help. We clunked in on the first prod and it was just a case of holding a good position while the fuel flowed. Ha! I make that sound like we were just walking to the shops. Between me hyperventilating and sweating and responding to Calvin who chatted away without a care in the world, I managed to fly a ropey close formation position on the small, badly lit basket and mostly nothing else. Not the most fun trip I had had, but hey. Once we were full, I tried a couple of dry prods with Calvin suggesting I do them au-naturel (i.e. on my own) which worked out well. I was happy to put it back on deck at Miramar, and yet another episode in Mr Tug's bizarre, shouldn't have really done that list of mad experiences, was ticked off. The debrief was a hoot with everyone taking a shot at the new guy, but all in good fun. I was happy and also a bit relieved to drive back that night, top down, in the dark warm air of Southern California.

OB was about 25 minutes from Miramar and there were three or four different routes to and from. My daily choice depended on time of year, time of day, and a whole host of other variables. It seemed that every house on our street was individually styled and although ours was a bit odd, it definitely worked for us. The upstairs was given over to one large bedroom with a fair-sized dressing room off it and a huge en-suite. There was also a walk-in wardrobe, but what made it was a small balcony that faced all the way down the hill to the Pacific Ocean. Hell's bells, we were spoiled. Downstairs had a big lounge and diner at the front, which we rarely used, three more double bedrooms (one of them en-suite again) and a galley kitchen. At the back of the house was a big family room which I think might have previously been the garage, and this is where we primarily lived. It was so big that we were able to set up two televisions.

One was the standard American TV through which we paid for cable, and at the other end of the room, we had our British TV that we brought out with us. Whilst we couldn't receive any signal on it, we had it set up with a video recorder (yes—that is how old I am) and had brought all of Holly's children's film tapes. Outside, we had a courtyard that led onto the large rear garden. Can you believe we had a lemon tree in the garden? The final bit of our American home was a monstrous concrete RV stand at the back inside the security gate. With my car being a soft top, I would park it in the back where it was much safer.

It was a 5-minute drive down to the beach car park where I could bodyboard in the surf for a while and then take Holly in the shallows and let the ocean splash around her legs. At least by now we were a nice shade of tan and people didn't need to put their sunglasses on, or shade their eyes from our pasty white bodies. Flying Hornets during the week and beach at the weekend. Surely it was all going to come crashing down, wasn't it?

Can you pass the paper down, Colonel?

Well, it didn't. It just got better and better. If it's all the same to you, I would prefer to gloss over the night bombing trip that came up next. That doesn't really fit with the 'things getting better' narrative, and yet another pair of pants got the brown stripe treatment. The next trip though? That was something that blew my mind. It was CAS, and if I am being completely honest with you, I was cacking myself as soon as I saw my name on the schedule for it the day before. My cack-factor went through the roof at met brief when Junk stood up and gave this little piece of advice: 'Nyaa, OK you guys, we are going into a live CAS phase this week so there are only three things you need to remember. One—don't kill a Marine. Two—don't kill a Marine. And three—don't kill a Marine. If you don't like the look of it—DON'T DROP!' Didn't fill me full of confidence on my first live CAS trip, that's for sure. Oh, did I mention we were dropping live 1,000 pounders, and I was going to be flying with the boss?

The plan was to fly up to the 29 Palms training area about 150 miles north-east from Miramar in the Joshua Tree National Park. Nearly 1,000 square miles of combined arms training facility, where armed forces could drive tanks around, attack towns and call in air support. There was even an expeditionary airfield that you could 'deploy' to and live in a tent city while flying your missions. Thankfully, we were just flying in, bombing, and coming home again. I had heard too many horror stories already about 29 Palms, even in my short time in the States. We were part of a combined exercise that included FAC training. We would launch out of Miramar as a 3-ship, and set up a pattern around the target where we would be passed the 9-line by the FAC. The jets were loaded up with bombs in a separate area on the airfield called the CALA (combat aircraft loading area). This kept all the dangerous stuff in one place away from the flight lines. My external checks now included checking the fuse settings and connections on the bombs. It all looked a bit mechanical with the fuse just stuffed in the nose of the bomb. You could set it for instant explosion on impact or delay it so that the bomb would penetrate the surface of what it was hitting and then go bang. When I say bang, I mean BANG!!! These were thousand pounders, and when they went off, all of the shrapnel and crap of the fragmentation pattern would rise up to nearly 3,000 feet! And I had three of these big fat bastards on board. It was a bit concerning that there were a couple of flimsy wires running down the outside of the bombs, but Killer wasn't fazed so I figured it was OK.

It took a bit more runway to get airborne, but as soon as we were cleaned up, the jet flew as normal except we were obviously using a bit more gas. This would become relevant later on in both this trip and another one some months later. We couldn't land back at Miramar with live weapons, so we definitely needed to sling them off up at 29 Palms. There was a bit of stuff to be done on the Stores page on the left-hand DDI. I had to set how many bombs would fall on each pass; which one would go first; interval between bombs; fusing etc. All the sort of stuff a Tornado GR1 mate would have had a wet dream over. I just wanted to make sure I didn't screw it up. The 9-line gave us the info that friendlies were only 500 meters from the target which freaked me out a bit, but Killer was uber calm and plugged it into the kit. I was fortunate that I was able to watch 1 and 2 drop first and as the FAC called DHs, I tipped in for my first run and called that I was visual with the target and 'in hot'. He cleared me hot and I felt a satisfying bump as the explosive bolt shoved my first ever live bomb into the shit and corruption of the leader's frag pattern. I pulled 4G to recover and stay above the min height of 5,000 feet and climbed back into the circuit pattern around the target.

We were then split off into singletons and handed off to our own personal FACs. Damn it—this meant I would have to get eyes on my own target without seeing Junk's hits first. My heart rate took a leap as our 9-line came in. This time we were holding at low-level and Killer put all the info I needed up in the HUD for me including the TOT. After a couple of minutes of holding, it was time to press for the IP and I shoved the throttles up for the run. The gas was getting a little low and we still had two bombs to loose off. We were also doing a hi-pop attack so lots of afterburner. No time to worry about that though, as I hit the offset point and pulled hard through 30 degrees to the right. After a short extension, it was full burner and pop hard. My eyes were on stalks trying to find the target while flying the aeroplane accurately to the tip-in altitude.

Killer saw it first and talked my eyes onto the tank (I bloody love WSOs!) and I tipped in to make the 45-degree dive. 'Combat 23 in hot!' I called as I dropped the designation on the tank and got cleared to pickle from the FAC. I adjusted the designation once and held the pickle button in as the aircraft vector flew right through the release line. 'Bump' it went and I was back into the climb.

'Drop the left wing, Tug,' said Killer. 'Man! Look at that!' Our bomb had lost its temper as advertised and a big black plume with fire in it slowly clawed its way up into the sky to try and reach us. I had never seen anything like it. One more to go, but we were definitely going to be out of fuel.

'No sweat, Tug. We'll land at 29 Palms and refuel after the last run.' This gave us a whole lot more gas to play with, and we were able to do the last run with similar explosive results. All good, but now I had to land at 29 Palms. The runway was made of interlocking metallic strips, a bit like the flooring you might put down in your house. Except this flooring was 8,000 feet long and had aeroplanes landing on it. The airfield seemed to be in the middle of nowhere, but we found it OK and I broke into the circuit and did an acceptable approximation of a landing. Landing is always a bit higher stakes when you have the boss in the boot, but he seemed happy as we semi-porpoised down the bouncy runway and taxied onto the flight line of sorts to shut down. We managed to grab some chow in the combined mess hall. The food was great considering everyone was living under expeditionary conditions, and then it was time for a visit to the little Marines' room before the 30-minute trip back to civilisation.

The toilet tent was an experience I have tried my hardest to burn out of my mind. The shitter was a very long metal trough with a wooden top. The top had about thirty holes in it and you just dropped them and then sat at the first free hole to do your business. Killer had seen it all before and set to, but I was horrified. Maybe this was where the famous Marine Corps brother and sisterhood was forged, but my fragile RAF officer constitution wasn't quite ready for it, especially when a corporal shouted, 'Can you pass the paper down, Colonel?' to Killer from about six holes away. However, despite my reservations, I had a thousand pounder of my own I needed to drop so I swallowed my pride/disgust/amazement and joined the brotherhood on the communal trough. Looking back, I suppose it was quite liberating, but it is something I never want to do or even witness again in my life. I couldn't wait to roar down the bouncy runway and leave the Hammer House of Horror Toilet behind.

I spent the whole of the next week on more familiar ground in the air-to-air environment. Almost straight away, I was up to 4 vs 2 intercepts and leading the trips so they could get me pairs and 4-ship lead qualified—and that after only fifteen trips on the squadron. I was loving the trust they were willing to give me and tried to repay that trust by going into full-on work-up mode, prepping in the evenings, and making sure my briefing and debriefing skills were up to scratch. Of course, there were some differences in how I briefed and conducted training, but they let me have my head so that I could show what I could do. Not everything went smoothly, but on the whole I think I showed plenty of promise as I got to grips with my jet. Flying as a crew came back to me in a heartbeat so I think my various work-ups progressed well. I was desperate to get my teeth into the air combat work-up though. I had had a taste of paradise doing ACM on the RAG, but this was the front line so maybe I could leave some of the academic bullshit behind and just see how gobsmackingly brilliant my exotic flower could be?

Before letting me loose with her though, she tried one more trick to seduce me into the ground-attack fetish club, but it didn't work. She took me strafing again, and as much fun as it was, the ball ammunition that we fired did nothing to stir my libido. The last time I strafed was with Hi-ex so ball just wasn't going to cut it. It was almost like she had put an overcoat and wellington boots on. No—if she wanted to stir my ardour, she would need to get naked again and take me upstairs to air combat heaven.

March in the cake!

Actually, re-reading that last bit, I have to correct myself. The Hornet only needed to pitch up with a pulse and I would be smitten. I was in awe of it and it had completely captured my aviation heart. Just before I started my air combat work-up, it was time for us to go to our first social event on the squadron. The Marine Corps had its birthday on 10 November, and they celebrated in style with the birthday ball. Miramar's ball was held in the Marriot downtown San Diego, and it was a chance to dress up in mess dress and party the night away. Holly was staying over at Muck's place and they had arranged baby-sitting with an Australian Navy expat who was on exchange over at Navy North Island. We had only been in San Diego a month, but were about to discover the huge Royal Navy and Australian Navy exchange community across the water on Coronado Island. They would become the backbone of our social life.

Anyway, I got together with Indy and planned out a nice little touch for the ball. In the RAF, we would wear a cummerbund and bow tie in squadron colours, but this was not a thing in the Corps. I bought two plain black cummerbunds and sewed the squadron patch onto them. They looked brilliant with the green against the black. I also bought a black bow tie and a dark green one, snipped them in half and then re-sewed them with a black half and a green half. I thought they looked even better than the cummerbunds once they were tied. Muck and his wife Suki turned up at ours in a stretch limo and we piled in with Indy for a champagne tour of the city before arriving at the Marriot. Yes, we stood up in the limo, looking out of the sunroof and popping the champagne corks—when were we ever going to get the chance to do it again?

The ball was great. Each squadron had booked a suite, and that is where we started. Free drink and a mountain of buffet food greeted us in the suite and we were absolutely plastered by the time we went down to the main event. After the sit-down dinner, there came a silence where we were asked to stand. It was all very solemn until someone shouted 'March in the cake!' I almost spat my drink out and had to stifle a laugh as this enormous cake was marched into the room. It just seemed a bit comical until the significance of the ceremony sank in. The first slice of cake was given to the oldest Marine who then passed it on to the youngest Marine there to signify the passing on of knowledge within the brother and sisterhood of the Corps. Marine Corps Order 47, written in 1921, was then read out detailing the history and the spirit of the Corps, followed by a personal message from the head of the Marines—the commandant.

All in all, it was very moving and matched any of our dining-in night traditions. At this particular ball, all of the Marine fighter crews then shouted the quote about USMC fighter pilots taken from the film *The Great Santini*, which went as follows:

> To the Corps elite. To that special breed of sky devil known and feared throughout the world, the Marine dogfighter. To the bravest men who ever lived. There's not a force who could defeat us, deny us victory, or interrupt our destiny. Marines! To Victory!

This ended with a rousing shout of 'OOH RAH!' The official part of the evening then ended with a chorus of the Marines hymn (which I made sure I had learnt beforehand). The end of the last verse summed up their ethos and beliefs:

> If the Army and the Navy,
> Ever look on Heaven's scenes;
> They will find the streets are guarded,
> By United States Marines.

It still gives me goosebumps today. I loved the Marines. I loved the Hornet. I loved my life. And then it got better.

The air combat work-up on the squadron was a formal affair a bit like the RAG air combat phase. In my case, it was to be accelerated up to full-up combat fairly quickly to get me ACTI qualified. That was assuming I would be any good at it of course. No guarantees there. I would have to fly each trip with an ACTI WSO in the back and fly against an ACTI pilot. There were about four Marine ACTI qualified pilots plus Muck who was just designated an ACTI because he was so bloody good. There were about five or six ACTI WSOs so plenty of choice. The ACTI course was a number of weeks long so it was an important qual.

My first work-up trip was against Junk and I would have Flame in the boot. Junk had an 'unusual' approach to briefing, that was completely non-standard. We loved him all the more for it though, as we knew that as soon as he was airborne, he was the epitome of professionalism and skill. He absolutely horrified Flame in the brief though. Junk was supposed to give a standardised brief on the yardstick Hornet and things I should be doing and looking out for. All of a sudden, he stopped and said 'Nyaa. I don't know why I'm briefing this shit Tug. You know what you are doin' so just do what you want OK?'

Flame's jaw dropped and Junk saw it. Quick as a flash he said, 'Nyaa, don' get me wrong! Don't crash or nuttin'!'

I'm not sure if that reassured Flame or not, but we launched anyway. A quick bit of offensive perch followed by a Guns-D saw off the academic side of the whole work-up, and then Junk and I got into the neutral splits. Flame was brilliant. He was a quiet guy on the ground, but had cuttingly sharp humour. In the air, he turned into Super-WSO and was right in the fights with me. There was no assessment here, just two people in a crew trying their best to shoot the other jet down. Junk was so good, he managed to engineer both offensive and defensive looks for me, and although it looked like a full-up fight, I knew he could have eaten me for breakfast if he had wanted. He was gracious in the debrief, telling me he was fighting his best most of the time (he wasn't) and then said he would tell everyone else to go all out against me. The official work-up was done in one trip really. The rest of my formal programme would be nothing more than plain old doggers.

Hot dog, Tug! How the fuck did you do that?

Later that afternoon, I flew against our training officer, Pepper. He had 1600 hours on the F-18 and had flown A6 Intruders previously. It was a bit of a mismatch putting my 70 hours up against him, but I had Buff in the back seat helping me out this time. Buff was huge and looked like he had just walked out of the gym. He was a major and a very experienced

F-4 and F-18 WSO. Not the most animated of guys on the ground, but just like Flame, he came alive in the air. Pepper obviously hadn't had the gouge from Junk and so detailed a bit of academic perch work first. I was already thinking that he might be underestimating what I could do, which might give me an edge when we got to the neutral splits. It did.

Everyone was expecting us to merge and go into a classic two circle rate fight with our yardstick Hornets. If I did that I was screwed, as Pepper would easily out fly me with his superior handling. I told Buff that I was going to take the fight vertical from the start and see what happened. Doesn't sound like much of a plan, I will grant you, but what I would then do is look at their reaction and decide my follow-on move from there. Buff was happy as he was ex-F-4 and we usually had to try something out of the ordinary. At the merge, I faked a turn across Pepper's tail and then slammed the burners in and pulled to flat plate the jet into the vertical at 7G. Pepper, and his WSO lost sight for a short time as they were expecting us to be mostly level with, or below them. That allowed me to rotate my jet towards their six and put them under a bit of pressure, meaning they had to ditch energy to pull back towards us. We then got to the endgame. This is going to be difficult to explain, so I want to try and turn you into fighter pilots in the bar for this.

Every fighter pilot relives their fights afterwards using their hands as aeroplanes, so let's have a go now and see if I can show you the situation I was in, and the move that I pulled. We call it 'hands in the bar', by the way. OK, stand up and put your left arm straight out in front of you, fingers together, palm down, waist height. Now rotate your lower arm clockwise (to the right) so you are thumb down. Pull your lower arm towards you slightly. Your left hand now looks like an aircraft on its side flying from left to right. That hand is Pepper. Hold your right hand with the thumb on top, right back into your belly button pointing at Pepper. That hand is me. If you move Pepper slowly across to the right and keep the fingertips of your right hand pointed at him while he moves, slowly but surely, your left arm has to come into your body and your hands would meet with them about 90 degrees off from each other. This is the position we found ourselves in.

From here, you will find that your right wrist cannot flex any more to the right. This is us hitting the G-limit. The jet cannot turn any tighter. What Pepper is expecting me to do is ease off my G and go through his tail to the outside of his turning circle (as your left hand moves further to the right, it gets closer to your body—now think of your right hand going under your left wrist). This is called mis-matching turning circles and I should unload to zero G while doing it so that I accelerate faster and then I pull back towards him. The problem with this manoeuvre is that it allows him to unload too (as I am not threatening him) and he can gain energy and zoom away from us. It then becomes a bit of cat and mouse where the one with the best handling skills will win. In that case, it wasn't going to be me, was it?

I didn't want to give up my advantage so let's go back to the starting positions with our hands. As Pepper (left hand) moves slowly to the right, quickly snap your right-hand palm down, point the fingertips upwards as far as your wrist will flex, and smartly bring your hand up in front of your face. It will now be blocking your view of Pepper, but move him slowly to the right. This vertical manoeuvre stops us from having to go outside his turning circle and is called a Hi Yo-Yo. Ordinarily, I would have to hold the Hi Yo-Yo until he separated away from me and then I would have to overbank towards him and pull into his 6 o'clock. As your left hand shows out to the right of your right hand (currently in front of your face) rotate your right hand clockwise so it is palm up and pull it in behind your left hand.

Now, this manoeuvre can allow Pepper to counter as we are not threatening him at the moment the nose comes off him. Enter the Hornet and its toy box full of batshit crazy moves. As Pepper flushed out to my right, he was continuing to unload, when he should have pulled up into me, so he made a little separation between us for me. He didn't pull up as he was full on expecting me to mismatch the turning circles. He realised his mistake and looked as though he was going to pull up into me, but it was too late. Instead of overbanking after him, we were so far nose up that I thought I would try and just keep the nose on him to freak him out. I pointed the stick at him—literally in the cockpit. I pushed the stick full forwards and hard right because that was where he was in space. The jet rotated around an axis that only existed somewhere in the space time continuum fantasy world and I found myself pointing at his jet pipes. I quickly selected the gun and the radar GACQ mode locked him up. Track his airframe with the gunsight while pulling the trigger and then the satisfying call of 'Guns, guns. Terminate' to finish it all off.

There was a second of silence in our jet and then Buff shouted, 'Hot dog, Tug! How the fuck did you do that?'

'No idea, Sir. I just pointed the stick at him.'

'Jeez! I have never seen a move like that before.'

'Trust me, Sir. I am as shocked as you are.'

We couldn't even figure it out in the debrief and Pepper was at a loss too. I had heard pilots before saying they felt their aircraft was an extension of their hands and feet. I had never felt at one with an aeroplane to be able to say that before. This jet though? I truly felt it was an extension of my imagination.

All bets were off now and it was no-shit full-up doggers against me. I got my ass kicked on some splits and kicked some ass myself on others.

Each time I flew and fought somebody, it added to the knowledge bank and filled my fighter pilot brain with what worked and what didn't. I flew with Flame on what should have been a 2 vs 1, but they decided to make me the 1, and I turned myself inside out trying to stay alive and then get some shots. The coordination from Flame was brilliant and he was as furious as I was when we got shot down. That trip ended with a couple of splits of 1 vs 1 vs 1. I have always described that exercise as the most fun you can have with your flying suit on. Everyone is your enemy so different tactics come into play, and the potential to cheat is rife. I cheated like a bastard and Flame was all over it with me. We were last man standing on the first fight, but the other two ganged up on us in fight two and we died bravely. Quickly, but bravely. Everyone was hooting in the debrief, calling us cheating bastards, but with huge smiles all around.

'If you're not cheating guys, you're not trying hard enough,' I casually stated to another chorus of howls and good-natured banter. What a hoot!

I had a peanut bladder

The next day was Friday and Miramar was having a safety stand down day. These happened from time to time and were designed to get everyone concentrating on safety issues while all the aircraft were grounded. I was going to be flying though. Indy had asked me if I fancied going on the road for the weekend. I had not done it before, but some of Indy's old mates from the Tornado GR1 OEU (Operational Evaluation Unit) were on a weapons test deployment at Eglin Air Force Base in Florida. He wanted to head over for the weekend and hook up with them. The Marine Corps had no issue with jets flying at the weekend so Indy planned it all out and handed me a set of maps to study a couple of days out. We would need to pre-position the jet at North Island, as there were no movements allowed on the Friday at Miramar. It was a 15-minute hop across the water to Coronado Island, so my first trip with Indy wasn't the most amazing for either of us. The following morning, we blasted off from the airfield where they had filmed a lot of the ground scenes of the film *Top Gun*, and climbed into the upper air to join the Jetways (equivalent of the airways in the UK).

We pressed east for a couple of hours and dropped into Cannon Air Force Base for a planned refuel and a bite to eat. Cannon was the last base to operate the F-111 Aardvark bomber and they looked like a real blast from the past out there on the flight line. As soon as we were full, on all counts, we pointed east again for another 2 hours. On the way, I pumped Indy for as much information about the radar that I could, and played with the controls, tracking all of the airliners, and generally trying to alleviate the boredom of the long transits. Approaching Cannon and Eglin, Indy talked me through the air-to-ground modes of the radar and the way that he manipulated them for the best picture. His capacity was off the charts. Yes, they were just transit sorties, but he was always so far ahead of the game, it was easy for him to teach me as well as we went. However, despite Indy's brilliance, there was nothing he could do to raise our interest levels when we were flying over the great fuck-all of Texas. Good God, it was huge and boring. Hundreds of miles of nothing to see. The only thing that kept us on our toes throughout both trips was trying to get air traffic control services to talk to us. It always took two or three calls to get them to reply. This would lead to an issue a couple of weeks after, which I will tell you about later.

All the way to Eglin, Indy had been telling me how great his GR mates were, and how I was going to like them. There was always some good-natured banter between fleets and so I said that unless they met us at the jet with a beer, then the weekend was a bust.

'Already told them, Tug,' he said, 'they know you were Phantoms so I've told them not to embarrass me!' Eglin was in the middle of some huge forested areas in the north-west of Florida, and I plonked it down and taxied in to find the four GR boys waiting for us—that looked promising. We shut down and climbed out, and I started to put the jet to bed while Indy hugged his mates. They were a brilliant bunch and I had even heard of two of them by reputation. Might as well open up with a bit of banter then.

'Where's the beers then guys?' I asked. Blank looks. I gave Indy a withering glance and he actually took them aside and bollocked them! It was only about 1300 body clock time for us, so the last thing I needed was a beer anyway. The guys took the banter to heart, especially when I heard Indy hiss, 'I told you he was Phantom!'

Thirty minutes later, I found myself in a roadside bar with a massive jug of margarita in front of me and a salted glass. We were all in flying suits and promptly got shitfaced. Except I didn't. Nobody knew at the time, but my body had always had a violent reaction to tequila—it still does. The guys must have thought I had a peanut bladder because I regularly went to the loo to throw up my margarita and then go drink some more. Why not just tell them, and order a beer I hear you ask? Basically, I had bantered myself into a corner and backing down would have destroyed my reputation in their eyes. I am such a knob head sometimes. What followed was the most brilliant detachment weekend I had been on in years. I knew Indy was great company, but so were his buddies. As they were on a long-term deployment testing bombs and clever multi-function fuses, the unit had a bonded store of booze with them for their personal use. They would have been borderline alcoholics at the end of that det if the bonded store was anything to go by. There was just so much of it. We were staying in a nice hotel block in Fort Walton beach near the larger town of Destin. The ground floor had been semi-destroyed by a recent hurricane and was strewn with sand and debris. It looked like it was derelict until you got up to the rooms and suites which were amazing.

We tanked up on free hooch and headed out into town for grub to soak it all up. At the end of the night, we ended up in an Australian themed bar called Kangaroo Jacks. The place has wild with live music, lots of audience participation and a river of booze. We were out of our faces that night and after some life-reviving brunch, we did it all again on the Saturday. I toned it down a little the second night as we were flying back on the Sunday. Only one of the GR boys managed to drag his sorry arse out of bed to give us a lift to Eglin, and it was two tired and somewhat shabby pseudo-Marines that did the reverse trip through Cannon to Miramar. Reports from the Eglin crew were that I was OK—for a Phantom mate. The flip side was that they were not dull and boring at all—for GR mates. Our love-in was such that they asked us back two weeks later for their final weekend in the States.

I only had one trip the following week, and it turned out to be my last ACM work-up. I was flying with a newly qualified ACTI WSO called Anal. He was a pedantic guy, hence the callsign. Very professional though, and he had only just arrived back on 121 after being away on his ACTI course. I was up against Pepper again, and so there was a bit of pride and reputation on this one given our last trip against each other. Once the sortie brief was done, I got together with Anal for a crew brief. Completely forgetting he had just done the ACTI course, and was therefore keen to impart all his new found knowledge, I started to tell him my game plan for the first fight and what I expected from him, when he interrupted me immediately.

'Right, Tug, I expect you to merge 2,000 feet above base height and fly a yardstick Hornet. 380 knots sustained speed. You can use the 2,000 feet to base height to squeeze more G and maintain speed, but I will only allow you a plus or minus 50-knot speed excursion from that.'

There was a bit of a pause and then I realised that this was the whole plan.

'And then what?' I asked.

'What do you mean?'

'What do we do after that? What do we do if he matches us? What do we do if he reverses single-circle to nose point? What if he goes vertical?'

'Erm ...'

'OK, here's my plan for the first fight. I am pretty sure he will be expecting me to go vertical, as I pulled that on him last time and shot him. He will want to match that so it doesn't happen again. However, he knows I ditched all my speed last time, so he will try and keep his energy high. It will be a lazy pull so that I top out before him and give him the advantage. However, I am going to turn in front of him pre-merge to make him think we are going two-circle. He will try to extend vertically to make separation for the shot. I am then going to reverse the turn and snap round to AMRAAM him. Plus or minus 50 knots just isn't going to work. I will be ditching a lot of speed in that reverse.'

Anal was quiet.

'Of course, he might not do any of that and we will be fucked, but if I was a betting man, I would say it will happen a bit like that. If it's any different, I'll just fight what I see. How's that sound?'

I'm pretty sure Anal was expecting to deliver an academic style ACM trip, and tried to push the yardstick Hornet again, so I did a deal with him that if we got shot on the first fight, I would do as he said on the subsequent ones. Now, you may think I am making this bit up to make it a good read, but Pepper did almost exactly what I predicted he would do. The thing is that for the best part of a week, I had bantered Pepper about how I had introduced him to the vertical. Him being an old bomber pilot, he only thought in two dimensions etc. It was just normal banter between fighter crews, but it always has a bit of an effect you know? I had been planting the seed for that first fight for a week.

The fighter pilot will cheat

Pepper was flying with Indy, so it would be the first time Indy would have seen me doing air combat. There was a bit of pressure on me then. I aggressively turned in front of Pepper. We would normally turn across someone's tail, so he probably thought I was trying to steal a march on him. Up he went, as advertised, and I reversed and hauled 7.5G, and my wonderful Hornet responded by snapping its eager little nose around. I got a VACQ lock and my AMRAAM shot off the rail (in my head anyway) and fight one was over in less than 20 seconds from the initial merge.

'Fox 3 kill. Terminate.'

Apparently, Indy's commentary went something like, 'You need to pitch back in! He's got separation! Come hard left! Come hard left!!! Chaff! Flares! Oh ... we're dead then.' The second fight, I faked a yardstick Hornet and turned across his tail. He did the same thing and dug in down to base height thinking he would out-rate me round the circle. Just across his tail,

I went vertical with the speedbrake out to ditch speed. If he had come up with me, I would have been poorly placed, but he thought he could power away with his extra speed, as I hadn't made enough separation in the vertical for the missiles. As he continued round the circle, I pirouetted the jet and it almost stall-turned to point directly down onto him. My main concern here was not to go through base height and kill myself, so I sacrificed a bit of nose advantage to avoid 'the ground'. Again, poorly placed if he powered out of it. He didn't though. He was so intimidated by my nose, that he broke hard into me and washed a lot of speed off doing it. I called a snapshot with the gun which he reacted to and washed even more speed off, and then it was just a case of nibbling away behind him to complete a proper guns kill.

We didn't have the gas for another fight so Pepper led us back to Miramar, and four sweaty aircrew climbed out of their fighting machines and walked quietly into the debrief. Indy was smiling so I guessed I hadn't let the British side down. However, the debrief took a bit of an odd turn when Pepper and Anal started discussing my energy management. On more than one occasion, I was asked what speed I had at various parts of the fight. My replies of 'I don't really know' were met with a shake of the ACTI head from Anal, and sighs from Pepper. It was starting to wind me up a little, as in my mind, it didn't matter what speed I had. All that mattered was that I was behind him and the SHOOT cue was flashing as I pulled the trigger. I was asked yet again what energy I had at a certain point, and I thought it was time to shut things down.

'I have no idea what speed I had, as I was too busy gunning you Pepper.' There really is no answer to that and Indy fought down a bit of a snort. Anal's argument was that we were poorly placed if another bandit came in and threatened us. On that point, he was 100 per cent correct. But this was 1 vs 1 and it was not real.

1 vs 1 against your squadron mates is not about being tactically sound and winning a whole campaign. It is about that moment; that snapshot in time where nothing else matters except you and the person you want to shoot down. Yes, it breeds trust in your own aircraft and your handling of it. It helps to embed radar and weapons handling in a highly dynamic situation. It also helps to develop decision making on the job and crew coordination. Honestly though? It is a bare-knuckle slugfest surrounded by an attitude of who wants it most. It is about revenge and aggression and above all, ego. It was two-nil and that was all there was to say about that. And they gave me the world's best dogfighting aeroplane in which to do it. Marry to that, a bit of RAF training and a lot of old tricks and deception, and I was well placed to bury my imposter syndrome and truly revel in my fighting. I was written up as an ACTI after that trip and was

over the moon that I hadn't embarrassed myself doing something I had a background in and really should have been good at. Don't get me wrong here—I was still making mistakes and getting my ass kicked, but I was learning all the time. I felt as though I had proved myself a bit, and the squadron had opened its arms to me. I was a bit of an oddity, but I revelled in the difference and like I said, I was nowhere near as odd as Muck. I just felt like I belonged on 121, and I belonged in the Marines. It was a wonderful feeling.

That weekend, Flame and his wife invited us over to their house to celebrate Thanksgiving with them. Thanksgiving is the biggest and most important holiday season on the US calendar. We drove over with Indy and they opened their house to us. Flame's wife, Mimi, cooked up the most amount of food I had ever seen on one family table. All of the traditional food was done, but at the end of the meal, Mimi made us a cup of tea. She had never brewed tea in her life and didn't even have a kettle (few American houses did). Despite that, she put a large pan of water on the stove to boil, and threw in about ten tea bags. Dear God it was awful, but the mere fact that she had tried something to make us feel even more welcome was just beautiful.

Back at home, I had become completely enamoured with Michael Jordan's rise back to the top of basketball, and watched every Bull's game that I could on TV. I even went so far as to buy a full-sized freestanding basketball net and set it up in the back garden. I had played a bit of basketball at school and then again in the RAF, so figured I would be able to emulate Jordan after a bit of practice. Have you seen how tall a basketball net is? Very quickly, my dreams of a late career in the NBA were dashed when I found out that even free-throws were difficult. Now, there are two methods for improving your performance in sports. The high-end sports star will practice skills, increase fitness, and try to improve any and every facet that can have an effect on their game. The fighter pilot will cheat.

I lowered the height of my net, and went out to buy a kid's half-size basketball. I could hold it in one hand like all my favourite NBA players. Then I set out to recreate all of Jordan's moves from the various slam dunk competitions that he blitzed. My ultimate was taking off from the free throw line (much closer to the basket on my court); 'flying' through the air for seconds just like Air Jordan (hmm—doing a little jump off the ground); and slamming the ball through the net one-handed (that bit is true). I looked like a basketball God—in my own head. Anybody watching would have seen a sad spindly loser, playing on his own with a set of kid's sports toys. I doubt Michael would have been impressed. Jordan was getting back to the top of his game, and that is how I was feeling with the F-18. The thing with flying though, is just when you think you have it cracked, it throws something at you to show you that you haven't.

I flew a couple of intercept trips with relatively new WSOs in the back and I was leading inexperienced first-tourist pilots. After only two months on the squadron, I was back in a semi-instructional/mentor role. One of those trips was the first time I had flown with Bluto. As I have said before, he was an experienced aviator, but on the OV-10. He was still pretty new to the F-18 and its multitude of roles. Unfortunately, he had flown with a lot of macho single-seat pilots on the RAG and had been little more than a passenger with them. Here on the squadron, he would need to get up to speed and become an active part of the crew. I had a crew brief with him, telling him how to build the picture for me using the intercom (rather than me using the radar myself) and things were going OK. The second trip I did with him? Not so good, for either of us.

Told ya, mate!

We were scheduled as the wingman of a pair led by Muck and Indy and we were off to 29 Palms to be on call for some FAC training. Bloody CAS again, but this time we were carrying four live 1,000 pounders each. If all ran smoothly, the trainee FACs would get four runs of section attacks for their training. We would be short on gas as soon as we got airborne, so if it didn't go smoothly, they would get less runs and we would pickle off a couple at a time. It was a late afternoon launch so any faffing about could well see us having to spend the night at 29 Palms, sweating buckets, and sleeping in a tent. I would do anything to avoid that and the horrors of Satan's communal toilet.

We arrived on station and checked in with the FACs and were told to hold down at low-level. I was trying to formate on Muck in a tactical battle position two miles line abreast to cover his six. Time passed and Muck pimped them for the 9-line. All we got back was a 'standby' call and we continued our tactical race track. I called my fuel state to Muck as things were getting a bit tight, but still no 9-line. OK, bear in mind that we can't take the bombs back to Miramar, we have to get rid of them somehow. There was a dumping ground called Sunshine Peak which was way up to the top of the area and that was where you dumped any ordnance you hadn't dropped or fired. Sunshine Peak must have had more metal in it than all the iron and tin mines in the world combined. We were getting to the point with the fuel where we would just have enough to get up there and still make it back to Miramar. As soon as it went below that, we were committed to dropping on the CAS run, or spending the night in purgatory. At last, the 9-line came through and we both wrote it down—or so I thought.

As we had walked to the jets earlier, Muck had asked me to do my own nav kit for the 9-line and not use Bluto. 'He's not up to it mate,' he told me. Bluto had pleaded with me to let him do the kit and as he had previously been a FAC in the air, I relented. Let me be absolutely clear here. I was still struggling a little with the whole CAS thing (It was only really my second proper go) and so any help to lighten my load was appreciated. Allied with that, it was twilight and just flying formation on Muck was getting hard even after I had closed in to about a mile. I was also distracted by the fuel load and the pressure of dropping live. All in all, then, nowhere near the top of my game. In fact, I was probably close to my limit. The FAC called for one bomb each on the run, but Muck called, 'Negative. Combats are one pass, haul ass!' On hearing that call, I pulled up the stores page and selected all four bombs to go at the same time. With Muck's bombs, this was going to be one hell of a bang.

We were due to push to the IP 30 seconds after Muck, and I asked Bluto to bring the IP up in the kit. All I got was silence.

'Bluto. Bring up the IP, mate.' Nothing. Muck pushed for the IP and I had a quick look at my watch just as a backup.

'Bluto! I need the IP now!'

'I can't find it, Tug,' he said in a quiet voice.

'What?!'

'I can't find it in the kit.'

'Well just type it in now!'

'I didn't write it down. I just typed it all in straight from the 9-line.'

'Shit!' It was almost time to push, so using my map in the semi-darkness, I cobbled together a heading and then got back onto Bluto.

'Man,' he said. 'This nav kit is kicking my ass.'

'That's nothing to what I am going to do to it when we land!' I shouted. 'Just plug the target in and I'll tackle it from there,' I said with absolutely no confidence at all, and pushed for an IP that I didn't really know the location of. I was way beyond my capacity as I was flying at low-level in the gloom; only going roughly in the right direction; no timing or steering; four shouty bombs; and the XO's voice in my head saying, 'DON'T KILL A MARINE!' Somehow, I managed to call the position of the target to Bluto from my 9-line, and he typed it in. I figured we were somewhere near the IP and set off on heading with another look at my watch. I heard Muck calling 'In hot!' to the FAC. Bluto was just a passenger at this point and was saying nothing. God, if this is what CAS was really like, you could bloody well keep it.

At some arbitrary point, I popped, and as I looked in the vague direction of the target, the FAC asked if I could see Muck's hits. You couldn't miss them. Four 1,000-pounders makes a hell of a mess.

'A-Firm,' I said.

'Right! Hit those!'

'Combat 72, in hot.'

'Combat 72 cleared hot.'

It was supposed to be a 30-degree dive profile, but because my kit-free navigation to the IP was a little dodgy, we were much closer to the target than planned when we popped, which meant I was in a much steeper dive. Bmf, bmf, bmf, bmf went my drag-inducing fuel-drinking ACME cannonballs, and my jet responded to the 6G slug on the stick, and soared into the darkening sky.

'Good hits!' shouted the FAC, but I didn't care. I was totally washed out and could barely speak on the radio for the join up with Muck. I couldn't even enjoy the fact that I had avoided spending the night at 29 Palms. Had I not seen Muck's hits, there was no way I would have dropped (it would have been too dangerous) and it would have been a very quiet transit to Sunshine Peak and then landing on the bouncy runway. I had visions of me sitting at one end of the shitter, as far away from Bluto as I could get. And not passing him the paper.

We discussed a few things on the way back and I did some mea culpa in the debrief. I was a bit shit on the trip. My major mistake was to let my awareness drop when I thought Bluto was picking up the load. I was experienced enough to know better than that, but probably not good enough anyway to have done everything myself. Rock and a hard place. I also had a reset to my ego which was probably long overdue too and definitely deserved. I imagine that was the last time Bluto typed the 9-line directly into the kit too. 'Told ya, mate!' was all Muck said to me afterwards with his all-knowing grin plastered across his face. He put his arm around me and walked me out to my car. I was shattered. Top down and drive back to OB in the dark cleared my head nicely. CAS was going to take a bit of work.

This is probably a good time to tell you about Muck. Whereas Indy was the nicest guy in NATO, Muck was definitely the oddest. I loved them both. That oddness fit Muck like a glove. I'm not sure the Marines knew what the hell to do with him, so they did what Marines always did—they cracked on with him anyway. He was a 1,000-hour Hornet guy and was very, very good in the air, and professional and capable on the ground. Despite his experience, he tried to learn something new every day, and kept a little black book on him which he wrote in constantly. After passing my ACTI work-up, the boss had asked me to give a brief on how we taught ACM in the RAF. I remember talking about mind-set and aggression a lot and then got onto a bit of weaponeering (QWIs look away now). The young guys on the squadron were missing shot opportunities due to not thinking ahead and anticipating when a shot was coming up. I used to teach a mnemonic at Tac Wpns training for Sidewinder shots of ARG WHOOOOOSH! This stood for aspect, range, growl. You pictured in advance the aspect of the shot that was going to present itself (head, beam, or tail on—or somewhere in between). This then led you into knowing the range bracket available for the missile (there were max and min ranges for each aspect). Once you were in range, if you had a growl (tone) from the seeker head in the missile, then the next thing you should hear is WHOOOOOSH, as you pull the trigger and the missile launches off the rail.

'ARG WHOOOOOSH, mate! Love it!' he shouted in his Aussie accent, then wrote it down in his book while chuckling to himself. 'ARG WHOOOOOSH! I'm gonna use that!'

Jesus Indy. I think I was asleep there ... Indy? ... Indy?!

We socialised a lot with Muck and his wife Suki. They had two boys around Holly's age, and a girl in the pipeline it transpired. Suki was the most laid-back woman I had ever met. She needed to be given how much of a free spirit Muck was. Their younger son, Nicholas was an even freer spirit and even Muck called him 'the terrorist'. They were great company for us and Muck introduced us to the huge Aussie Navy expat community over on Coronado Island that we shared fortnightly social events with. He was a man of hidden talents also. He asked Indy and I out one night for a few beers, but was a bit secretive about where we were going.

The cab pulled up outside the San Diego Yacht Club which was an elite, members only club. It had won the Americas Cup for goodness' sake so they weren't going to let in three relatively poor and scruffy oiks like us. Unperturbed, Muck, who had more front than Skegness, walked up to the door and said 'G'day David' to the doorman who replied with 'Nice to see you, Muck,' and let us in. Indy and I were gobsmacked and we went into the busy bar to see lots of posh people shake Muck's hand and buy us a load of beers. And then the story came out. One Saturday afternoon, Muck had blagged his way into the bar and ordered a beer. The barman had said it was a members' only club and everyone turned to see who the pleb was that didn't belong. The wall behind the bar was covered in those plaques that yachting people have with the side relief of the hull of their yacht on it. Muck pointed to a golden-hulled plaque of a boat called the Kookaburra, and said, 'No worries, mate. I thought I could get a beer here seeing as you have my boat on the wall.' It all went a bit quiet. This boat had taken part in the Americas Cup and Muck had worked at the boat yard in Australia that built it so he had been hands on it during its manufacture! From then on, he had free membership to the club (and a bit of celebrity status), and he and Suki regularly sailed there with the kids. Muck and Suki practically lived on the water back in Oz and he had skippered boats all over the world before joining the RAAF.

His handling of the jet was superb, and he seemed to have capacity coming out of his ears. I soaked up as much as I could from him and he was always patient enough to explain things in detail for me. All the way through my flying career, I have come across some superstars. Muck was one of them, but for the life of me, I don't know how or why. He just was.

Not content with being horribly shitfaced for a full weekend once in Florida, Indy and I went off and did it all again for the OEU's leaving party. Cannon was closed on the Friday so our refuel took place at Dyess Air Force Base in Texas. This just happened to be one of the two homes of the B1-B Lancer supersonic bomber—an all-round gobsmackingly beautiful looking aeroplane. There were at least thirty of them on the line as we taxied in, and they were probably worth more than all the jets in the RAF put together. On arrival at Eglin, the GR boys met us at the jet with a beer which Indy was buzzing about. I was too, given that we wouldn't have to stop at some dodgy roadhouse for a margarita again. The weekend went as advertised with lots of partying, bad karaoke and not much sleep. We had barely dented the bonded store, so the guys loaded us up with bottles of spirits to take back to Miramar. God alone knows what the groundcrew thought of us as our bags clanked when we put them in the video recorder hold, and Indy secured some loose bottles in the space behind his ejection seat. Maybe he thought I was such a ropey pilot, he would need a stiffener or two to calm his nerves when flying with me?

Remember I told you on our last trip to Eglin that most of the air traffic services wouldn't talk to us straight away because of our accents? Well, on the way to Eglin this time, we got so sick of it that we stopped checking in when we changed frequency. Very unprofessional, but we were just fed up with repeating ourselves when nobody responded. Eventually, after we had moved into their airspace by about ten miles, they would call us.

'Combat 51, are you on this?' We would then reply with:

'A-Firm, Combat 51. We've been trying to call you for the past ten miles. We are level at four zero zero.'

'OK, Combat 51. Continue.'

That seemed to be the standard sequence, and it worked, so we patted ourselves on the back and continued like that. On the way home that

Sunday, we were very tired and still a bit hungover. There were almost no other aeroplanes up there on the jet routes for us to play with on the radar and very little stimulation all round—autopilot, autothrottle, autoroute. And we were heading into the vast nothingness of Texas. We were handed over to Fort Worth centre, and Indy switched frequencies. I didn't check in and we waited. The next thing was, I was dimly aware of someone shouting at me.

'Combat 51, are you on this?!'

'A-Firm, Combat 51. We've been trying to call you for the past ten miles,' I answered automatically.

'I've been trying to call you for the past 40 miles, Sir!!!' he replied. Holy shit! I was instantly alert and alarmed.

'Er. Roger centre, we are level three eight zero.'

'Are you sure you are OK, Sir?'

'A-Firm. Must have been a comms issue,' I lied.

'OK, Combat 51, continue.' I had a cold stab down my spine.

'Jesus Indy. I think I was asleep there ... Indy? ... Indy?!'

I looked in my mirrors to see Indy's head up against the side of the canopy, and he was fast asleep. I waggled the stick to bang his head on the window and he woke with a start.

We had planned to press all the way to Cannon again, but I asked Indy to find us the nearest suitable air base that we could use and still make Miramar in one hop afterwards. Dyess came to our rescue, and as we were familiar with it, it was a good choice. I had never been so awake in my life getting that jet on the ground. We both looked a bit pale as we wandered into the ops building, but a Burger King while the jet was refuelled would hopefully maintain us back to Miramar. Indy went over to file the flight plan, but as we tried to leave ops, we found the door was locked. The ops officer looked over to us and said, 'I'm sorry, gentlemen. We are now on exercise and moving the shape.' For those who are unaware, 'the shape' was the code word for nuclear weapons. The whole of the base was on lock down for an hour while this huge convoy of very serious looking trucks transported real nuclear weapons from one bomb dump to another. It gave us a chance to get some power nap style shuteye and I doubt we looked like professional aviators while sprawled out on the chairs snoring our heads off. We spoke constantly to each other on the second hop to Miramar, and just sucked up the frustration of having to check in twice each time with the various ATC agencies. As it was Sunday, there were no ground crew to see us in at Miramar, so we put the jet to bed on the line and clanked our way back to the cars for the drive home. Like I said—not very professional.

The green-looking wheezy man

After a couple more trips, I had a week of leave in the two weeks before Christmas. We had splashed out and booked a short holiday in Hawaii. Once again, when would we ever get the chance to do something like that? At my first baseball game, Sharpe had told me that the USAF owned a hotel right on Waikiki Beach on Oahu, called the Hale Koa. You could stay there if you were serving personnel and it was relatively cheap, so off we went. Hawaii is the definition of paradise and we fell in love with it. The Hale Koa was amazing and had a great big Christmas tree in the foyer. I could write a whole book about what we did that week, but, suffice to say, we did all the standard touristy things such as the cultural centre; a luau (traditional feast with music and dancing); Pearl Harbour which was as poignant as it was stunning and historic; and Waimea Bay with its giant surf. The surf at Waimea Bay was thought to be too big to tame all the way up to 1957. I was determined to have a go in some way. I couldn't surf, but I was getting OK at bodyboarding in Ocean Beach. There was nowhere to hire a board so I decided to body surf in the shallows. The beach fell away very quickly so the shallows became the depths within 20 or 30 metres of the shore.

I body surfed for about 20 minutes only. When I say body surfed, what I mean is I got tumbled around in the ultra-violent salt water washing machine. All of my tubes and orifices were jet hosed out, and once it was bored of me, the surf dumped me face down on the beach gasping for air. Not quite the Beach Boys 'Surfing USA' picture I had in my mind. I was absolutely exhausted and nauseous, and Holly must have wondered who the green-looking wheezy man was, stumbling around, knocking her sandcastles over. On the flight home from Hawaii, we were sitting next to a very nice American woman who was chatting away, but looking closely at Holly's face. She hoped she wasn't being too forward, but she was an optician and noticed that one of Holly's eyes was drifting a little as she nodded off to sleep. She recommended we have her seen by a paediatric optician, so we did. My wife took Holly to her first appointment and came back in floods of tears. It appeared that Holly had a condition where her eyes were different sizes and so her dominant eye had taken over leaving her left eye to atrophy a bit. It meant a regime of patching her right eye until her left 'woke up'. It also meant she would need glasses. My wife was upset as she had been the kid at school with glasses and all that entailed, but the lack of compassion from the optician had tipped her over the edge. With Holly only being two years old, how were we going to stop her pulling the patch off her eye? The optician's advice was to wrap stiff magazines around her arms and speed tape them so Holly couldn't bend her arms enough to reach the patch! I called the optician to get some detail and she patronised me so much that I vowed we would find another. One of the Marines on 121 recommended his daughter's optician and he was brilliant. We got Holly fitted for some tiny spectacles and patched her glasses instead of her face. I threw the magazines and speed tape away.

Back at work, I had two very pleasant trips with Hoover and then it was time for our first California Christmas. I have always been a Christmas person. This would be Holly's second Christmas, but the first one she would be aware of at the time of it. It was a bit odd opening presents with the Californian sun streaming through the windows, and even more strange having a full roast turkey dinner, after a stroll on the beach. It was even more odd when we visited a particular street a few blocks from us. What had probably started out as a bit of good-natured competition on Christmas decorations, had exploded into a winter wonderland in every home on the street. You could barely see the original houses for the decorations and it attracted visitors from all over the county, raising lots of money for charity. At night, it looked spectacular, like you were in Lapland. During the day in the sunshine? Hmm—not so much. We only had Christmas Eve through Boxing Day off, and then it was back to work and straight into a night flying programme on the 27th. Miramar had another safety stand down on the 28th, so we flew out of North Island for the night.

I flew with a young, but experienced WSO called Pilgrim, and we launched as a 3-ship with me being the only one not on NVGs again. We were providing targets for some F-16s who were working out of Yuma, and we were all going to land there for the mass debrief. When I say mass, I mean MASS! We were going against ten of them so it wasn't really a fair fight. Ten was a bit overkill, and how they coordinated everyone at night was a thing of beauty. I had never seen so many blips on the scope. The second trip into North Island was much more manageable as we used our 3-ship to do an internal 1 vs 2 intercept trip. The most amazing thing on both trips was that we saw the Hale-Bopp comet as it made its way across the Universe. It would only become visible from the ground with the naked eye a few months later, but for us at 30,000 feet above all the light pollution, we had a grandstand view.

OK, enough flirting. It was time to dance

My last trip of 1995 was something special. I had just over 100 hours on the jet and I was scheduled to fly 1 vs 1 dissimilar air combat training (DACT) against an F-14D. The D-model Tomcat was bloody enormous and powered by two engines of climate change proportions. It was going to be a difficult fight as this thing could power itself out of most situations, and the swing-wing aspect gave it good manoeuvrability too. Therefore, it had a reputation, and folks were wary of going up against it. My mindset was that it wasn't a Hornet. So, it couldn't do some of the things we could do. There were a lot of things it could do that we couldn't, but why focus on those?

I got all sorts of advice from the other pilots on 121 about how to fight it, but most of it relied on handling the aircraft really well and managing energy. No way I was good enough to do that so I instantly thought deception would be the key. I would need to do something they wouldn't expect. To be honest with you, I didn't think my 100 hours was going to be good enough to take them, but it wouldn't stop me from trying, and I would turn myself inside out if we ended up defensive. They put the boss in my boot, and together we walked across the hangar to the VF-2 Bounty Hunters to meet the crew we would be flying against. Their squadron spaces were full of Tomcat pictures and plaques, and to be quite frank, it looked bloody awesome, and I was desperate to have a go in one of their jets. The RIO (radar intercept officer) of the crew met us and offered us a coffee which was all very pleasant. Crikey—this guy was enormous—another American football player type. He took us into the briefing room, and we waited for his pilot. It was all being staged for us and I gave the boss a quizzical look as the RIO dramatically announced that his pilot was Grizzly. Killer just rolled his eyes and sighed as this man-mountain strode into the room adorned with 2,000-hour Tomcat badges and huge WestPac (West Pacific) cruise patches on his flying jacket.

Apparently Grizzly was well known and had a reputation as big as his jet. It was almost an 'Elvis has entered the building' moment. Anyway, once the shock and awe moment had passed, we got down to briefing. Their confidence in their jet and their own performance was astounding, and it was almost like they were saying 'when we beat you' and treating our little jet like a bug that needed swatting. It rubbed me up the wrong way immediately and I was desperate to take them down. The worst thing was that Grizzly briefed it all up with a huge smile on his face like the outcome was inevitable. As we wandered back to 121, Killer said to me, 'I really wanna kick his ass, Tug.'

'Me too, Sir—believe me.' We found a briefing room and I laid out my gameplan for the first fight. It was similar to the stunt I had pulled on Pepper so needed a bit of deception, and I would also be giving away a bit of advantage at the start to tempt them into pulling a move I could capitalise on.

'What if it doesn't work, Tug?' he asked.

'Well, Sir, I will be working my nuts off to claw it back again if he doesn't bite.' I told Killer I didn't think my handling was good enough to start with a yardstick Hornet so this was our best bet. I also told him I thought Grizzly was over confident and would be expecting what he had seen before from the F-18. I must have sounded convincing enough as the boss went with it.

The upcoming combat aside, just taxiing out and lining up on the runway next to the Tomcat was a life event for me. Once again, I was speechless at how big it was and as they powered away from us on the runway, our jet was buffeted to buggery as the inferno of their burners single-handedly torched us to a crisp. Ten seconds later, we rolled and slipped airborne behind them like one of those sucker fish that sniffs around the arse of the big shark. I carried out my weapons checks, and after they had done theirs, I dropped into close formation on the right wing. I didn't need to be in close with them. I just wanted to! I had to pinch myself yet again. I had watched *Top Gun* at the cinema in York while I was learning to fly on the Jet Provost Mark 3, and here I was, in close formation with the star of the film. And I was in a Hornet!

OK, enough flirting. It was time to dance. The F-14 had the Phoenix active missile, but it was nowhere near as agile as our AMRAAMs. Therefore, we were only using Sidewinders and the gun each. It was their brief and lead, so their prerogative on weapons choice. I had no problem with that, but it did remove one of the big advantages we might have had. At the outwards turn call, I climbed a couple of thousand feet as I would need it for my opening move. If he dived for base height, he would have 4,000 feet of turning room as we passed. This was quite an advantage if he took it, but he didn't. We watched him climb to match us, which is just what I thought his ego would get him to do. He knew he could out-rate us round the circle, so obviously didn't feel that he needed the vertical turning room I was giving him. I kept the burners in as we turned towards each other and head-on we must have had 450 knots. His Rio should have seen that on the radar so it would be obvious we were going for a 2-circle rate fight. Just as we merged, I faked a hard turn towards him further cementing 2-circle in his mind, but instead of pulling, I held the jet on its side while pulling the throttles back to idle and popping the speed brake.

Timing was critical here to make sure he was going 2-circle. I then reversed and hauled 7.5G to ditch speed, then used the height above base to pirouette the nose down and round into single-circle. Grizzly pulled his nose up to power out of it into the vertical. Their logic was that a move like that meant there was no way I could get the nose on to threaten them. However, that's why I merged at 450 knots and had 4,000 feet of height to play with. I had ditched a lot of energy to get the nose around, but I hadn't started with the yardstick speed. I had been much faster so still had enough in hand. The 4,000 feet gave me room to pirouette the nose and also maintain a little bit of energy. I had just enough to snap the nose up for the Sidewinder. Just as with Pepper, I got a VACQ lock, a Sidewinder tone followed immediately with a SHOOT cue. I pulled the trigger and the fight was over. I terminated over the radio, then fell out of the sky a bit as we were pretty slow at that point, and then got ready for the next one.

I always say this—losing the first fight is demoralising. The next fight doesn't count as you are already dead. It is difficult to think clearly on the subsequent fights, especially if your ego has told you that you are going to win every one easily. Grizzly and his RIO were all over the place on the next two splits and it was easy kills for us. The little bug that they thought they were going to swat turned out to be a Hornet, and it had stung them to death. It was a lot of fun flying back on the Tomcat's wing and it must have looked awesome as we broke into the circuit at Miramar with me hanging onto the F-14 with his massive wings swept back looking like a dart.

Killer was overjoyed and slapped me on the back as we walked in. The ready room was buzzing as he relayed the story to everyone about how we had three kills to zero. What he failed to mention was his part in it all. He was way too modest, but I could not have pulled off that first move (or any of them come to mention it) without his commentary during the fights. I have never got to grips with how back-seaters were able to endure the violent moves and the constant changes in G during air combat, yet still provide the essential service that was a huge part of our success. Taking just my first move, I needed to drill my eyes onto Grizzly's jet and commit nose down while doing it. Not once during that move, did I need to look at the HUD which meant I could concentrate all my attention on Grizzly. Not only was Killer a talking HUD, he was also sharp enough to know if we had enough space to pull out for the altitude the aircraft was at, and was advising me of it throughout. On the subsequent fights, when I was losing sight of the Tomcat, he padlocked his eyes on and fought the aircraft himself by talking me into rolling and pulling until I had sight again. As soon as I called 'Tally', he was straight back to being a talking HUD. He was just brilliant. Any navs/WSOs/RIOs reading this might be thinking 'So what? That's the job, mate.' Well, take it from me—there is at least one pilot who truly appreciated what you did and how you did it.

Oh my God, kill me now

Grizzly and his RIO were gracious enough to accept full on defeat in the debrief, so no problems there. The score was 3–0 so it would have been a ballsy move to go on the offensive. It was even better when we put our tape in and they commented on how good Killer's commentary was and how well we coordinated as a crew. What a way to end my first year in the United States. It might not seem it as you have read this, but 1995 had gone in the blink of an eye. I also finished the year getting something I had wanted for a long time—my name on an aeroplane. I always wanted it on a Phantom, but the squadrons I was on didn't really go in for that kind of thing. But there it was on the side of an F-18 Hornet for all to see. Flt Lt R A Wilson, and underneath it—MR TUG.

1996 started with some run of the mill intercept stuff (if anything could be considered run of the mill in a Hornet), but also with me being fully employed in the ops office. I joined Muck and Indy in writing the flying schedule and coordinating the annual training programme. Every time we flew, we would log training codes dependent on what we had actually done on the sortie. There was a yearly currency on everything and these currencies fed into an overall measure called the CRP, or combat readiness percentage. We would work this out for Hoover, and the boss would present our figure at the group meeting every month. Our group commander was Major General Bolden so a bit of pressure, as you don't want to disappoint an astronaut. You were also showing your tail to every other squadron at the presentation.

It was time for us to work out our CRP and it came in around 82 per cent. We told Hoover and he looked like he had been shot. 'Oh man! 82 per cent? Oh no!' We asked him what the problem was and he told us that the absolute minimum was 88 per cent (I forget the actual numbers, but this gives you an idea). Hoover was devastated as this would seriously embarrass the squadron and the boss. My take has always been to expose the problem and be truthful. If we did this, then surely the group would have to allocate more flying to us and solve the problem. This was not how it worked in the Marine Corps, or indeed in any organisation world-wide in my experience (including the RAF). It was awful to see Hoover so upset, so Muck said we would run the numbers again for him. He asked Indy and me to come and look at the data with him. We were nonplussed. Doing the numbers again would give us the same result. We had already checked them twice. We didn't look at the data again though. We went for lunch. Muck drove us to the golf club on base and we had lunch out in the sunshine at the club's restaurant. We asked Muck what he thought the data was going to show, but all he said was, 'Leave it to me guys. I've got a plan.' We enjoyed a very leisurely lunch and headed back to 121 to enact Muck's plan, whatever the hell it was. The three of us trooped into Hoover's office and Muck said, 'Hi Hoover. Look, we've run the numbers again and the CRP came out at 92 per cent not 82. It was just a mistake so we are all good.' Ah, so Muck's plan was to just lie about the CRP then. Hoover's face lit up and he beamed a smile at us. Disaster averted. We filed out thinking that was the end of it. A week later, Hoover announced at met brief that 121 had won a group award for having such a high CRP. Not a flicker on Muck's face.

About this time, Nellis Air Force Base was running one of its Red Flag exercises. Air Forces from across the world would congregate in Las Vegas and have a big two-week punch up in the Nellis ranges which were wrapped around Area 51. They were massive exercises and usually had an RAF bomber squadron as well as a fighter squadron on them. The bomber squadron had loads of Indy's old mates on it and he knew the boss really well. I knew a couple of the guys on the Tornado F3 squadron, and that unit had one of Muck's best mates from the RAAF on exchange. It would have been madness not to take a couple of jets in for the weekend. So, we did. I flew Indy and we led Muck who had the flight surgeon in his boot. Every squadron in the Navy and Marine Corps had a flight surgeon attached to it, and they flew as much as they could. It only took 40 minutes before we were breaking over more aeroplanes than I had ever seen in one place. The pan at Nellis was vast and it was covered in metal of all shapes and sizes. It was proper fast jet pornography.

We had no accommodation booked as we just figured we would bed down in our buddy's rooms. The RAF contingent was staying in the Alexis Park Hotel just off the strip, and we arrived to find the bar awash with two squadron's worth of aircrew, most of whom were well on the way to being drunk. I saw lots of familiar faces, but was looking for Plop, my old mate from 92 Squadron Phantoms. Out of nowhere, Muck stood up on the bar and shouted 'JIMMY!' at the top of his voice. An Australian voice at the far end of the bar shouted 'MUCK!' and a very short pilot leapt up onto the bar. They walked towards each other with glasses flying everywhere and embraced in the middle of the bar. Nobody batted an eyelid and more drinks were ordered to replace the broken ones. All of the RAF guys had suites so sleeping arrangements were easily sorted, and I hit the town with Plop.

I had never been to Vegas before and it took my breath away. What a place! Plop and I did all the touristy bits at the time and marvelled at the sheer, over the top madness of places like the Luxor—a bloody big black pyramid at one end of the strip, and the MGM Grand with its almost 7,000 rooms. Apparently, it cost over a billion dollars to build, and they had made it all back in gambling revenues within six months or so. The whole weekend was a nice pre-cursor to my first proper detachment with 121. We were due to be deployed to Nellis for two weeks to support the USAF Fighter Weapons School. This was their equivalent of TOPGUN I suppose and would see us providing targets for the F-15 and F-16 schools.

Just before that though, the Wilson family had another trip abroad to fit in. This time, we were off to Blighty for Mitch and Maggie's wedding. He had asked me to be his best man, which I saw as a huge honour and I was delighted to step up. We arrived back into Manchester to find Britain socked in with snow. I had only been in the States a year, but I was already a California beach bum and the cold shocked me to my core. Poor Holly didn't know what had hit her, as she stood knee-deep in it in my parents' garden after we arrived. Mum and Dad were overjoyed to see her as I am sure they had thought it would be at least another two years after they returned from their holiday. After a week with them, we made our way over to Ormskirk for the wedding. It was a brilliant time, watching two people who were so obviously in love, pledging their lives to each other. I had known Mitch's parents and brothers for years, and had even flown with Hitch (his eldest brother) when he was a student at Valley while I was instructing. He had just graduated from Valley and was due to start the Jaguar OCU shortly after the wedding. I didn't banter him at all of course about how underpowered the Jag was. Maggie's family were delightful too and the whole day went off with a bang. As much as we enjoyed a taste of home, I can't lie and say that I wasn't over the moon when we boarded the plane back to San Diego and the sunshine.

I had one trip to get back into the swing of things and then it was off to Nellis for two weeks. My shakedown trip was loft-bombing with Buff. What a cosmic waste of fuel that was. The 26-pound practice bombs we lofted went nowhere near where they were supposed to go, but I hoped it was all about the technique, and full-sized bombs would be a lot more accurate. It's the hope that kills you, so they say. Well, it certainly wasn't going to be my bloody lofted bombs, that's for sure. We flew all the jets in and decamped to the officers' club to meet our hosts. Nellis O-Club was legendary and had a pool table in the middle of it, but not for playing pool on. The USAF played a semi-violent game called 'Crud', which was a cross between billiards, tennis, and all-in wrestling, without sticks, rackets or wrestling trunks—thank God. Anyway, the fighter weapons staff gave us the big ignore for some reason, so we made our way downtown to our hotel. Yeah, that was a loose term. The USAF had put us up in a lower market motel type of place. It wasn't bad, but when you consider how cheap the rooms were in the big resort hotels, it was a bit of a slap in the face. Marines are a hardy bunch, so just set-to, but I did think it was a bit off given that we had two lieutenant colonels and a few majors with us.

It turns out that this was not unexpected. The USAF regularly treated the USMC as the bastard stepchildren of military aviation and didn't rate them. From what I had seen so far, the USAF must be superstars if they were better than some of the guys I had been flying with. Maybe they just hadn't come across 121 yet? That was about to change—in a big way. Killer and Hoover had briefed me up that I was going to be flying with the junior and inexperienced WSOs to bring them on in the air-to-air arena. I would also be designated as a 4-ship leader, helping to develop a crew who were due to attend an upcoming ACTI course. To kick off with though, I flew a low-level familiarisation trip with Hoover so he could show me all of the features in the Nellis range complex. The main two things to look out for were Tonopah airfield, which was super-secret (housing the F-117 Stealth Fighter that wasn't really there), and the big one—Area 51, known as 'the box'. That place didn't even exist, but if you flew into it, you would be detained after landing, and taken away for a serious 'debriefing' involving a brutal internal examination. Which kind of means it did exist after all?

So, with all of 40 minutes' experience in the ranges, I led the next trip which was a 4 vs 4 against the F-16s. Bluto had won me in the raffle and was in my back seat. My plan of showing him the ropes in a nice controlled manner went to a sack of shit straight away as my number 3, the other element leader, went unserviceable on start-up, so we had to launch as a 3-ship. I was working like a one-armed paper hanger on that trip. Just getting in and out of Nellis was like flying an instrument rating test with all sorts of entry points and gates to fly through. No chance of just busting back into the circuit in a clatter of bits here. This was the US Air Force and therefore completely anal and inflexible. We were providing target profiles on that trip so not allowed to use AMRAAM or our full up radar modes. We had to pretend to be a MiG-29 with limited sensor capability and carrying dummy Sparrows to simulate the AA-10 Alamo, and the AA-7 Apex heat seeker. I had two junior crews up there with me and coordinating them to provide the correct target profiles and spacing between our groups took all of my capacity. Blimey! I hoped I wasn't looking at two weeks of this otherwise I would be knackered. We played our part and got royally shot down, then did it all over again for them. Job done. And then we debriefed.

'Oh my God, kill me now' was all I was thinking throughout that debrief. Their 4-ship was made up of two weapons instructors (the equivalent of our QWI staff) and two guys on the weapons instructor course. The lead pilot was staff and was as anal as any RAF QWI I had ever met. We went through the usual domestics of getting out and back, and then it was time to debrief the intercepts. He drew arrows up in blue on the whiteboard to signify their formation, and then declared that he was using a '10-mile marker pen'. I had no idea what he meant until he measured out 6 marker pen's distance on the board and drew our formation up in red. He then elicited the radar picture from each of his formation and drew us up on the board, with all of us moving 5 miles closer—sorry, I mean half a pen closer—as he developed the intercept. He made a point of calling us bandits which is the NATO codeword for hostile aircraft. I was OK with that until he kept saying it to our faces.

'Bandits. What did you see here?' and 'Bandits—picture?' which was a bit rude. It was especially galling when he asked us twice what we saw at range. Given that he had limited us to a 40-mile radar scope in the brief, we couldn't see anything outside of that range. He snorted and sneered a bit the first time I told him we had no picture at 60 miles, but when he did it again at 50 miles, I had to say something.

'Can I just check you remember that you limited us to a 40-mile scope?' There was a bit of Marine snorting then. He looked a little embarrassed, but tried to style it out.

'Yeah of course,' he said with a look of disdain on his face.

'OK, well it's probably not worth asking us what picture we had outside of 40 miles then. Just trying to move things along for you, mate.'

Being a weapons instructor, he had probably never been challenged or put on the spot before, and certainly not while he was staff, but I loathed QWIs, especially the ones with the superior attitude. Even though we were providing targets for them, and expected to be shot down, there was no need to treat us like shit.

You are invited to the merge

Anyway, the debrief took on a bit more of a chippy mood and I was glad to see the back of Captain Attitude and his 10-mile pen. It turned out that they all had 10-mile pens and elitist attitudes, and it was obvious that it wasn't just my experience. All in all, they were treating us as second-class citizens. I was looking forward to the second week where we would be able to fly full-up Hornets and redress the balance. In the meantime, we had to suck up being the punch bag. Again, I had no problem with that so long as the chosen ones showed a bit of respect and grace in the debrief. Was that too much to ask? Later that day, I was number 3 of our 4-ship and had a similar experience to the morning. At least I was able to do some work-up on Bluto's radar work close to the merge so not a complete loss. I needed a beer and a moan that night I can tell you. A few of the Marines told us expats that they were used to that treatment from the USAF. I wasn't though, so it was time to dig in.

The following day, I was pretty much flying solo. I had the flight surgeon in the back so everything was on me. He had plenty of Hornet hours, but it was still a passenger ride and all of the responsibility that comes with that. Oh, it was also another 4 vs 4, although they put me as number 4 so nowhere near the lead. The lead F-16 was a grade one arrogant prick who treated us appallingly in the brief. I mean, he had some stones on him given that our boss was in the lead, but it didn't deter him at all. I made a point of asking for clarification on a couple of things. I knew damn well what he meant, but wanted to throw him off his game by showing that his brief wasn't clear. His brief should have been perfect as he was demonstrating to his students, so it was a tiny dig at him. Killer, being the immensely mellow dude that he was, remained completely unfazed and grinned at me as we walked out of the brief. He took me aside and said he appreciated what I was doing, but there was no need as it would make no difference with these idiots.

So, up we went, and down we came, having all been shot down about 20 miles away from the F-16s. We were not allowed to do any hard manoeuvring as they took their shots, so it was all a bit misrepresentative. However, according to the debrief, the USAF's asshole of the year claimed a stunning victory against the forces of evil and I was left wondering why he wasn't chief of the air force already, seeing as he was surely the greatest fighter pilot of all time. A couple more beers and a lot more moaning that night, saw me needing a bit of a reset, and the next trip was set up to give me just that. There was a half squadron of F-15s at Nellis, also providing opposition for the weapons school, and we had found out over a beer at the O-Club that they were getting the same reception from the QWIs, so we sorted out a 2 vs 2 against them as a bit of a loosener to remind us how much fun flying fighters actually was. I was leading our pair with Bluto, and sent a little jokey letter to the F-15 guys in the morning. They received a small envelope in their crew room which contained a hand written invitation from me and Bluto. It read:

You are invited to the merge. Please bring your Sidewinders and gun.
Briefing room 4, 1030hrs.
RSVP to Mr Tug and Bluto, 121 Squadron

They turned up with big smiles on their faces and I briefed up that we would only count shots once we had passed each other after the merge happened. I had Billy and Brock as my wingman. Billy was a newish guy and still on work-up, and Brock was a good solid ACTI WSO. Bluto and I would lead the whole shebang, but if we went down, the F-15s would assume the lead and take Billy out for a 2 vs 1. If it went to a 2 vs 1, the pair of fighters would need to get two kills on the single to win the fight. We were looking forward to a proper punch up rather than being killed from 20 miles away, and I almost skipped out to the jet. Nellis was one of those bases where there was a red line painted the full length of the pan.

There were breaks in the line where you could cross to get to the flight line. You could actually cross anywhere as it was only a bloody painted line. If you did though, you ran the risk of being gunned down by one of the many armed guards that patrolled the area. I kid you not. It was even painted on the ground that the use of deadly force was authorised if you crossed the red line in the wrong place.

On start-up, one of the F-15s broke, so I rebriefed on our tactical frequency that we would switch to the alternative exercise (altex) of the 2 vs 1, but also added that the F-18s would go gun only. Both Billy and the Eagle driver acknowledged, and off we went. Billy and I did a pairs take-off, and as soon as we were airborne, I waved him out into fighting wing formation. The Eagle joined on our other wing and I turned us to the west this time. Our play area was away from the Nellis ranges over in R-2508, otherwise known as Death Valley. It is an area of outstanding beauty which is saying something for a stinking desert, but it is also awesome for doing intercepts and air combat. Lots of high ground to fly around and through, and just spectacular views. Yeah, yeah. Enough of the documentary, let's get to the big punch up.

UTTER FUCKING BUFFOONERY!

We separated out to opposite ends of the range and I called 'Fight's on!' over the radio to get things going. This was going to test Bluto's radar to visual skills as well as his commentary in the visual fight. It would test Billy's ability to stick on my wing in a tactical formation while listening to Brock, and also trying to get eyes on the F-15. A good workout all round. Once we got into the visual fight, we should easily be able to tie up one F-15 in our turny-burny championship jet, so long as we kept him close and denied him his Sidewinder shots. I called that I would be the eyeball, and therefore went for the closest head-on pass that I dared to do to tie up the Eagle, while Billy hooked in as the shooter. If Billy took a big enough height split from me, he should get in unseen for the first gun shot. That all went to plan and I got the F-15 to turn away from Billy and present his arse ready to receive some 20mm suppositories. The Eagle driver's head must have been on a swivel, and he must have seen Billy enter the fight, so forgot about me and flat-plated his jet back towards Billy. The F-15 is enormous for a single-seat fighter—as big as a tennis court. He must have had ultra-confidence in his jet and his own handling of it to pull off a move like that. It was at the same time, both beautiful and breathtaking. I couldn't just sit around and marvel at how good he was all day though. I used the opportunity to climb out of sight and set up my own re-entry to the fight. I powered up vertically to sit about seven to eight thousand feet above them.

The Eagle's break had left him low on energy with Billy just about saddled up behind him, a little out of range for the gun. And then the strangest thing happened. The F-15 was in a slowish turn close to the base height and Billy was just following him. All he needed to do was cut the corner to get the gunsight on and we would be one shot to the good with mine to go. I floated over the top of the fight and thought that Billy must have been on the limit of performance. If that was the case, then I needed to re-enter and take the first shot.

'Have you shot him, Billy?' I called. No answer, so I rolled over and committed my nose into the affray.

'Break out high and left!' I said. He was in the piece of airspace I wanted to be in so the procedure was to break him out first before I could enter. He didn't move!

'Shit!' I shouted to Bluto and flat-plated our jet back to the vertical to power out of there before I hit Billy.

'Jesus! What is he doing?!' Bluto was as nonplussed as I was. OK, I needed to end this.

'Have you got a shot, Billy?' No answer, so I put my nose in again and bawled, 'BILLY! GET OUT OF THE WAY NOW!' just trying to break through to him. I was expecting him to break left away from the right hand fight he was in, but no. He broke right, to the inside of the circle, and somehow managed to fly out in front of the F-15!

'What is he doing now?!' I locked the Eagle in GACQ and got the sight on just as he called, 'Fox 2 kill the Hornet,' and I gunned him twice to terminate the fight. It had not taken long, but that fight had been long enough to burn everyone's gas down to minimums. We gathered up the troops and led them back to Nellis via a million reporting points and instrument flying rules. I think it looked pretty cool breaking into the circuit with our mixed formation, but for the life of me, I couldn't work out what the hell had happened in that fight.

Bluto and I stepped off the pan without being shot in the head, and I waited for Billy to show up before we debriefed with the F-15. Brock was on his own in the debriefing room and there was no sign of Billy.

'What was going on in that fight, Brock?' I asked. He had the weirdest look on his face, almost disbelieving.

'Tug. I have no explanation for it.'

'Why did he break inside? Why didn't he take the shot more to the point? He obviously had the performance.'

'He was looking for the other F-15.'

'What?!' said both Bluto and I together.

'He thought we were doing a 2 vs 2.' My jaw was on the floor, and it was at this point that Billy walked in.

'OK, before we bare our arses to the F-15 guy, tell me what you were thinking, Billy.' Not a word from him, but an intensely surly look to me and Brock. Wow! This was going a bit downhill.

'Come on, mate. I need to get to the bottom of what you were doing, otherwise we can't sort it.' Still nothing, but he was looking downright aggressive. I tried being a bit more direct.

'Did you hear the rebrief on the ground?' Silence.

'Well, you acknowledged it. Did you notice only one F-15 on our wing all the way out to Death Valley?' Silence. Just a hard stare. Now, I had made a fool of myself numerous times in aeroplanes, especially when I was at Billy's stage. I always put my hand up to my shortcomings (many and varied as they were). In fact, if I had shown Billy's current attitude on the Phantom, they would have knocked my block off. I just didn't get what his act was. Brock then said they had a communication breakdown in the cockpit which was a polite way of saying Billy hadn't said a word throughout. I could excuse being maxed out, but not knowing we were only fighting one aeroplane was inexcusable. There was no explanation for him not taking the shot either. Brock was as bamboozled as me, and he had been in the same jet as Billy! Maverick ... er, Billy just wouldn't get the sight on and take the shot.

Despite everything, I had to cobble together something to say for the debrief with our adversary quickly, as he walked in shortly afterwards. What I came up with was not my finest hour as an instructor or mentor, but it appeared to do the trick. We went through the usual domestics and I asked if everyone was happy with my re-brief of the 2 vs 1. Nods all around except for Billy who stared at the floor in silence. Then we got to the fight. I drew it up on the board, deliberately not marking it out with a 10-mile pen, but just eye-balling it. When it got to the gravy strokes, our friendly Eagle driver asked how the number 2 ended up in front of him. This was my chance to get Billy to talk.

'Do you want to run us through that, Billy?' I asked. Dear God, he just sat there staring me out. If looks could kill, I would be a goner. Except I wouldn't. Billy's look would probably have floated out in front of me aimlessly and I would have shot it down. Our F-15 guest looked confused so I stepped in.

'This is why it happened,' I said, and on the whiteboard, I wrote, 'UTTER FUCKING BUFFOONERY!' in big capitals. 'Can we leave it at that?' I asked him.

'Sure thing, Tug,' he replied, and we called it a day. I shook his hand, told him how awesome his opening move was and we both agreed we should do it all again sometime.

As soon as he left, Billy was up on his feet, furious. At last, I had a reaction from him. I got him to sit down and he eventually admitted he had been totally maxed out. I told him I had no problem with that, but he must own up to it as we can then work together on a solution, or a plan to make him better. Not speaking to his WSO in the air and sulking in the debrief by not taking any part in it was just unacceptable though, so I gave him a bollocking for that. We then spoke about using a WSO to relieve some of the load and freeing up capacity. He had to leave the single-seat macho bullshit aside while he was learning. The poor guy was almost in tears and he looked on the edge of a breakdown. The humiliation of being called out in front of the F-15 had almost been too much for him.

'Billy,' I said, 'we all have shit trips. God knows, I have had my fair share of them, but look at me. I am flying one of the best fighters in the world, so they never did me any harm. One trip does not make you shit mate—OK?' He nodded, but it was obvious he was still hurting.

'It's only you that drags this into the next trip, Billy. Nobody else gives a fuck, so what do you wanna do? Let it destroy you, or move on?'

'Move on,' he said.

'Ooh Rah!' I replied which made him smile as I probably sounded as un-Marine as you could get. That night, Brock and I plus a few others had a beer with him to see where his head was at. He was still mightily embarrassed, but on the mend, ready for the next trip, where hopefully he wouldn't waste any time trying to fight a bandit that wasn't actually there.

Bluto got a well-earned rest from my back seat the next day, which was a shame as we were working well together by that point. My next victim was another ex OV-10 Observer called Prof. He was a nice older guy, but struggling a little with the increase in speed and roles and capabilities of the Hornet. Our first trip ended quickly as I experienced my very first engine failure in the F-18 during climb out from Nellis. It was a proper bang that sent the engine temperature through the roof, so I shut it down and we called for the cable and landed into it with no drama. This was a carrier aeroplane so taking the cable at an airfield which wasn't as violent as landing on the boat was no big deal for it. Next up with Prof was a big trip for me. 1 vs 1 ACM against Muck. That was going to be a real indicator of how well I had progressed. Muck was exceptionally handy and had a proper bag of tricks up his sleeve so no amount of cheating was going to help me. That's not to say I wasn't going to cheat, but I fully expected to have my ass handed to me. He also had Indy behind him who was just an awesome air combat WSO. I wanted to use the trip to get Prof up to speed on ACM commentary and awareness too, so we did a little bit of defensive perch work first and a bloody Guns-D. After that, we had gas for one split. All I remember of that fight is that it was relatively long, and the only shot taken was a snapshot guns by Muck that he couldn't call a kill on. Had we had more fuel, I have no doubt he would have nibbled away at me and got me. I was overjoyed nonetheless that I had made it hard for him. We landed at March Air Force base, east of Anaheim off that trip, and hired a car so we could drive home to San Diego for the weekend. Indy's girlfriend was over for an extended stay and we all needed a break from the bright lights of Vegas, and the disdain of the weapons school instructors. It was only about a 90-minute drive from March to San Diego. The only thing I remember about that drive was being overtaken by a man in a car doing about 90 miles an hour. Not unusual in itself, but I forgot to mention he was eating noodles out of a bowl with chopsticks while driving. It's odd the things your brain remembers sometimes. Only in California, huh?

We flew back in on the Sunday afternoon and used the trip to sharpen up Prof's radar to visual commentary from the intercept phase into combat. The weekend away from Vegas had left me nicely refreshed and ready to take on whatever the USAF threw at us. Unfortunately, the first thing they threw at me was Captain Arsehole and his 4-ship of F-16s again. Bluto's respite care was over too, and the schedule had us leading our 4-ship against them. The F-16 was called the Fighting Falcon, but was known by everyone flying it as the Viper because it looked a bit like a snake, head on. There was also some banter about it looking like a spaceship from the TV programme Battlestar Galactica called the Colonial Viper or something like that. Either way, they revelled in the name which I can understand. I had flown the Phantom (I might have mentioned it before) which was a very cool and hard name, and now I was flying the Hornet which sounded just as cool.

We'll call that four–nil then

So, week two started as week one had finished. Viper 1 treated us like shit from the off, and the brief became a little adversarial as I started to question him a bit more directly and aggressively. It was my 4-ship this time so it was time for him to show a little respect. The promise of us being allowed to be a bit more proactive and aggressive in the air turned out to be bullshit also, and once again our hands were tied. Unusually, it was a tough day weather wise, with lots of multi-layered cloud to contend with, so the base height was quite high. We were up in the contrails as our height block was above the F-16s. This meant we would be easy to see. That might sound a bit unfair, but if I was leading the whole mission, I would have put them up in the trails too—dealer's choice and all that. We would just have to deal with it. We couldn't see the F-16s trailing so even at 60 miles from them, I knew they were below us.

We were getting information from a ground controller, and when they called a rough height block, I questioned the controller to check the actual heights of the F-16s. At the same time, I got Bluto to open up the range on his radar scope, and sure enough, he got hits on them below the hard deck. All four of them were ground kills. The ground controller called that the F-16s had terminated the fight and were resetting. We were up at high level and supersonic at this stage so spewing fuel out like you read about. After the reset, we only had fuel for one presentation and then I had to take us home through all the clouds back to Nellis. I had two junior pilots as numbers 2 and 4 so we split into pairs for the recovery, then managed to join up again as a 4-ship below the cloud for a neat run-in and break from echelon formation. I couldn't bloody wait for that debrief, and neither could the rest of the guys in my formation. This was a major mistake that Captain Fantastic had made so we wanted to see how he dealt with it.

His plan was to ignore it altogether! He began as always with any safety points. Not a single Viper spoke up. The young Marines looked at me, but I shook my head slightly to see where this would go. After the domestics were done, he took his 10-mile pen and started drawing up the second intercept. That was when I stopped him.

'Do you want to talk about the first presentation?' I asked.

'There was only one.'

'No. I mean the one where you all flew through the hard deck.'

'I terminated that one.'

It was a minute after the fight's on call so we had started. 'Congratulations. You terminated the split after you had all died. Can you tell me how you all ended up below the hard deck?'

'Like I said. I terminated it so lesson learned.'

'Lesson obviously not learned though is it? All four of you were below the hard deck. For real, let's say in cloud or at night, the three of you,' and I pointed at the other Vipers, 'followed your leader into the ground and died. And yet none of you brought that up as a safety issue? I've got young aircrew here in my formation, and we are trying to teach them about professionalism and honesty in the air. You are an instructor. If you can't own up to a major mistake like that, how do you expect them to do the same? You screwed up, so admit it and accept it and let's move on.'

His face was purple, but he wouldn't budge. It was Vegas so he was doubling down, I guess?

'OK,' I said, 'we'll call that four–nil then,' and just shut down for the rest of the debrief. That was until it came to them putting their tapes in. They had another weapons instructor in there running the films as Viper 1 debriefed. He had spent the whole debrief sat at the front dipping, and had a huge lump in the side of his mouth which he constantly chewed on. He spat into a coke can, so each time he did it, the sound echoed, and it was putting my teeth on edge. As we all had to marvel at one of Viper 1's shots, this foul creature reached into the very back of his mouth, while pulling his cheek out with his other hand, and brought out what looked like a wet turd which he then systematically and with precision, tried to push into the coke can with his now wet, brown index finger. It made me retch, and I couldn't take it anymore.

'For the love of God, mate! We are trying to debrief here!' He looked up, completely bewildered, and a bit of brown gob dribbled from his brown speckled teeth onto his flying suit. That was it for me and I just got up and walked out with the rest of my formation. I got the eight of us together and gave a short debrief on integrity and owning up to our mistakes. The bottom line was that anything that happened on that trip after the hard deck bust was meaningless. If he had come in with a humble mea-culpa attitude, or any of the other three Vipers had brought it up as a safety point, it would have been a two-minute learning point. As it was, his attitude of ignoring it and trying to cover it up made it the most important lesson of the det so far.

The arrogance of the instructor staff was becoming fatiguing, but I didn't know why I was surprised. I had come across awesome QWIs in the past, but the natural default among a lot of them was to take an elitist attitude. Multiply that by ten for the USAF and you had the weapons instructors at Nellis. It was really grinding me down. Indy came to my rescue. He had set up a fun trip for us later that afternoon. Nellis had the very last operational Phantom squadron in the USAF and Indy had arranged a bit of a punch up for us with them. It was a reserve unit so manned by a load of retired senior officers who basically flew just for the fun of it. On that squadron was a USAF guy who had done an exchange on Indy's Tornado GR1 squadron. In fact, I also knew him as he had been doing a UK orientation course at RAF Brawdy while I was working up to be an instructor. It was a 2 vs 2 with the F-4s leading.

We wandered over to their squadron and it was like Phantom pornography for me. I spent ages looking at the pictures and boring Indy and our two Marines with tales of adventures past. They were gracious enough to listen as they knew it was therapy for me. We went into the brief and the flying suits on the F-4 crews were full of 3,000- and 4,000-hour Phantom badges. These guys were very experienced. Old, but very experienced. A full-bird colonel was leading their pair and he gave a relaxed brief that was short on detail but brimming with promise. Basically, we were heading out to Death Valley and just going to have at it. They could have stacked the odds in their favour, knowing we had a much superior jet, but they didn't. They just wanted some fun. The only concession was that pre-merge shots didn't count. These guys wanted to turn and burn. And turn and burn they did! They had briefed that we could manoeuvre at any height pre-merge, but we had to be at least 5,000 feet above ground level to engage in full air combat. Below that, it would be limited manoeuvring—something we called 'day tactics' in the RAF. Even though their jets were old, their G limit was about 7G I think, so pretty close to ours. No way they could match our airframe though, or so I thought.

In a fight, I was usually all about the moment. How do I get the kill and/or stop them from killing me? It is an immense amount of fun, but you don't really have the time to appreciate it. This was different. I was absolutely awestruck at what these guys were doing with that aeroplane. It was pulling G and swapping ends like a Hornet. They pirouetted and stall-turned the thing around the sky. If the moves they were pulling were not illegal, then they were certainly against all that was holy or good. And I loved watching them. They were doing things with the Phantom that I could only dream of doing when I flew it. What an absolute hoot and a much-needed tonic. Sometimes in the melee of military aviation, we can lose sight of just how much fun it can be and how lucky we are to be doing it. Indy had given me a gift by organising this, and the F-4 guys had given me a front-row seat to a spectacular show. Of course, we shot them down on both fights, but that wasn't the point. Even Billy would have won that fight, despite probably thinking there were three of them up there. It was just a whole lot of fun.

They would have a choice of arseholes to poo out of

Eight huge smiles in the debrief, and the main learning point was 'Can we do it again?' Smiling was off the menu the next day as I suited up for a 4 vs 2 against the twin-seat F-15E guys on the course. We were providing canned target profiles for them and the F-15 student crew were leading with their staff on the wing. Once the coordination brief was done, we split off for own formation briefings. Our 4-ship was being led by Handy and Rabies. They were a couple of young guys who had been selected to go on a Marine Corps tactical leadership course and so were working up for their 4-ship lead qualification. I was number 3 with Prof, so was the duty adult assessing them. They were great guys and very likeable, but had been working really hard to get up to speed, and had had a couple of bumps along the way. Tons of potential though. The brief was good, but missing an altex which I got them to come up with. If the F-15s broke, we would use the same domestic set-up for the sortie as briefed (start points, comms frequencies, height blocks, weapon loads, etc.) and flex to an internal 2 vs 2 with me leading the pair of targets against Handy's two fighters.

Above: Alaska glacier.

Right: Hawaii beach.

Above: From Yorkshire to Disneyland.

Left: Hornet pilot.

Right: With Indy at the Marine Corps Birthday Ball.

Below: I finally get my name on a jet!

In my Hornet.

In my Mustang with Holly.

Mum and Dad at Disneyland.

Ocean Beach baby!

Not looking cool in my cool flying suit.

On the way to Alaska.

Proudly showing Dickie Duke my jet.

Seating Ron in my jet.

The Hornet's Nest.

Sorry Holly, she is here to stay!

The legendary Dickie Duke.

The poo and puke machine tests out her pipes.

Farewell from 121. They set us up for this one!

The view from our bedroom in Ocean Beach.

With Holly at Lake Mission Viejo.

The foreigners: Muck, Indy and me.

My farewell present from VMFA-134.

Me, College Jimmy, Cousin Jimmy, and Harry O at the Bull's game.

Above: Just when I thought I had seen my last bomb!

Left: Two more trophies. My Sidewinder umbilicals.

My American wings.

Right: Look at that sinister red eye!

How cool is this badge?

VMFA-134. The Smokes—best flying I ever did!

Above: Somehow the F-15 guy didn't twig I was British despite these badges!

Left: Now that is one cool flying helmet!

A slick herd go saw us blast airborne with our beautiful jets and we set up to the north-east of the training area to wait for the fight's on call. We had been floating around for a bit when I pimped Handy to ask our ground controller for an update on the start time. After a bit of a pause, they came onto the radio to say that the F-15s had cancelled as the student crew had failed the brief. I did a double-take and then jumped in to confirm they hadn't even got airborne in the first place. It was true. The F-15E instructors had failed the students as their brief had not been good enough, but didn't think it was necessary to tell us and stop four expensive jets getting airborne, when our whole reason to do so was to provide targets for them. What a pair of bastards! It was a massive lack of respect. OK, I would sort that out later. All Handy and Rabies had to do was re-brief the altex and then at least I could assess how they managed the 4-ship.

Badly, as it turned out. We flew all the way to the other start point as a 4-ship, and then turned around and flew back. All the time, I was getting more and more frustrated that they weren't getting on with it. I pimped them over the radio to re-brief the altex parameters, but they came out with a ton of confusing comm showing me they had no idea what to do. We already had the parameters on our kneeboards, but we still needed them to confirm what they wanted to do. I waited as long as I could and then took control. I split their pair off to the west and took my wingman east, telling Handy to change to the fighter frequency and confirming their height block. It was a quick intercept and merge and then another faff after the termination as they tried to join us up as a 4 and take us back to Nellis. They were obviously phased by the trip, and it was like trying to hang on to a runaway horse on the way back. No stable speed control in the descent; in and out of cloud rather than flying through the gaps; rough corrections onto headings etc.—all the stuff that made being on the wing, tough.

As we walked in, I told Handy and Rabies to take their time and prepare a proper debrief while I went to see the F-15 instructors. OK, I have sworn a fair bit in this book already, and there is a bit more to come, so I will spare you chapter and verse on that conversation. Suffice it to say, it was all one-way, and they would have a choice of arseholes to poo out of afterwards. It might be a while before they could find their 10-mile pens too. Handy and Rabies looked like they were waiting for the guillotine as we started the debrief, but their saving grace was that they ran it professionally and held their hands up to their mistakes. The major point was all the gas we wasted flexing to the altex, and me having to take control. They looked gutted, but I stood up and told them that all they had to do was use the details from the trip we had briefed, and split us off as a separate element. All of the work was already done. They had just been thrown by the F-15s cancelling in such a disrespectful way and everything had snowballed once it hadn't run on rails. 'Been there, done that myself,' I told them to lessen the sting. I had been very direct with them, so wanted to build them up again.

I needed some air afterwards as I was still fuming at the F-15s, so I went outside and sat down on the steps in front of the building. I had flown about ten complex missions in seven days and pulled a lot of G in them, and with the intricate briefing and debriefing, the pace was catching up with me. Handy and Rabies came out and sat either side of me and started to apologise for the last trip until I cut them off, telling them not to dwell on it, but concentrate on what came next. They were honest enough to admit they were worried about their upcoming course. They were also feeling the pressure as they had led almost every trip they had flown on the det. Unless you have been there and done it, it is difficult to imagine how fatiguing leading missions can be. I told them we would schedule a down day for them so they could recharge and then see if I could organise something a bit more fun for them. They were good honest guys and I wanted them to do well. I went to see Indy and asked if he could set up another fight with the F-4s, and then we took Handy and Rabies off the programme the next day to give them a rest. They would be back to leading the day after though, as they needed the 4-ship lead tick before their course started. Indy and I spent a bit of time with them over a beer or two in the evening to help them get over the bad trip.

I only had one mission the next day thank God. Prof and I were number 3 of a 4 vs 4 against the F-16s again. Our lead was Astro who was towards the end of his first tour and a new 4-ship leader. For once, it was going to be a fair fight with full-up weapons and radar, and it was about time. At last, we would have a chance to kick some Viper ass. The problem for us was that the F-16 was mega-quick. Much quicker than us at top speed, so this would mean their missiles would go further than ours. That should result in them getting the first shot away. When you are 'out-sticked' like that, you must do some sort of manoeuvre out at range to get inside those first shots and even-up the weapons deficit. Astro planned to fly straight towards them, but separating us out into two pairs. We would drift away from each other, which would induce the F-16s to split and try to get outside of us. His plan was for us to cross target the bandits. So, the left-hand pair of us target the right-hand pair of theirs on the scope, and vice-versa. It meant that we would be turning across the nose of the nearest pair of bandits (albeit quite a few miles away from them), but then we could keep turning to run away from them while supporting our AMRAAMS to Pitbull on the ones we shot. Confused? Of course you are. Against some threat aircraft and missiles, it can be a valid tactic, so long as it is executed perfectly with accuracy. Against a very supersonic

AMRAAM capable F-16? Not a chance we could do that perfectly. We had two junior crews in number 2 and 4 and it was a big responsibility to get things just right.

Of course, there are times to practice these things, but this was the first chance for us to get some satisfaction out of the F-16s and give them a bit of a kicking. Even if we got it absolutely on point, it still relied on them not being very good. Love 'em or hate 'em, the USAF were insanely disciplined on pre-merge radar handling, and with their superior speed, we were either going to be marching onto a face shot from them, or we were all going to die in the turn across the formation with an AMRAAM in our side. I challenged the tactics at the end of the brief, but Astro dug in. He was adamant it would work, but I knew that as a collective, we just weren't good enough. I was absolutely convinced I wasn't good enough, that's for sure. When there is a disagreement like that in the brief, the leader makes the final decision on what will happen. Even though I was against it, it was then my job to try my very best to make it work, so long as safety wasn't compromised, and that is exactly what I did.

We all got shot down in the turn before our own AMRAAMS started to track. Twice. It was badly humiliating all round. Our first chance to fight full-up and we had capitulated in the worst way. Astro was non-plussed in the debrief. The F-16s were cock-a-hoop. We had been bleating about using our F-18s to their full capability, and they had destroyed us the first time we were set free. In our 4-ship debrief afterwards, it was time for a bit of home truth.

'I just don't understand how we all got shot down,' wailed Astro.

'Because the tactics stink.' I replied.

'Well, it worked perfectly last time,' he countered.

'Where was that?'

'Against the F-5s at Yuma.'

'Jesus, Astro!' I cried. 'These weren't F-5s mate! These were F-16s—one of the most capable jets in the world!'

He had used the tactic against a jet that had little or no head-on threat against us, and certainly didn't have AMRAAM. We checked our tapes, and sure enough, we were awful on the first split—me included. The second split, we very nearly nailed it, but still got out-sticked and shot down. Cross targeting got binned after that.

To quote Yogi Berra (very famous New York Yankees baseball player and manager) the next day was, 'Deja-vu, all over again'. Handy and Rabies were in the hot seat leading our 4-ship with me as number 3. It was two F-15Es again, but thankfully it wasn't the instructors from last time as that would have been a touch awkward. All good through our formation brief so I guessed the day off had re-energised them nicely. On start-up, one of the Eagles went down so they scrubbed. We were still going to launch so Handy and Rabies could get another lead check under their belts. Quick as a flash, Handy came on the radio and re-briefed the 2 vs 2 altex. It was clear, concise, and direct, and at the end of it he demanded acknowledgement from us.

'Two copied.'

'Three copied.'

'Four copied,' we all replied in staccato fashion. It was a beautiful thing and I was ecstatic. Off we pressed and as soon as we got to the play area, they cleared us off to act independently as the targets and we were ready to go straight away. They controlled everything between them, and I could hear Rabies jumping in on the radio to coordinate the exercise with the ground controller. They were like a different crew to the one I had seen a couple of days before. A nice controlled recovery saw us safely on the ground, and after shut down, I headed straight over to their jet with Buzz, my WSO, so that we could walk in together. I think they were a bit worried as I approached them, but when they saw my beaming smile, they relaxed. I was out of control happy with them and punched them both in the arm.

'See how easy it is?! That was awesome guys! Just fucking awesome!' I was just as effusive in the debrief, giving plenty of praise where it was due. I had come from an air force where predominantly, we debriefed what went wrong. If you did something right, well that was your bloody job. But if you did something wrong? Oh my God they would flay the skin from your back. I learned fast when I became an instructor that praise was a much better motivator than shame.

Nah, son. That would be illegal

After the debrief, I got them to one side and said that Indy had arranged a little present for them later that afternoon. We were going to take on the Cold War Warriors on the Phantom. We were crewed up with me leading the whole thing and Rabies in my boot. Indy would jump in with Handy. The idea was for them to relax and just go along with it and try to recapture some of the pure joy of flying that gets a bit lost when you are on an assessed work-up. It was four different guys from the last trip against the F-4s, and two of them were retired generals. I briefed it up, trying to match their relaxed manner from the other trip, and everyone seemed up for it. When it came to weapons, we went for post-merge kills again, but I stated that the Hornets would go guns only.

'OK, we'll go guns only too,' said the lead Phantom pilot.

'That's OK, Sir. You can have heaters as well if you want?' I replied.

'Nah. We'll stick with the gun,' he said with a huge grin on his face. Four-thousand-hours F-4, retired general, and still trying to psyche-out the opposition! We all just fell about laughing.

'OK, General. Guns it is.' I smiled, and we made plans to meet out at the runway. Rabies was gobsmacked with how casual the brief was. His own briefings recently had been pulled apart and scrutinised to the minutest degree, but this trip was all about putting the fun back into flying and fighting.

It was a breathtakingly beautiful afternoon in Death Valley, as two Hornets led their grandparents into the range and split to opposite ends. I had given Rabies the option of just sitting there and soaking up the atmosphere—just getting his head out of the window and enjoying himself, but he wanted to be an active part of the fights. It was the first time I had flown with him, and I was very impressed. His cockpit work was really good, but what set him apart was his unbounded enthusiasm. He just loved flying and he loved the F-18. Speaking of which, I had been harbouring covetous thoughts since my last trip against these guys. The F-4 was my first love, and seeing the way its pilots had thrown it around had me stirred up. Was my head being turned away from my current squeeze, back to the Phantom? If it was, my Hornet would soon put a stop to that.

Everyone was playing a bit fast and loose with the hard deck for combat and slipped into a case of what I would describe as 'spirited day tactics'. Death Valley had lots of high ground, and valleys to hide in, so the first fight saw us sitting high and trying to look down to break out the F-4s. They stayed together on the first run and we committed down from on high. It was clear sky above us and although we had a bit of sun behind us, they had eyes like shithouse rats and saw us. They powered up to meet us, but stayed together so that they could threaten across the fight to the aeroplane that was fighting their partner. It was only a matter of time until we got in behind and gunned them to end the fight and reset for another.

The next fight had them splitting up and hugging the ground in and out of the valleys. Handy and I separated out to try a wide bracket, then we hit the deck to try and prevent them getting tally on us. Nothing on the scope due to the terrain masking them, so I went through a mental plot of closure and where I thought my bandit would be, and got Rabies to go completely heads-out. I hugged the ground to try and skyline him, and as we came around the corner below the ridge line of the valley we were in, Rabies called, 'come hard right, Tug!' And there was that wonderfully brutal shape of the greatest jet fighter in history, coming onto my nose as I turned. I rocked back for the gun and GACQ automatically locked them up. Sight on as they broke right, but it was too late and I gunned him.

'BREAK LEFT, TUG!' shouted Rabies and I immediately flat plated the jet while looking over my left shoulder to see a face full of the other Phantom. Once we had committed low and lost them on radar, they had engineered a join up to try and gang up on one of us. Handy was steaming over towards us, but at that moment, I was 1 vs 1. The new threat went close aboard over the top of us and zoomed up into the ether. I was already reversing in full burner, but not pulling as hard as I could. I had lost a bit of speed in the break so just came back in a slight climb to get low and deep in his six. The gun was useless in this position, but I just wanted to stay behind and build energy so I could use the vertical. He ran out of speed a long way up and rolled towards my six as I started to ease my nose up. We were in a classic rolling scissors, but bottoming out at about 1,000 feet above the ground. We really should have been above the hard deck of 5,000 feet at that point. As he came down, I turned across the fight and rolled again for his six. I now had enough energy to change the shape of the fight into the batshit crazy F-18 rolling scissors.

I stood my jet on its tail and feathered the stick to keep us climbing and moving back behind the Phantom. He started to flush out in front of me and I held my nose up at about 100 knots to make separation for the killing move. What about Handy you might be thinking? We had been coordinating with him throughout the split, with Rabies trying to help him back into the fight with position and height updates. I was busy fighting what appeared to be the greatest Phantom pilot that ever lived, so let Rabies get on with it. Hell's bells, this guy was turning himself inside out, but it was almost like my Hornet was dissing my ex-girlfriend. Whatever the Phantom did, she wasn't a patch on Miss Hornet. I've said it before—I bloody loved this jet!

'Combat 61, break out right and low now!' called Handy, and off I went away from the fight, as Handy and Indy slotted in and gunned the life out of the old girl thereby cementing my relationship with my F-18. I cannot articulate the feeling we had in the cockpit on the way back. Adrenalin buzz? Endorphin rush? Just totally bloody ecstatically happy? Yes, yes, and yes. The smiles on our faces were something to behold, and when the Phantoms broke out the beers for the debrief, we were able to escape the shackles of modern-day professionalism and live for a moment in the fighter spirit of the past. Even then, there were some limits ...

I was loosely debriefing the second fight when I asked who was in the rolling scissors with me at low-level. There was only silence.

'Come on, guys. Who was it?' I asked.

'What? A rolling scissors?' asked my favourite general.

'Yes, Sir.'

'At low-level?'

'Yes, Sir.'

'Nah, son. That would be illegal,' he said while looking at me straight in the eye and winking! So that was the end of the debrief and we just sat with them a while and drank our beers.

That trip was a great way to go into the weekend. My wife was flying in with Holly, and I had booked us into the MGM Grand for three nights. Hoover had thought I was looking a bit raggy from fatigue so told me to take an extended weekend, which was great of him. I borrowed one of the squadron cars and drove to the bottom end of the Las Vegas strip, which was where McCarran airport was, to pick them up. The flight was delayed by a couple of hours, but they eventually arrived. Everyone who got off the flight looked a little ashen, and when I saw the state my wife was in, I was shocked. The 737 they had been on had suffered a sudden pressurisation failure out of San Diego, and the oxygen masks had tumbled down. People were screaming, and Holly had freaked out, not unsurprisingly. They had landed back at San Diego and swapped jets out, but you could still see the stress on people's faces. That changed to a look of disbelief on my wife's face when we drew up at the MGM Grand. What a place! The room was brilliant, but still relatively cheap. The casino made all the money it needed from gambling so they could afford to keep the food and room costs down. It had a mini beach resort out the back which we used a lot, swimming with Holly while looking up at the lurid green and gold colour scheme of the hotel building all around us. You were not allowed to stop and stand still in a casino if you had a child with you, and we were moved on a couple of times with Holly in her stroller. There was plenty of child friendly entertainment though, with Circus Circus at the top end of the strip and the full-sized pirate battle that took place every couple of hours outside Treasure Island.

All too soon, my long weekend was over and the cockpit called me back for one last trip before we ended our Nellis adventure. It was a 2 vs 2 against the F-15Es and I was leading it with Hoover. On my wing was a young pilot called Tom-Tom. So called, because he marched to the beat of a different drum. Basically, he was an odd kid—a bit off the wall. He seemed a decent enough guy, but had a reputation of just doing random stupid stuff. I got to see it first hand on this trip.

No doubt that was going to come to an end sooner or later

As the intercept began, Tom-Tom was on my right wing in a wide battle formation. I was running the radar on the first split (I had asked Hoover nicely again) and as soon as we got contact, I called the picture over the radio. All I was expecting from Tom-Tom was a call of 'Two. Same' to tell me they had the same picture on their scope. What I wasn't expecting was for Tom-Tom to go hard right through 90 degrees and bugger off into the middle distance. I want to try and give you a flavour of what this sounded like in my cockpit so anything in italics is over the radio from both me and Tom-Tom, and normal text is in our cockpit:

> '*Combat 3-1. Single group bullseye 2-7-0 ten, low, fast.*'
> '*Where the fuck are you going Tom-Tom?!* What is he doing Sir?'
> 'No idea, Tug.'
> '*Two is blind.*'
> '*No shit, Tom-Tom!*'
> '*Copy. Come hard left heading west. Single group bullseye 2-6-0 ten, low, fast.*'
> '*Two is blind, no-joy.*'
> '*Right! We'll just fucking attack them on our own then, shall we?!*'
> '*Copied. Combat 3-1, Fox 3 Southerly. Fox 3 northerly. Flanking north towards you.*'
> '*Blind. No joy.*'
> '*Fuck's sake!*'
> '*Combat 3-1 pitbull southerly. Pitbull northerly. Bug out east.*'
> '*Combat 3-2 visual—joining on your left.*'
> '*Well fucking done Tom-Tom. Two minutes too late, but what the hell?!*'
> '*Combat 3-1 visual. Time out kill southerly and northerly. Terminate.*'

Or some such like that. Hoover was cracking up in the cockpit as I had now experienced first-hand what it was like to have Tom-Tom on my wing.

It was almost impossible to be mad at Tom-Tom though. It was just who he was. The embarrassing relative in the family who is a social hand grenade, but you love him all the same. The debrief was OK until the F-15s asked me to put my tape in to check my kills. I stopped dead in my tracks and Hoover started to laugh out loud. Everyone was a bit perplexed until the speakers burst into life with 'Where the fuck are you going, Tom-Tom?!' and continued on through my angry and sarcastic commentary. Poor Tom-Tom was horrified and I had to explain that raging was how I dealt with my stress in the air. From that moment on, my tape was the star of the show in most debriefs, as everyone wanted to know what the crazy Brit thought of them each day. As the weather began to improve to the classic San Diego climate, we began to get more and more visitors from the UK. First up were my second set of parents, Ron and Meg. I had met them years before during my flying training. Their eldest daughter, Annie had been going out with a guy on one of my earliest courses called Bonk, and I had been in their guard of honour at their subsequent wedding. Annie had become like a sister to me over the years, and despite Bonk being chopped from flying training and then leaving the RAF, I had always kept in touch with them. Ron and Meg had practically looked after me when I went through fast jet training at RAF Valley in north Wales. I spent most weekends with them during that course and it galvanised a friendship that endures to this day, thirty-five years later.

They were visiting the States with their best friends and doing a train tour that ended with them staying with us in Ocean Beach for a few days. We took them over to Coronado Island and had lunch at the Hotel Del Coronado. The Hotel Del is a beautiful colonial style luxury hotel where they filmed *Some Like It Hot* with Marilyn Monroe, and sitting in the sun on the terrace made us feel like film stars. Ron and Meg were Holly's godparents, so it was lovely for her to spend some time with them. In essence, they treated Holly like she was their grand-daughter. On the Saturday, I took Ron and his friend Geoff up to Miramar to show them the F-18. Ron was ex-RAF and aeroplane mad, so getting him to sit in the cockpit on the line was just magical. He was a private pilot himself and was gobsmacked at the displays and controls. I had sat him in a Phantom years before, but the Hornet just blew his mind.

As I was closing the canopy and getting ready to drive them back to OB, I noticed one of the other jets had a canopy up and someone in the cockpit. I wandered over to find Rabies in the front seat going through some drills. He jumped down and I introduced him to Ron and Geoff. He was absolutely charming with them, answering all of their questions (Ron would talk to anybody and everybody about anything and everything) with a grace and a big smile on his face that made me like him even more. He had come in at the weekend to familiarise himself with the front seat controls prior to going on his tactics course with Handy. He had also booked a couple of simulator rides to do the same. Talk about dedication and professionalism. It also turned out that Rabies' family history led all the way back to north Wales, so Ron was overjoyed and told him he would send out some Welsh flags and paraphernalia to remind Rabies of the 'homeland' (which he did as soon as he got back).

Back at 121, we embarked upon a programme of DACT against the F-5s, so most of March saw us fighting, then landing away at Yuma and fighting again on the way back to Miramar afterwards. The pace was relentless, but I was lapping it up. I couldn't get enough of the jet or the Marines. The Nellis det had really solidified me within the USMC brotherhood in the squadron, or so it felt to me, and I felt like this squadron and the guys on it were my spiritual home. I was very tight with Indy and Muck, and now it felt like I was the same with everyone else. No doubt that was going to come to an end sooner or later. And it did.

Unfortunately, it was announced that our boss, Killer, was being posted out. So be it. Turnover of personnel happens, but this was to have much more of an impact. Generally, on a USMC squadron, the boss handpicks his own XO and OPSO. Killer had picked Junk and Hoover. Therefore, when the boss changed, so did the other two posts. All three of those guys were quality Marines and men, and I had loved serving under Hoover, so we were all a bit upset with them moving on. 121 was due to deploy to Iwakuni that September so the new boss and his team would have about six months in post before taking the squadron away. The guys got even more upset when it was announced who was taking the squadron. Nutmeg was a WSO who had a poor reputation as an aviator. He had risen to lieutenant colonel on the strength of his ground tours and was coming back to the cockpit to lead 121. That is probably being a bit direct—of course he had to be competent in the cockpit, but all I heard was that he was more geared towards the admin side of things which was a 180 from Killer's approach. Coming back from a ground tour was hard enough, but to take command of a fighter squadron at the same time would be a steep learning curve.

I hated the F-16

Nutmeg has chosen Speed as his XO. Speed had been on 314 with Alf and had a poor reputation as an aviator (seeing a pattern here?). He was renowned as a weak player on 314 amongst his peers. Finally, there was the new OPSO. Slop had just returned from an exchange with the RAAF so should have been fairly handy. He also knew Muck from Oz, but when Muck heard his name, his inscrutable face told us nothing. When we pressed him about Slop, he just shrugged. That told us all we needed to know. Anyway, we had a month's grace before the terrible trio arrived so we made the most of it. Hoover and an experienced pilot called Wally had been shafted to drive up to Monterey for a combined arms table-top exercise colloquially known as the 'Puffer Board'. I might get some of this wrong as I wasn't there, but Hoover told the tale beautifully, and it is worth recording here. It was a 3-day exercise run by the US Navy, and involved representatives of lots of flying, ground, and sea units, standing around a huge table called the Puffer Board. It had a 3-dimensional landscape with airfields and tanks and SAM sites, and each rep had a control board. At any time during the exercise, you could push some buttons on your board and simulate an attack on a target. The target would light up and I think a puff of smoke/sand went up (not sure about the smoke element, but I am guessing that is why it was called the Puffer Board? I am sure some nerd reading this can correct me in a review on Amazon or some such). The idea was that the advance continued over the three days and any engagement would be debriefed as they went.

Bearing in mind that this was a 3-day event, we were a little surprised to see Wally and Hoover back with us so soon. Hoover stood up after met brief and told us this story. The exercise was being run by a crusty old admiral and his directing staff. Almost as soon as he got things running, a tank column lit up.

'Stop the exercise! Who was that?'

'F-18D, Sir. We have called in a 4-ship of F-18s to attack the tanks,' said Hoover.

'Very good. Note that down, Commander. OK—no more F-18s in the area from now on. Start the exercise.'

Another light on the tanks. 'Stop! What was that?'

'F-18D, Sir,' said Wally this time. 'We have called in a package of AV8Bs to attack the tanks.'

'OK, very good. Noted. No more fast air packages from now on. Start the exercise.'

Another light on the tanks. 'God damn! Stop! What is it now?'

'F-18D, Sir,' said Hoover who was tag-teaming with Wally. 'We called in naval gunfire.' The admiral was a little wound up that his golden exercise had been stopped three times in as many minutes.

'Right! There are no more assets of any kind that you can call onto any target, OK? Now let's get this thing going again.' He was muttering under his breath by then. Another light on the tanks.

'God damn it, stop! You don't have any assets. How are you attacking it this time?!'

'Our own bombs, Sir.'

'OK—you have no more bombs!' he seethed.

Another light.

'GOD DAMN YOU FUCKERS! WHAT IS IT NOW?!'

'Zuni rockets, Sir. We use them to mark the target, but we can attack with them too.' He just stared them down and restarted the exercise. One more time, the red light. The place was deathly silent as he turned to look at Wally and Hoover.

'So, we have the gun, Sir and ...'

'OK YOU TWO—FUCK OFF!!!' and he pointed to the door. 'FUCK OFF NOW!!!' and off they trooped. So, the F-18D lasted all of about 15 minutes of the three-day exercise. Hoover was the most gentle unassuming guy, but he could tell a story and we were howling with laughter at the end of it. Everything else aside though, it really brought home the amazing capability of the F-18D. It seemed that there was nothing it couldn't do.

Saying that though, I did have my ass handed to me by some F-16s one day on the way into Yuma. It was a 4 vs 4, but not a 10-mile pen weapons school 4 vs 4. This one had us mixing things up at the merge and Prof had his head on a swivel in the fight, trying to keep track of them. My wingman died pretty quickly and I was 1 vs 1 against my bandit. I could hear our lead pair taking on their own bandits, over the radio, with shouts of 'flares!' and shots being taken. My Viper was doing his 9G monster energy rate fight, and I was defensive from the off. No way I could beat him in a rate fight, even without starting from a poor position, so my only hope was to drag him slow. I turned myself inside out to nose point, but he was smart enough not to buy it. It was sickening to watch his nose come around, and it was all I could do to keep unloading for speed and then snap the nose around again. The nasty bastard just watched me like a cat with its nose up against the fish tank, waiting for me to finally give up. I was willing him to run out of fuel and leave the fight. Before that miracle could happen, his mate creamed in and shot the living daylights out of us. I hated the F-16. It was our hardest fight, especially against someone who knew their jet like these guys did. I would have killed for a go in it as well, but you know ... love the one you're with and all that? Once we had pulled all of the F-16 bullets out of our ass on the ground at Yuma, Prof and I launched into a 1 vs 1 and beat the shit out of our opponent just to get all the frustration out. We were still humbled by our F-16 spanking though. That would take some getting over, I can tell you.

Following a night out at a local restaurant to say farewell to Killer, Junk and Hoover, the day finally came for our change in command. There was a small parade of squadron personnel and Killer officially handed over to Nutmeg, and a new era began. Slop was not Hoover, by a long stretch, and he immediately set to work telling Indy, Muck, and I that things were going to change on his watch. He thought Hoover was too soft so we needed to get used to his style. His style turned out to be him being a knob. Muck had invited him round to a BBQ the weekend before that little chat to introduce Indy and I on a personal level and start things off on the right foot. Slop was full of himself and particularly ungracious towards Muck, given that this was a welcome party for him. At work, it meant we had to justify every single sortie on the schedule before he would sign it off and send it to Speed and Nutmeg. They would then send it back requiring the minutest of changes before they would sign it off also. The schedule on a Marine squadron constitutes orders, so as ops officers we could not leave work until they were signed. I finally lost my rag when I was kept on the squadron until 8pm one day because Speed thought there was a spelling mistake that needed correcting (there wasn't) and he had gone back and forth since 4.30pm without telling Slop what was wrong and therefore what needed correcting.

Nutmeg was trying to run the squadron from an anal admin point of view. I think he truly believed that great performance in the air came from having all the admin squared away. Whilst that can be true in some minor cases, it might have done his credibility a favour if he had concentrated on being a better WSO in the first instance. When you sense that a squadron is leaning that way, it affects your decision making as an aviator. Covering your ass becomes all important.

Let's get back to me covering my arse

We had entered a bit of a bombing phase, which included a bombing competition at El Centro. As a fighter pilot, I am proud to say I came nowhere near winning it, by the way. After that, there was some high-angle Stuka madness stuff up in the China Lake ranges, about 150 miles north of LA. I managed to not scare Bluto too much during my dive attacks, thereby lulling him into a false sense of security of him thinking I knew what the hell I was doing. We weren't far away from the air combat trip I mentioned at the start of this book where I would prove otherwise. We bobbed into China Lake airfield for a refuel and then back out for more steep-angle, flinging ourselves at the ground stuff before being vectored over the ocean to meet a C-130 tanker.

Mouse was the young pilot leading our 4-ship as part of his work-up. He was the only pilot on the squadron I was wary of. Not a great aviator, but he was convinced he was one of the best. There are just some pilots out there that always get their ambitions mixed up with their abilities, and he was one of them. He had almost been sent back to the RAG for further training at one point. The tanker was bloody miles away and we were on the cusp of being down to minimums when we joined up with it. The C-130 could stream two hoses and had the most stable basket of them all, so everyone got in first time and filled to full. I have had some 'adventures' with tanking in the past and always said a little thank you to the aviation gods whenever I plugged in successfully, and that day, I needed to. I was number 4 so last to tank and the pressure was on. Just once, I would have liked to have tanked with no pressure on me at all, but that day, I was on vapour as we plugged in.

We were so far away from Miramar by this time, we just turned for home and Mouse plugged the burners in and started to climb. It was a beautiful bright afternoon as we just climbed and climbed into the ether. Back to full dry power and Mouse announced that we would just see how high we could get. I think we finally topped out at 60,000 feet which was as high as we could get in the fit we had (pylons and bomb racks). We then did another of the Hornet's party pieces in the descent by feathering the jet pipes. The jet pipes would get wider or narrower depending on the power you set. The 'petals' at the back of the pipes would move in and out to do that. With full burner, they would be at their widest. We went into an idle power descent which had them almost at their narrowest. By touching a tiny bit of power on above flight idle setting, they would close even more giving the sleekest aerodynamic profile, and reducing the drag and fuel flow. Coming down from 60k cost us almost no gas at all and it blew my mind. OK—it didn't really. I just put that in for all the tech geeks and aerodynamicists who are into bollocks like that. Let's get back to me covering my arse.

Rabies and I headed off to the range in El Centro for some bog standard low-angle dive bombing. It was late in the afternoon when we started, so early evening as we dropped our last bomb. Just as we were clearing the range, the alarms went off and I looked down to see a right-hand OIL caption. I went through the drills, but it persisted so that meant an engine shutdown. Another alarm went off showing a full flap failure on the flight control system (FCS) page on my DDI. Damn it! The nearest diversion was right below us, but El Centro was the arsehole of the universe and not somewhere we would want to spend the night. OK, it wasn't the nightmare of 29 Palms, but it wasn't far off. We were only 25 minutes from Miramar, but it was over the mountains. Rabies said he was happy to press and claim we had lost the engine the other side of the hills. I guess he wasn't looking forward to spending the night with me ... er at El Centro either. Maybe professionalism kicked in for once, but more likely, it was arse covering, and I said we needed to do the right thing, and we diverted into El Centro having declared an in-flight emergency.

Rabies was heading off for his course the following day, so he was driven back to Miramar while I stayed overnight with my poorly jet. There was no food available as the chow hall had closed, so I sat in my room with no TV, eating a power bar from the vending machine. Ever had a power bar? It was a bit like eating my own flying boot. I fucking hated El Centro! The troops had driven over that night and after an engine run and the largest breakfast in NATO (because I was starving by then) I was able to blast airborne solo this time, to nurse the patient back to Miramar. I walked straight into a grilling from Slop. He wanted to know why I had diverted as it had caused them a headache having to send Marines to El Centro. I was squeaky clean though. I had lost an engine and gone to the nearest diversion to land ASAP, exactly as the drill had said. Textbook procedure. Trying to fly across a range of mountains was completely against all common sense when you had an engine already dead and other bits going wrong. Odd that I seemed to be in the shit for doing the correct and professional thing for once.

Baseball season had started again and I had my first of many outings to what was then called Jack Murphy stadium, to see the San Diego Padres. This outing came courtesy of one of the Australian expats. He was Navy and a bit of a spiv, and had somehow secured a private box with food and drink included. It was up behind home plate and so had a brilliant view of the game. Baseball is my favourite spectator sport and I adore the history surrounding the game. I was absolutely hooked and went regularly to see the Padres, always trying to take any visitors we had to give them a taste of the national pastime. As baseball started, the NBA finished with Michael Jordan completing his return to the game by leading the Bulls to the title (his fourth).

I guessed that the boss wanted a closer look at me, because he requested that he fly with me. I am sure he wasn't expecting to lead a 4-ship low-level strike mission, but we thought we would turn the tables on him a little. It was even higher stakes when we got a call from Group HQ that Major General Bolden would like to fly with us. So, I was going to have an astronaut on my wing and the boss in my boot. Yes—I was shitting myself. However, it was low-level so I figured I was probably the expert compared to the others (I hoped) and Indy slotted himself into the formation to help with the planning. I don't mind admitting to you that I was completely star-struck in the brief. I tried to be as professional as possible, but in my head a voice was shouting, 'there's a bloody astronaut in your brief, Tug!' I ended up flying the sortie as if I was solo. Nutmeg sat there for most of the trip just quizzing me on what I thought of his squadron and the guys on it. I suppose I was happy that he called it 'his' squadron, as I think ownership and pride in that is really important. I made sure to tread carefully with my answers, as I had Nutmeg pegged as the classic smiling knife. You know what I mean? Pleasant to your face but ready to stab you in the back when it suited them. Most of the guys were hanging out in the ready room later that day when Nutmeg and Speed wandered in. Nutmeg told everyone about the chat we had had in the cockpit (I wondered where the hell that was going), and so he wanted to ask what us Brits did when we got a new CO. I said we would put a couple of barrels of beer on in the Mess and show off our new boss.

'OK, Tug,' he said, 'let's do that. You're in charge so pick a couple of guys to help you organise it. We can book rooms in the O-Club and make a night of it.' Looked like I had made an impression then. So why did I feel like I had put my foot into a bear trap?

Thursday night was supposed to be the big night at Miramar O-Club so we set a date and I asked a couple of Marines to help out. Fizz and Buzz booked the accommodation for me and secured the beer using squadron funds. I then asked Billy to take the mildly amusing invitations around to all of the resident squadrons, telling them there was free beer to be had. The date chosen coincided with both Indy and I having visitors out from the UK. Indy's guest was Flea, who was a well-liked GR1 back-seater and a bit of a drinker. My guest was a legendary drinker. Bobby was one of my favourite navigators from the Phantom and one of my best mates. He was staying with us for a week with his wife and two sons, but I managed to spring him for the night.

IF HE FLIES THE CORRECT BLOODY PROFILE!

I had formally briefed up the squadron on how we would conduct ourselves, likening it to a 1 vs 1 air combat split where we had a gameplan to destroy the other squadrons by out-drinking and out-singing them. Basically, we wanted everyone to leave the bar wishing they were on 121. A bit of a hard sell with Speed and Slop in tow, but you know—we had to try. Flea and Bobby had brought flying suits with them especially for the occasion and we proudly entered the bar en masse to find it was completely empty. I fully expected tumbleweed to drift through the doors, it was so deserted. Not to worry though as it was still early, so we set about getting some speed on. I think maybe six other guys turned up and we pounced on them and forced a free beer down them. We showed off our new boss. They had all heard of him so I was getting a bad feeling that everyone had stayed away because it was him. Luckily, it was much worse than that. I was quizzing one of the guys who was on my RAG course about why there was such a poor turnout from his squadron. He looked a bit confused.

'Did you see the invitation?'

'What invitation, Tug?' he asked.

'The one inviting you here to meet our new boss?'

'Didn't know about it.'

I collared Billy and asked if he had gone round with the invitations to the other squadrons. He replied in the negative.

'Why not?' I asked, incredulous.

'Well, we don't want those other squadrons drinking our beer.' Insert long pause here ...

'That's the whole point you pillock!' I shouted. So, Billy hadn't invited anyone and the whole thing was in danger of falling flat. Luckily, Bobby had hit his stride so we started singing some fighter songs. Indy and Flea replied with a couple of bomber squadron ditties and even the Marines joined in with a couple, including the Marines hymn. Muck sang an Australian Air Force song that was bordering on criminal let alone offensive, so we kept him quiet after that. Billy was in another chastened mood, but I made it up with him. To be fair, he had probably invited some random F-15 pilot that we couldn't see, to the club (there—I've definitely milked that joke enough now). Sore throat from the singing; sore head from the immense amount of beer we had to get through; job done.

Good grief, I needed a skinful of beer after what happened the following week. Everyone was out of currency for air-to-air gunnery so we scheduled a few trips to sort that out. Once again, this was a first for me on the Hornet, but it looked like the Marines did it the same way the RAF did—in principle anyway. Some poor sap would launch out over the Pacific towing a flag and four of us would set up a carousel style pattern around it. Now, given that nobody had done it for a while, it was a ballsy move putting four in the pattern straight away. It was a fairly bum-clenching event anyway without over complicating it by squeezing four of us into the pattern. The whole thing hinges on the leader of the 4-ship flying a consistent pattern of speed, G, and altitude, with the rest of us taking our timing and position in the pattern from him. Slop was leading, so with all of his experience and confidence in himself, we should have been OK. Of course, we weren't (tell me you saw that comment coming?). I was pleased that Indy was in my jet. I really needed somebody sharp that I could rely on and he was the absolute best.

Each of us had 578 bullets with the noses painted a different colour for each jet. This meant that whatever holes I could drill through the flag, would have a tint of colour around them that I could identify as my hits. Slop led us out to the flag and we did the big dance in the sky to separate out around the pattern. The way it works is that the flag flies in a lazy circle and we dive down onto it from on high to shoot at it. As one guy shoots, the next is in the dive. The third is on the perch waiting, and the fourth is climbing back up to the perch. You know there is a book called *Confessions of a Flying Instructor* that explains all of this in detail? You could have saved yourself the last 20 seconds if you had read it. With four of us being in close proximity, you can see why the leader's pattern is so important to maintaining order. All I can say is that it was a shit show of epic proportions. I was number 3 which put me opposite Slop in the pattern. Trust me—that's how the geometry works out. Number 2 is shooting as I am in the dive and 4 is behind me. The only one I should need to avoid is the leader as he is climbing to the perch as I am diving and vice-versa. It should work out OK—IF HE FLIES THE CORRECT BLOODY PROFILE! After my first near mid-air collision with him, I had to break away and make up random manoeuvres to make the pattern work. I was grabbing handfuls of stick and throttle and using up the gas like you read about, trying to catch back up to number 2, who I then almost had a mid-air with as he broke away from number 4.

I was convinced it was me screwing everybody up. I asked Indy time and again what I was doing wrong, but he couldn't figure it out either. Every time I tried to fly the right pattern speeds, I either closed up too tight on number 2 or fell back into number 4's airspace. I was sweating buckets at the end of it and only had enough decent looks at the flag to get off half of my rounds. The rest, I had to blat off into the sea in a very satisfying 3-second buzz fest of hot bullets and gas. After the most enjoyable 3 seconds of the whole trip, my mind turned to what the hell I was going to say in the debrief. On the way home, I just resigned myself to thinking I would have to do a bit of mea culpa and then apologise for being shit and spoiling everyone's fun. As we walked back from the jet, Muck, who had been the number 2, ran over to me and immediately started apologising for screwing me over.

'Sorry mate. I was working my nuts off trying to hold onto Slop! Fuck knows what he was doing!' he said.

'Jeez, Muck. I'm sorry too. I just couldn't get the pattern right.'

It turns out that Muck, I, and the number 4 pilot all ended up apologising to each other for our poor flying, so something was up. It all became apparent when Slop put his tape in at the end of the debrief. His speed and G in the runs and altitude up on the perch were wildly different from run to run. Muck was thrashing around trying to keep a proper spacing so the rest of us stood no chance. When Muck challenged Slop about his tape, Slop went thin lipped and bollocked us all for not making the pattern work. At least his own WSO had the good grace to look embarrassed.

Even though I was in the clear and not as crap as I thought I was, I hated trips like that. Any time I couldn't get things to work out, it knocked my confidence and I had to wait for the next trip before I could prove to myself that I really could do this flying stuff. When the flag was delivered and rolled out in front of the squadron building, we all went out to watch Slop pat himself on the back at how many hits he got. The rest of us picked up some hits here and there, but nowhere near where we should have been with 578 rounds. Shame they couldn't mark my hits on the ocean surface—I scored at least 300 in that last blast. My next two rides were in the back seat. There were a couple of air tests that needed doing on jets that had come out of maintenance. They were mostly conducted solo, as there was nothing for the WSO to officially do, so I asked if I could jump in as a sort of work-up to me becoming air test qualified. The first one was with Speed. He was the only one of the terrible trio that I hadn't come across in the air, so it would be interesting to see what his act was. The only thing I remember from that hop was what happened on the ground before we got airborne. We had to give way to a 4-ship of straights from 314 Squadron, and we waved to each other as they crossed our nose.

'Man!' said Speed, 'Look at those guys. All of them are looking at us thinking thank God I'm not in that shitty tub. I'd rather have the extra fuel than a WSO.' So, he was the XO on a twin-seat squadron and that is what he truly thought? It told me everything I needed to know about him. Thank God I wasn't a WSO having to fly with him every day.

That afternoon, I jumped in Muck's boot for the second air test. I've said enough times already how off the wall Muck was, but as he stepped into the aeroplane, he became a different person. He was straight, disciplined and thoroughly professional. He talked me through the air test procedure from start to finish while demonstrating it all perfectly. As soon as we shut down and started to walk back in, he was back to the usual mischievous and unpredictable free spirit that we loved him for. We had a large-scale exercise coming up at Naval Air Station Fallon, up in the north-west bit of Nevada, near Reno. It was a good 200 miles north-east of San Francisco so at least an hour's transit time from Miramar. We were to deploy there for a couple of weeks to work up with the other squadrons that would be joining 121 on its next WestPac deployment that September. Muck was due to be posted back to Oz when that happened, with Indy and I expecting to move to another F-18D squadron, possibly 225—the Vikings.

At the end of May, I took a couple of weeks off and we headed up north for a trip to San Fran. What a beautiful city. We stayed in the US Marine Corps Memorial Club right in Union Square, and did all the touristy things including Alcatraz, the Golden Gate Bridge and riding the famous cable cars. It was a wrench to leave after only a few days, but much better was to come. We drove across country into the Yosemite National Park and stayed in the Yosemite Falls Lodge for another three nights. That place took our breath away—literally. The air was so clean and clear that each time I breathed in, I felt like it was cleaning my lungs, ridding me of all the stale air I had breathed in my life up to that point. It was downright beautiful and I felt like I never wanted to leave. We really could have dropped out of life there and then, and disappeared into the wilderness, eating our own earwax, and wiping our arses on dock leaves. When I got back to 121, I wished we had.

Send another XO. This one's broken

I was prepping for a trip with Indy when Muck came into our briefing room with a face like thunder. He had tried to sign out one of the secret weapons documents to check on some fuse settings or something, and was told by the security clerk that he couldn't have it. It was a new directive from the boss that the three of us were banned from signing out the secret documents. Been here before haven't we, Tracey? The three of us went to see Slop and he told us we had no clearance to look at them. The fact that we had been clear to look at them the day before and had previously pored over them on numerous occasions was lost on him apparently. The three of us were summonsed to Nutmeg's office for a pow-wow. He sat at his desk with Speed and Slop standing either side of him like evil henchmen, and the expat collective sat opposite. The news was that none of us had official security clearance, and he also wasn't happy that Muck and I didn't have an official ACTI qualification. So, the upshot was that we weren't allowed to look at any of the weapons manuals and Muck and I were not allowed to teach air combat anymore. Operationally, this was madness. From an air-to-air point of view, we wouldn't be able to build an accurate or effective intercept timeline against various threat aircraft. For air-to-ground, we would be diving towards terra-firma dropping loud bangy shit with no access to the Z-diagrams.

Speed's clever solution to this was that we would have to trust the Marines in our formation to check that stuff for us. I would test that theory later in my brief. Of course, we asked about the fact that we had already seen the secret documents, but Nutmeg's line was that he hadn't seen any admin that we were cleared so that was that. Speed's clever solution to this was that it was down to us to chase it ourselves through our embassies. The point about not being ACTIs was valid so we asked if we could both go off and do the course. However, you needed security clearance to do it so we were screwed there. I pointed out that we had both been teaching air combat for many years by then, so why not use our expertise? Our results had borne out our experience, surely? On this point, Nutmeg then had a brilliant idea. Muck and I would fly individually with an ACTI WSO in the back on 1 vs 1 trips against Speed, to prove our worth. If we were any good, he would consider reinstating us. The whole thing got a bit heated, and Speed's final clever solution was for the three of us to 'shit, or get off the pot'. In essence, get security clearance sorted ourselves from the embassy, or just mellow out and enjoy the sunshine in California and stop whining.

'So, if I hear you right, Sir,' I said, 'if we are not able to do all the regular things a fighter crew would do, such as reading manuals etc. [OK, I was laying it on a bit thick here], we should just go to the beach and stop moaning?'

'Exactly that,' said Speed, with Slop nodding like a ... er, nodding dog. And that was that. No solutions from them. The Emperor of Admin had spoken and so shall it be. I was fuming.

My number 2 on the intercept trip was a nice young guy on work-up called Hero. The poor kid didn't know what hit him and neither did 8-Ball, his experienced WSO. I laid it on in the brief, testing their knowledge of the air-to-air weapons. It was shockingly poor. I am no QWI (thank God) so I don't care if somebody can't build the bloody weapon. However, I do care if they don't know how to use it and the rules of thumb for max and min ranges. So much for Speed's clever solution number 1 of trusting our wingmen to know the critical stuff on our behalf. I wasn't a bastard on that trip or in the debrief, and Hero did really well. I did overhear him telling one of his buddies in the ready room, 'Man! Tug just gave me a class on the AIM-9!' By this time, word had got around about our situation and the proposed showdowns with Speed. There was even a bit of a book going on who would win and how easily. I had no idea how good Speed was, so the pressure built over the week until the fateful day arrived. In the meantime, I had a very pleasant day out to Yuma as number four of a 4-ship with a brilliant WSO from group. Penguin was a half colonel doing a ground tour, but tried to fly as much as possible, mainly for his own sanity, I think. This meant that every time he did fly, he was incredibly happy and grateful. He was the perfect companion in the cockpit. Pepper was leading, and saw us through an internal 2 vs 2 to land at Yuma. After a bit of lunch, we briefed up with a 4-ship of USAF F-16s that we were going to fight with, prior to going home to Miramar.

For some inexplicable reason, Pepper had us walk for the jets about an hour sooner than we needed, and we taxied out in the stifling heat of early June to wait at the hold short of the runway. The ORP (operational readiness platform—a bit of concrete near the end of the runway) was a bit narrow, so we folded our wings and parked up close to each other to leave space for other aeroplanes. And that's where we waited. For ages. In the baking sun. Penguin was chatty and jolly and I asked if he had seen the film *The Battle of Britain*. He loved it so I thought I would try a bit of hold short banter over the formation radio frequency.

'Is there any chance of us getting airborne?' I said, à la Michael Caine's character, 'The engine's overheating and so am I. Either we stand down or I blow up! Now which do you want?' I said it in my best plummy English accent. I could see Indy laughing in the back of his jet, and as soon as I finished, he transmitted, 'Must be these X-Wing fighters, Tug. No reliability.'

Penguin was hooting. He was loving it. Pepper didn't understand that we were bantering though and obviously thought I was being serious. He called us over to the Tower frequency and requested take-off. 'Oh hell!' I said to Penguin, but it was too late, and I spread the wings and off we went airborne 45 minutes early. By the time the F-16s arrived on station (a good 10 minutes late, as was their wont) we were completely out of fuel and just toddled off to Miramar having achieved absolutely nothing. Not totally convinced that one was my fault, but I will hold my hand up to it anyway.

High noon was finally at hand. Our showdowns with Speed. I was first up late morning, with Muck just after lunch. I guess Speed wanted to loosen up with me first before he took on the much harder fight against Muck. There was a buzz in the squadron as it was big news. I had gathered as much int on Speed that I could, but it was a bit scarce. Word was that he wasn't all that, but I made sure I was completely up for it. Flame was the ACTI in my boot, and he was fairly nonplussed as to why we were having to prove ourselves in the first place. I did everything by the book in the brief and onto the play area, to show I could do the procedural side of being an ACTI, and then it was time for the punch ups. I went vertical on the first one. He lost sight straight away and I shot him with a heater less than 15 seconds after the merge happened. That just made me cross. The second one, he went vertical, and I just went single-circle, nose pointed and AMRAAMed him as he floated over the top, about 10 seconds after the merge. So, this was the guy they were putting me up against to check if I was good enough? It would have been laughable had I not been so incandescent with rage.

He lasted longer on the last fight, but only because I couldn't be bothered to kill him with a missile. I wore him down and finally put my boot on his neck and gunned him. I took zero satisfaction from it. I hadn't won a single one of those fights. He had lost them by being shit. The ready room was full as we arrived back on 121, and I literally kicked the door open and burst in to sign us in, I was so spectacularly angry.

'How did it go, Tug?' asked one of the young Marines.

'Send another XO. This one's broken,' I said. Muck wandered over with a smile on his face and asked me if I had any int on Speed.

'Honestly, Muck? Just pitch up with a pulse and you should be OK.' I took him into a briefing room to give him chapter and verse, and about 2 hours later, he pummelled Speed into mush. Neither of us got a debrief, and our ACTI status remained rescinded.

I was wholeheartedly in love

A week later, 121 flew into Fallon with every other squadron deploying for the upcoming WestPac. It began with a mass arrival briefing in the conference facility. As we checked in, Muck, Indy and I were barred at the door by security. Apparently, Slop had neglected to tell us that we wouldn't be allowed access—I mean we only worked directly for him in the same office every day—so we went through the humiliation of being turned away in front of about two-hundred aircrew. What made it even more galling was that the RAF Harrier guy on exchange with the AV8B at Yuma wandered in with no problem at all. I had been through officer training with him back in '85 so asked him what the deal was with his clearance. Apparently, he didn't have it either, but his boss took the view that if he was flying the aeroplane, he needed access to everything. My first trip was a range familiarisation ride with Indy. The Fallon range complex was huge and varied and brilliant. There were all sorts of targets including a full-sized airfield with jets all over it. We would be bombing stuff like that all week. Our ordnance would include specialist weapons such as Rockeye cluster bombs and napalm. Hell's bells—napalm!!! There were a load of old napalm canisters hanging around and I guess the Department of Defense wanted it dropping before it was outlawed. It was easier to drop and explode it rather than dispose of it any other way.

We had not used these weapons before so it was imperative just from a safety point of view that we were able to read up about them. We pleaded with Nutmeg to allow us access just for the exercise, but he wouldn't budge. Out of nowhere, Muck announced that as of then, he wouldn't conduct any air-to-ground missions as he felt it was too dangerous without access to the information in the manuals. Indy nodded and so did I. And that was the final fracture between us and them. In the evenings, we drowned our sorrows in downtown Reno. It was a bit like a poor man's Vegas with cheap casinos and an altogether 'don't go down that street' vibe, but a lot of fun nonetheless. We seem to have been branded as bad boys, but everyone wanted to hang out with us which only polarised our newly minted bolshie attitudes. I mean, who the hell did we think we were? Three flight lieutenants (although Indy had just found out he was getting promoted) thinking we were more important than the reality suggested. However, no way we would have acted like that if Nutmeg, Speed and Slop had not been utter knobs. Even our maintainers were in on it, and a couple of our gunnery sergeants who were shift leaders took us out one night to commiserate. Gunny Tinker even tried to teach me how to play craps one night in a very seedy casino, but the immense skinful of alcohol I had in me meant I instantly forgot all of his advice. I might have well have chucked the dice onto the roulette wheel.

Despite not doing any air-to-ground, I banged quite a few trips in at Fallon, managing to tank from a C-130, and go against an EA6B Prowler which jammed the living daylights out of us. Rabies was working his nuts off dealing with the jammer on the radar. I just closed my eyes as I wasn't allowed to look at all that secret stuff on the scope. The only other thing that happened at Fallon that week was while I was briefing up a 4-ship intercept trip. One of the WSOs was an older major from group who was going to be posted onto 121 for the WestPac deployment. He had been partying every night so burning the candle at both ends. Half way through my brief, I noticed he had fallen asleep! It may well have been a charisma failure on my part that caused it, but kipping during a sortie brief was bad form at best. At worst, it was downright disrespectful and unprofessional. I stopped talking and just stared at him. One by one, the other six guys turn to look at Sleepy and started grinning. They wanted to see what I would do. I walked over and bent down so we were face to face. I swear to God, he was lightly snoring.

'AM I KEEPING YOU AWAKE, SIR?!' I shouted, and he reared up and fell over the back of his chair. He was very apologetic, but his credibility was blown. He wasn't a sharp guy, but this was the only calibre of aviator that Nutmeg was able to attract into the management positions on his squadron.

I have to take stock here. Reading the last few pages may give the impression that my California dream had turned into a nightmare. It hadn't. Nutmeg, Speed and Slop were minor irritations in the continuing wonder of this exchange tour. I had dealt with crappy bosses and flight commanders before, but what really mattered were my brothers in arms. Everyone else on 121 shone brightly and I still felt that nailed on Marines Corps camaraderie with them. Multiply that by ten and that's what I felt about Muck and Indy. And underlying it all, no matter what crap and drama came down the pipe, I was able to flush it all away as I climbed Jacob's ladder into the cockpit of heaven each time I went flying. The Hornet was my saviour over and over again. I had only been flying it for a year, but it already felt like it was the only aeroplane in existence. My first love, the Phantom, was long gone; my little fling with the Hawk was fun, but was over for now; my torrid affair with the F-18 was in full swing and I was wholeheartedly in love.

One final night in Fallon saw us hit Reno hard. We needed to. Speed had got hold of us and said that Nutmeg was planning to make a formal complaint to our embassies about our behaviour and performance unless we wound our necks in. Bollocks to him. We only had a short time left on his squadron and if he had the balls to report us (which I seriously doubted) it would expose the whole exchange programme from a security clearance point of view. Nutmeg was not a man to rock any sort of boat so we knew it was an idle threat. Anyway, down town, Muck suddenly decided that he better ring home having not done so for the whole det, and used a public call box on the street. His wife gave him a fair amount of shit so we sidled closer to earwig his bollocking. Their middle child, Nicholas, who had Muck's feral free spirit in him, had been playing up so it was time for Muck to step in and do some parenting. Bearing in mind that Nicholas was only about two and a half, this is the half of the conversation we heard:

'Nicholas. Mate. You have to listen to Mummy while Daddy is away, OK?'

Some toddler speak.

'Yes, mate. I understand, but ...'

More toddler speak.

'Yes, Nicholas. I hear what you are saying mate. But what you have to understand is, you can't go around acting like a raw prawn OK? Just do what Mummy says, and I'll sort it out when I get home tomorrow.' With that, Muck hung up, nodded his head, and ticked off parenting for another week.

We weren't flying out of Fallon until the next afternoon following the wash-up debrief that the three of us were banned from, so we tied one on and hit the sack, a bit tired and emotional. At 0500, there was a banging on my door which just wouldn't stop. I staggered to open it to see Muck and Indy in their underpants.

'Come on, mate. We're going to watch the sun come up over the desert.'

'Christ almighty, Muck! Just let me sleep!' I wailed looking to the zombie that was Indy for support.

'It'll be worth it. Trust me!' said Muck and he toddled off around the balcony of the block we were staying in. Indy just shrugged and followed, so I traipsed out too. It was already warm as we stood there in the semi-dark, semi-naked waiting for the sun to do its thing—which it did every bloody day anyway.

'This better be good, Muck. I'm knackered.'

'Just wait,' he whispered. As expected, the sun came up. As not expected, it took our breath away. The enormous ball of fire and fury lit up the boring lifeless desert floor and turned it into a dancing frenzy of coloured lights. As it shone on our faces, I turned to Muck and saw he had that annoying, but incredibly charming self-satisfied smirk on his face. We just burst out laughing and watched the sun some more. It was a truly magical moment spent with the best of friends, and was a wonderful gift from Muck to us. I could have hugged him.

He walked out of the squadron and never came back

As soon as we got back to Miramar, there was another magical moment for us. 121 held a squadron ladies' dinner night, so we dressed up in our Mess dress with our wives in fancy frocks, and headed out to a restaurant that was used to hosting these events. Being the Marines, the dinner night was written up in orders and the traditions were followed to the letter. A bell was rung and the many battle honours were called out. There was a single place setting on a separate table honouring those lost in battle. Being a traditionalist myself, I was actually moved by the solemnity of it. Guests of honour for the night were Major General Bolden and his wife. At the end of the dinner, when the toasts had been done, Muck stood up and asked to be recognised. Nutmeg was as nonplussed as the rest of us, but hey! It was Muck after all.

'I wonder, Sir, if General Bolden would be kind enough to share with us what it was like flying in a real rocket ship?' he asked. We banged the tables hard and eventually, he reluctantly stood up to speak. He was modest to a fault. It was the most unassuming yet enthralling speech I had ever heard at a dining-in night, and his humility, and the fact that he mentioned what his wife had been through also as he shot off into space, cemented our deepest respect for him. This was a man I would have followed to the ends of the Earth. And he was a bloody astronaut!!!

Muck was in his last couple of months before returning to the RAAF, and his replacement was due to take up post over at Beaufort in South Carolina rather than with us at Miramar. Zulu was everything that Muck was not. Tall, handsome, stable, polite, and eminently promotable. Despite being practically perfect in every way, you couldn't help but like him, and we instantly became friends. He came to us on 121 for about a month of US orientation and handover from Muck. What better way to introduce him to life in the US than take two jets to Nellis for a night out in Vegas? Indy and I led us out for an intercept trip which saw us land at El Centro. Having shown Zulu the dead zone of El Centro, we assaulted his senses by launching on a nav trip up to Death Valley and into Nellis. Somehow, Muck had persuaded the USAF to give us a van and book us into a nice hotel, just off the strip. Muck had no shame when it came to wheedling these things out of people. He had once flown into Reno for the air races with a young Marine WSO in his boot. As he taxied in, he told his charge to call him 'Sir' all weekend and to trust him. Before climbing out of the jet, he had swapped his name badge to one that had colonel on his rank, thereby promoting him upwards by three steps. The organisers saw that he was a senior officer and instantly bumped them up to VIP status for the weekend. Free drinks, better hotel and food, as well as VIP seating for the air races. So, a van and hotel in Vegas were nothing for him to sort out.

What happens in Vegas, stays in Vegas. Probably no surprise that we got shit faced, so hardly a secret. A late flight out the next day had us flying a nav route in and around the Grand Canyon, which was something else. Being able to do that in two Hornets was a massive privilege, and looking back, yes, I do realise how lucky I was. We spent the night at Colorado Springs which still looked a bit like a frontier town. We were almost 7,000 feet up in elevation, and although it was July, the air we were breathing felt ice cold and clear. We barely made it to a saloon type bar, our chests were heaving so much with the altitude, but being the athletes that we were, we managed to down a few ice-cold beers before turning in early. We had peaked badly in Vegas so this was recovery. Zulu headed off to the East Coast almost as soon as we returned to Miramar, and we got ready for our last month of flying on 121 before the Green Knights headed the long way west.

But, fly we didn't. Fallon had screwed our relationship once and for all with Nutmeg, and an edict came down that we were to get minimal flying. Slop told us not to schedule ourselves so we asked what he wanted us to do instead.

'You heard the XO. Fuck off to the beach!' So that is what we did. However, he neglected to tell us that there was a squadron parade to present some medals to some of our troops later that afternoon. Ordinarily, we would have lined up with the aircrew as we knew how important these 'formations' (as the USMC called them) were. Apparently, Nutmeg went mental that we weren't there and after met brief the following day, Slop stood up in front of everyone and said, 'I want to see the foreigners in my office now!' Having humiliated us in front of the guys, he then proceeded to bollock us rigid in his office. Look, I am happy to take a bollocking when I deserve one, but he told us to go and didn't tell us about the formation, so I think we had a case. Apparently not though. I tried to argue, but got shut down. Indy and I were pissed, but took it on the chin (Slop was a knob after all). Muck though? He stayed silent throughout, and when we were dismissed, he walked out of the squadron, and never came back.

Muck's disappearance caused some consternation on 121. Slop bollocked me for some reason and told me to get Muck's sorry ass back into work. I told him that I wasn't Muck's keeper, but the fact that we were socially tight meant I had to pass the message on. The Aussie embassy had backed Muck completely and told him to stay off work until his moving date. I just told Slop that Muck had gone silent and deep and I couldn't get hold of him. I only flew one trip in August, and that turned out to be my last on 121. What a crying shame. I had loved life under Killer, Junk and Hoover, and then Nutmeg's rule had ripped the guts out of it. Hopefully, it would be back to normal when I switched squadrons.

That would prove to be more than problematic as it turned out. However, following my last trip, Slop hauled Indy and I into his office for what I assumed was one last bollocking to send us on our way. We then entered the realm of the bizarre as he told us, almost in tears, how hurt he was that Muck had just left without saying goodbye to him! He thought they were friends and couldn't understand what had happened. Our meetings with Slop had turned into 'Yes, Sir. No, Sir. How high, Sir?' affairs, but I couldn't stop myself this time.

'Maybe telling us to fuck off to the beach and then bollocking us for fucking off to the beach might have something to do with it, Sir?'

I ventured. He just nodded, sighed, and looked down for a while. We then left the realm of the bizarre and ran head first into the downright surreal. Slop looked up and announced that Nutmeg wanted to hold a farewell for the three of us!

'So, what do you think?' he asked. I looked at Indy who shook his head ever so slightly.

'Well, Sir. Given that the boss wanted to report us to our embassies just a week ago in Fallon, I doubt that would be a good idea, do you?' I didn't tell him that all the young guys on 121 had already organised us a farewell lunch at the golf club later that day. Slop had to agree with us, and that was that.

The drunker we got, the more the F-4 stories came out

Indy and I headed out to the golf club and had a very pleasant and slightly emotional farewell, with the guys telling little stories about us before presenting us with our squadron plaques. It was lovely to think that we had made a good impression on them in such a short time. Afterwards, we headed back to 121 to pick up our flying kit and leave the Green Knights for the very last time. They would deploy to Iwakuni a month afterwards. Diplomacy moves slowly and my situation of not having a declared squadron to move to was small beer in the grand scheme of things. It was everything to me though. I only had a limited time on this exchange, and I wanted to fly as much as I could. The air attaché at the embassy must have been sick of taking my calls, and in the end, I just got with the programme and spent every day on the beach with my family for about a month. As idyllic as that sounds, I was desperate to fly and was really missing my Hornet. Indy had taken a job in HQ, picking up the odd bit of flying here and there, but he only had a short time left on his tour and had done all the flying he wanted to do by then I guess. Lucky for me, he had bumped into Hoover over at HQ, who had asked for my contact details. That night, I got a phone call from Hoover asking if I fancied going on the road with him one weekend. I had not flown for a month so told him I could do with an emergencies simulator and a shakedown flight for currency, which he organised for me with 242 Squadron.

It was brilliant to be back in my jet, even though all I did was a bit of general handling, instrument flying, and about 10 minutes of low-level. It got me current again, and that Thursday, Hoover and I checked in with 242, ready for our weekend away. We made a point of going to see the skipper and thanking him for the jet. He was a very well-liked guy and I hoped that now they were just back from WestPac, they would have room for Indy and I to join them. That was for the near future though. I had a long weekend's worth of flying ahead of me with Hoover. As I was starting up and taxying out, we slipped into a very natural routine together, and it was like the last few months with Slop had never happened. Hoover was so happy that I had mellowed out enough to call him Hoover in the cockpit, rather than Sir. A couple of hours saw us landing into Cannon for a refuel and then two more had us arriving at Naval Air Station Pensacola, in the western-most bit of the Florida panhandle. We were closer to Mobile in Alabama than anywhere substantial in Florida. Hoover had booked us into the O-Club for the weekend, and that first night, he took me on a walking tour of his time at Pensacola during his flying training. I have already said that Hoover was a great storyteller, and he regaled me with a load of outrageous tales that sounded remarkably like my experiences through flying training. Military aviators are the same the world over, but there is an even more deep-rooted similarity among fighter crews. We drowned our sorrows a little in the bar afterwards, lamenting the changes on 121, but rather than get maudlin, we swapped stories of the six months we had spent together on the Green Knights. Obviously, with us both being Phantom aircrew, the drunker we got, the more F-4 stories came out. I really should write a book about my time on the Phantom.

It was essentially a working trip for us, so the Friday had us starting up and heading out across the great state of Texas into Sheppard Air Base for a lunch stop. While the jet was being refuelled, I bumped into a German Air Force (GAF) instructor called Drumm. He had been on exchange with the RAF at Wattisham, and I had served with him on 56 Squadron. He had moved to the States to support the European and NATO joint jet pilot training (ENJJPT) programme, as part of the GAF contingent. Unfortunately, the RAF had stopped using the ENJJPT programme so there was no way I could just smooth across to Sheppard after my Hornet tour, and prolong my American adventure. I still had eighteen months to go on my exchange, but the clock was ticking. Anyway, whatever plan I came up with to stay in the US, the RAF probably had my future mapped out for me. I was almost certainly looking at a Tornado F3 flight commander tour after that, assuming I got picked up for squadron leader rank. Indy's promotion and my average, but successful performance in the service writing course should see that as a formality. I mean, almost nobody returned from exchange still as a flight lieutenant. You had to be a dead loss for that to happen (anybody have a sense of foreboding here? Hold that thought).

We landed back at Pensacola mid-afternoon, and Hoover asked if I fancied a look around the museum before dinner. The National Naval Aviation Museum had just undergone a refurbishment and it was nothing short of spectacular. On one of the floors, it felt like we were standing on the deck of an old aircraft carrier. The aeroplanes were beautiful. Hoover was a naval air nerd and he properly gave me a guided historical tour through the life of US Navy aviation. I was enthralled listening to him, but the best was yet to come. Hoover had done a number of WestPacs, and had passed through NAS Cubi Point in the Philippines, lots of times. The bar there had been a legendary venue and had been chock full of squadron memorabilia and trophies. When Cubi bay closed, everything in the bar had been photographed, catalogued, and sent back to the museum to be reconstructed. As we walked into the exhibit, which doubled as a café, Hoover's breath caught in his throat and he stood stock still. Apparently, it was picture-perfect from what he remembered the last time he had been there in the Philippines. His eyes lit up and he told me story after story, related to the trophies and pictures, and then he came upon a trophy that brought back a story of a crew that died in a Phantom crash. He told me all about the crew and what great guys they were, and at the end of the story, the tears were streaming down his face. It killed me to see him so upset, but I felt so honoured that he had shared that immensely personal moment with me. What a man. I was actually a tad emotional the day after, when we returned to Miramar knowing that I wouldn't get to fly with him again. After we put the jet to bed, we shook hands and he thanked me for a great weekend. I couldn't believe it. All I had done was drive him around the Southern states, but he had entertained me with stories for two solid days. I think I got the best part of the deal.

 I then spent the next two months on the ground while the USMC and the embassy decided what to do with me. I went completely feral and grew a beard. All of the cool baseball players at the time, wore Van-Dyck beards (just on the chin and up to a moustache), so I did the same and took on the persona of a California beach bum. We headed out to the Grand Canyon for a couple of days and it was awesome to see it from ground level having raged over it in a Hornet. Speaking of which, I almost forgot about my jet completely! The embassy wasn't bothering me so I thought, 'sod it!' and went even more off the grid. Talk about bad attitude. Eventually, the phone rang, and the air attaché told me they had sorted out a new squadron for me. VMFA-134 was a reserve unit in MAG-46, flying the oldest F-18A models, and they worked out of the next hangar along from where I had been on 121. That hangar had 'Hornet's Nest' written on the side of it in big letters. 134 flew brown camo Hornets, and was manned by airline pilots who came to fly F-18s when they weren't down route with their day jobs. The ops officer was the only full-time Marine, and I would be working alongside him, basically running the squadron day to day. It was going to take a little while to sort out the funding before I could fly, so I was asked to go and do some paperwork for MAG-46 in HQ. I had so much attitude by then, I gave that the big ignore, and by the time I was tracked down again, the details had been sorted out and I arrived on VMFA-134 on a Saturday. The reservists had a mandatory muster weekend once a month, so it was a good time for me to arrive and meet everybody. The rest of the time, they popped in and out when they were free. They had a minimum number of days they needed to do each month, but most of them did more than that. Right—it was time to join my new squadron.

5
VMFA-134 Squadron: The Smokes

I cheated, he cheated

The first thing I did was meet the skipper, Chilli and asked permission to join his squadron. He was as mellow a man as I have ever met. We then went to met brief to meet my new squadron mates. Well, that was an education. What an eclectic mix, but all of them still with that underlying Marine ethic. They were all older guys, very experienced, and mostly ex-Phantom with a smattering of Hornet babies. As soon as Chilli introduced me, and mentioned my F-4 background, I was in the club. Hannibal and Salsa, who were like two massive bookends, started bantering me immediately, and I had to be on my toes from the off. I was going to be working alongside Harry O, who was the only permanent Marine, and he was about my age and a very likeable guy. We hit it off straight away. As permanent fixtures, Harry O and I would rarely fly at the weekend, as we piled in our flying when times were quiet during the week. When Chilli was away flying a 747 for Northwest, Harry O was the de-facto skipper. All of the groundcrew were reserves also, and it was nice to see Gunny Tinker from 121 on the staff, having just retired from active service. I was dead keen to get airborne again, but also shitting myself after all that time on the ground. I had also been flying twin-seat for a year and now had to hack flying a single-seat fighter. You know, one of these days, I am going to have to deal with this bloody imposter syndrome once and for all. The day finally came, and I briefed up for a 1 vs 1 intercept trip as a shakedown.

My leader was an older guy called Hedge and he calmed me down right at the start, telling me we would walk for the jets in slow time so that I could get all the nav kit and other stuff sorted without rushing. I couldn't stop myself from smiling as I walked out to a sand-brown single-seat F-18A. It was all mine for the next 3 hours. We would do some intercepts, refuel through the hot pits, and then I would try my hand against Hedge in air combat. The guy had 3,000 hours Hornet, so I expected to have my ass handed to me, especially as I wasn't particularly current right then. I shook hands with the ground crew and had a bit of chat while I did the external checks. This was more to keep me calm if I am being honest, and eventually, I reached the steps and climbed up into my golden chariot. I had loved spending all that time on the beach with my family, but just sitting on the ejection seat again washed away all of my bad attitude and I was ready to reignite my love affair. Without the pressure of rushing, I found that I had everything ready almost straight away. My left thumb was like a little dancing worm inputting the waypoints I would need. Setting up the radar and stores was just as easy and I relaxed a bit and thought, 'Yeah. I can do this.' I was only 15 minutes into my 3-hour extravaganza so God knows where that confidence came from. I had to go through the salute, wave, odd look thing again, as none of the ground crew knew about my idiosyncrasy. Hopefully Gunny Tinker would sort them out with that. Hedge led me out and I lined up on the runway next to him. I had gotten (US speak there!) somewhat lazy in my twin-seat jet, so just changing radio frequencies and nav points was a bit of extra tasking which made me appreciate Hoover, Indy, and the swathe of great WSOs I had flown with even more. It was all down to me now. No pressure then.

We conducted a formation take-off which seemed to go well from my cockpit—I didn't hit him so that's how I am judging it! Off we roared into the bright blue of a crisp November day in Southern California, over the dark blue of the vast Pacific. Hedge gave me the first three intercepts and my radar handling seemed to be on point. No TWS and no AMRAAM, so it was back to AIM-7 Sparrow shots, keeping the target locked throughout, then converting to the stern for AIM-9 kills. After the first one, Hedge was happy that I knew what I was doing, and wound things up a bit so that by the end, we were doing almost full-up Hornet vs Hornet. I can't tell you how happy I was that firstly, I wasn't shit, and secondly that Hedge rated me enough to just have at it. I flew the whole of the recovery back in close formation just for the practice, and we broke into the circuit for a couple of touch and goes before landing and heading for the pits. Hedge debriefed the sortie on the back radio and as soon as the tanks were full, I started up the left engine and followed him back to the runway to do it all again.

The air combat splits were a hoot. I cheated, he cheated and I fell in love with my jet and my life all over again. It was honours even and I didn't even think to complain about having to do a Guns D at the end.

I didn't want the trip to finish and even volunteered three circuit patterns rather than my customary one and land fighter pilot frame of mind. I have said a lot about debriefing in this book, but all I want to say here is that Hedge debriefed the sorties. I would later come to find that on 134, that was not always the case. He heaped me with plenty of praise and I couldn't wait to fly with him again. So, having proved I could do the air-to-air academic stuff, I had to do the same thing with bloody bombing didn't I? A 4-ship into the pattern at El Centro saw that off, and afterwards Chilli told me I was full-up and ready to go. Oh, and I was free to look at any of the documents in the secret cabinet. That was handy, as I was responsible with Harry O for the cabinet itself, and knew the combination to the safe! No wonder Chilli had a smile on his face as he told me that. I was just in the mix now as another squadron pilot after the shortest work-up in history.

Back in at the deep-end then as my next trip was a pairs low-level, with us popping up to drop live 500-pounders. They went off with a bang and so did the rest of my tour on 134. The trips came thick and fast and were so varied, I barely had time to catch my breath. It was just what I needed to get my mind back on track after my enforced grounding. In only two weeks, I managed to fly alongside every pilot on the squadron, and against what seemed to be the whole of the US Military's aviation inventory. Our Hornets were mostly brown camo as I have said, so everyone wanted to fight us over the desert as if we were an aggressor squadron. They soon found out that we weren't, as we didn't fly set Soviet or Iraqi tactics, but full-up in your face combat God Hornets. I found myself getting swept up in the euphoria of it all and revelling in the fact that we were Marines, yes, but we were a bit fast and loose also. As ops officer, I was responsible for writing the schedule which also meant organising other units to fight alongside of, or against. I found myself one day taking a call from an F-15 unit that wanted to do some 1 vs 1 against us.

'What? You want to do 1 vs 1?' I asked.
'Yeah,' he replied.
'Against us?'
'Well. Yeah!'
'You don't want to do that, mate.'
'Why not?'
'Well, it will just be ugly. You ever fought an F-18?'
'No.'
'Yeah. Ugly.'

I was turning into a right arrogant son of a bitch; you might be thinking? This was part of 1 vs 1. The fight begins way before you get airborne. Everyone knew the F-18 was a tricky opponent, so why not up the ante before we start? The other issue they won't have been used to was our fake canopy. The Hornet had one of those shapes that lent itself to looking the same from above or below, so we had black paint underneath the cockpit in the shape of the canopy. At range in a fight, the way you tell which aspect the other aircraft is can sometimes just be down to shading and shadow. That false canopy saved my ass lots of times when opponents I hadn't seen in multi-bandit fights had missed the split-second opportunity to shoot me because they thought I was turning hard towards them, effectively coming inside the minimum range of their missiles. In actual fact, I had been turning away from them and they had seen my false canopy. Anyway, it all added up with our incredible airframe and air combat radar modes to us being a right bastard in a fight. Add a bit of fighter pilot arrogance and we were good to go. We always beat up the F-15s and F-5s, but it was generally a score draw against the F-16. I bloody hated fighting them. It was always a sweaty G-fest with those guys and if ever you found yourself 1 vs 2 against them, it was miserable.

So, no kid's books then?

About this time, Holly was old enough to start play group and we found one that was local, with a lovely old lady running it alongside two younger women who were absolutely hyper. Holly was quiet and reserved at the best of times, so I figured they would freak her out, but they really brought her out of her shell. We met another British couple whose son, Matthew, was also at the play group and we got chatting. She was a nurse and they were in California on the strength of her work visa. Anyway, we seemed to hit it off and all was good. I was picking Holly up one day which always seemed to cause a furore with the two excitable supervisors. I guess they just weren't used to fathers picking up their kids.

'OH MY GOD!!! DAD'S HERE HOLLY! DAD'S HERE!!!' they shouted when they saw me, which was a little embarrassing. Not as embarrassing as the next few minutes for Matthew's dad though. I got talking to him and asked him what he did for a living. He was mostly a house-husband, but he also worked in a book shop.

'Great,' I said, 'we buy tons of books, especially for Holly.' He went a bit quiet.

'Which one are you in? We'll come and boost your sales.'

'Er, you probably won't find what you want in this book shop,' he replied.

'Why not?'

'It's an adult book shop.' I still didn't twig.

'So, no kid's books then?'

'Er, no books at all really,' he sheepishly said.

'So ... what ... oooohhh! I see!' as the penny finally dropped. He worked in a bloody sex shop! I didn't know what to say. When I got home, I told my wife and she then told me that she had accepted a dinner invitation from his wife for the next night. We had a bit of a chuckle thinking dinner would be interesting with our new found knowledge. We had no idea just how 'interesting' it would be.

While Holly and Matthew played in his room, the conversation over dinner started very normally about our backgrounds and how we ended up in California, but quickly the subject of his job came up. He had no shame about it so good for him, I thought. It was fascinating when he spoke about it, but I didn't need as many details as he was willing to share with us. I tried to crack a poor joke about him getting free samples or staff discount, but he shared a decidedly odd look with his wife, and she went to get dessert while he continued with his tales from the 'not a book shop at all'. I was not drinking as I was driving, but they tried and tried to get me to, saying we could stay the night. I went to check on Holly and go to the loo, and when I came back, my wife had eyes as wide as dinner plates. As our hosts went off to mix some cocktails, insisting I try them and we stay the night, my wife hissed at me that we needed to leave immediately. They came back to the dining room with a jug full of margarita (oh shit, Tug) and a plan that Holly could share with Matthew, we could have their bed and they would kip on a camp bed in the living room.

I was not a sharp man at the very best of times, but I knew that look from my wife and announced that we couldn't stay over as I had the Marine Reserve muster weekend the next day, so we had to make tracks. They looked horribly disappointed, which I took as a compliment, and tried one last time to persuade us to stay. We packed up the mountain of paraphernalia that you have to take everywhere with a toddler, and drove off with my wife silent, but me telling them what a great night it had been and they should come to ours next time. Holly dropped off immediately on the drive home and my wife turned to me in the car and whispered loudly, 'Tug! They were bloody swingers!'

'Huh?'

'Swingers!'

'No!' And then it all dawned on me as she raised her eyebrows.

'Holy shit! No! I can't believe it!' Told you I wasn't very sharp.

I had only been on the squadron a month when half stories and rumours were fed to me about the recent history of 134. Red, the previous boss still came to fly with us from time to time. I loved flying with him. He was a nice old guy who obviously still enjoyed his flying and he was a genuinely friendly man. However, I started to hear that the squadron had fractured under his command due to some personality clashes and the whole thing had got out of control with openly hostile factions splintering out. All had come to a head at the end of a practice bombing sortie at El Centro. Harry O had been tail-end Charlie of a 3-ship (I think) and instead of joining up over the target to return to Miramar, the reservists in the other jets just pressed back over the mountains leaving Harry O to play catch up. He plugged the burners in and powered up to them, but instead of joining in close formation as planned, he sailed right past them. Trust me—we have all screwed up a join before! However, it happened again, and Harry O came in for some abuse on the back radio. Nobody figured there was anything wrong, even when he did it again, and also overtook them on the downwind leg in the circuit. It so happened that he had one engine stuck in afterburner. The other guys didn't do anything to work out what was wrong, and just landed, shut down, and left the squadron without debriefing, as they all had airliners to catch to pre-position for their day jobs, leaving Harry O still airborne.

As far as I recall from the story I was told, Harry O landed with the burner still engaged and slewed off the side of the runway into the dirt. He ejected and landed in a clatter of bits in front of his Hornet, taking a starring role in his own HUD film footage. That story might not be wholly accurate, but you get the gist. The lack of team work and support, and the fact that Harry O was still airborne while the others had sloped off was a major cause for concern in how the squadron was functioning. The investigation also exposed the toxic culture in the squadron itself, and so things had to be sorted out.

There were two definite cliques on the unit, but I tried to judge everyone on the strength of the interactions I had with them and formulate my own opinions. All told, out of about twenty-five aircrew on the books, there were only a couple I was wary of. Not a bad average, I guess? I was particularly wary of our maintenance officer. He was a warrant officer engineer called Watt and was a prickly character at best. He stormed into our office one afternoon, and took me to task in front of Harry O about me waving to the ground crew and not saluting. If he had asked me what was going on, it might have resolved easily, but he came at me with fire, so fire is what he got back. Apparently, no one had complained. In fact, when they spoke to Gunny Tinker about it, he had explained it was just the crazy Brit and that I was a bit odd, but OK with it. By all accounts, it put a smile on people's faces, so all good. Watt had a bug up his ass about it and thought he would try his luck at the last chance RAF saloon. I let him rage a bit about me showing a lack of respect, and then calmly asked him why he hadn't saluted me on entering my office. Harry O stifled a chuckle as Watt floundered, and I lectured him on the rank structure; respect for rank; and just overall general attitude. He didn't say another word to me for the rest of the tour, using Gunny Tinker to communicate through. Once Watt left, I just checked with Harry O that I hadn't overstepped (I was still a bit worried that I hadn't shaken off my feral attitude).

'Nah. He's a bit of an asshole, Tug.'

'Right you are.' And that was the end of that.

Hey, Tug. Wanna see something cool?

Christmas was on us again, so we thought another trip to Hawaii might be a good idea. This time, we took a longer break and spent the first half on the heart-stoppingly beautiful island of Maui. It's no wonder rock stars live there. If I had the cash, I would too. The second half, we went back to Oahu, but struggled for a hotel as the Hale Koa was full and the rest of the hotels in Honolulu were astronomically expensive. Salsa had recommended the Bellows Beach Air Force Base cabins. These were right on the 3-mile beach near Turtle Cove on the south-east side of Oahu and were probably wonderful in summer. However, they were somewhat 'rustic' let's say and the winter wind battered them at night. In the morning though, the crystal-clear turquoise surf was straight out of a holiday brochure, and I bodyboarded to my heart's content. Being a full-on California surf dude (as if), we took my body board back up to Waimea Bay to go play in the big waves. As I strode onto the beach with my board under my arm, the life guards took one look at my spindly arms and legs and immediately banned me from going in the water. I was outraged for all of a minute until I saw the size of the waves and watched them recover a professional surfer on a stretcher towed by a jet ski. He was put straight into an ambulance and driven off to hospital. I put my board back in the car and built sandcastles with Holly for the rest of the day.

1997 started with a couple of shakedown trips and a crazy 1 vs 1 vs 1 during which I chased my own tail for about 40 minutes. It was the most fun I had had in an aeroplane in a long time. At one point we were in a 3-ship rolling scissors/tree/batshit mad tumble. Amazing to think these guys flew civilian airliners during the week and were doing manoeuvres in the Hornet that would have got them sacked or even arrested in Delta, United or Fed Ex. We went straight from those easy shakedowns into a 6 vs 8 bloodbath against an Air National Guard F-16 unit that had dropped in to play with us. They were also doing some special weapons stuff and deployed with more kit than I think the RAF as a whole owned—and this was only the National Guard! One day, I was passing by the briefing spaces we had allocated them, and one of the guys saw me and said, 'Hey, Tug. Wanna see something cool?'

I wandered in and they had a bank of six TV screens showing a live special weapons mission. Whatever weapon they were launching had an electro-optical head, and its pictures were being data-linked back to us in real time. We watched as it raged towards its target, and then there was a big flash as it hit. Yes, very cool, but so what? Ah, we now watched the second weapon follow it in, and the guys did their own battle damage recce looking at the live TV pictures sent back by this weapon. Analysis done swiftly, and they were able to re-target the weapon to a different point of impact. One thing we excel at as human beings is that we always come up with new and innovative ways of killing each other more efficiently. No apologies for that—it is what it is.

After a week of turning myself inside out shooting down some F-16s (hooray!) and also getting shot to bits by some other F-16s (boo!), I needed a change of pace. That came courtesy of the newly promoted Squadron Leader Indy. He was almost finished on his tour, so this would be a bit of a swansong for him. He had arranged to take a jet on the road for the weekend to the East Coast to visit Zulu at Beaufort. Again, we would be scabbing a jet from 242, and got ready to launch first thing. Unfortunately, due to unserviceability, we didn't get the jet until late afternoon, so after only an hour airborne, it was dark as hell over the vast sand and dirt of New Mexico. We landed at Cannon again for the well-worn refuel plan and then blasted off into the big dark across Texas for a night stop at Navy New Orleans. I had never been to the 'Big Easy' so we were planning a big night out at this legendary party town. My room in the O-Club was perishing cold. It was the middle of January, and some idiot had left the windows wide open. My heater didn't work either so I had a quick shower and dressed in the freezing cold with my teeth chattering uncontrollably. I met Indy in the bar, which was shut, and we tried to book a taxi downtown. That didn't arrive, so after an hour of waiting (it was 10pm by this time) I got in a bad mood and slunk off to bed. I slept in my clothes under three blankets and froze my bloody cobs off. I tried to shake off my bad mood the next morning as this was supposed to be a jolly for Indy and we were getting to meet up with Zulu.

Beaufort was closed that day, but Zulu had told us to land at Charleston Air Force Base anyway as that was actually closer to where he lived. Charleston had about a thousand ginormous C17 Globemasters on the pan. OK, it was about thirty I guess, but holy hell, they were big. Our little Hornet looked er ... little in comparison, and I reckoned we could have taxied up the ramp and parked inside one of them. It was great to see Zulu again. He was as handsome and cool as ever (bastard!) and picked us up in a 1960s classic-shaped Mustang (double-bastard!). Zulu and his wife Lizzie, who was an awesome and accomplished cook, plied us with amazing food and a skinful of an Australian beer called Victoria Bitter or VB as it was known. The Aussies got a booze allowance while on exchange and they all had VB shipped in by the container load. On my return to Miramar, I would tap up the Aussies in the expat community and get in on the act. VB would become my staple diet for the rest of my tour.

Wary of the time we both fell asleep over Texas, Indy and I were sensible-ish and had an early-ish night before jetting off on the Sunday to turn through Barksdale AFB in Louisiana and Holloman in New Mexico. Barksdale had about fifty B52s on the pan as we taxied in. I though the C17 was big, but you should have seen these monsters. Basically, if you loaded our Hornet up with 8 x 1,000 pounders, you could then strap us to the bottom of a B52, and it could drop us on the enemy—aircrew and all. Indy had only planned the turn through Holloman so I could see the German Air Force Phantoms from the training squadron they operated there. He knew how to please his pilot! All in all, it was a wonderful trip, despite my paddy somewhere near New Orleans (I still haven't managed to visit to this day). I had one final night out in San Diego with Indy and then he was off back to the Tornado GR. He was absolutely wasted on that jet, but we didn't have a joint air-to-air, air-to-ground machine in the RAF (all you Harrier pilots out there calm down—nobody cares). That final night in San Diego didn't really go as planned. We had invited the expats over from Coronado Island to come and say farewell, but in the end, it was just the two of us left standing and we headed for a club/bar called Jimmy Loves. Now, the story goes that Jimmy Loves was part-owned by some Marine Corps pilots. When you dug into it and asked around, there must have been hundreds of owners because almost every pilot claimed to have part ownership. However, it meant that if you could prove you were a USMC aviator, you didn't have to queue to get in and the $15 cover charge was waived. After a couple of nights there, the doormen seemed to recognise us, and in we went. It was heaving with people, and as we fought our way to the bar, we bumped into our old sergeant major from 121 and he bought us a drink. I was all beered out at that point so ordered a gin and tonic. This was where I discovered that the Americans have no idea how to make a gin and tonic.

RIP, you Devil Dogs

They fill a plastic cup with ice, and then simultaneously fill it with cheap gin, and tonic from the machine. At best, you get a 50–50 split which is strong, but even worse when they put the 'well' gin in it. 'Well' drinks were what you got if you just asked for a vodka, gin, whiskey etc. They were the cheapest spirits in the bar. If you wanted something more refined, you had to ask for the branded spirit specifically. Anyway, my gin and a bit of tonic stripped away the skin at the back of my throat and I went to get another round in. I swear to God that the barman, who was talking over his shoulder at the time, didn't press the tonic button, and we 'enjoyed' neat ethanol over ice. Even Indy's eyes were watering at that point. It was time to visit the little Marines' room, so I went downstairs past all the cool photos of Hornets and Phantoms, and did my thing in the restroom. At that very moment, the watery American beer and my two poisonous gins did an absolute number on me as I staggered back upstairs. The bouncers saw a man looking confused and barely able to stand upright, and immediately ushered me outside. I would have protested, but my chances of getting back in were non-existent, and also my homing device had kicked in telling me it was time to go. Somehow, I found a cab and managed to mumble my address to him. He made me pay up front which was fair enough, and I then endured twenty long and distressing minutes trying not to throw up before reaching Ocean Beach. Somehow, I made it and crashed out into a deep sleep.

I was woken up by hissing and clicking noises, and the feeling that I was in the shower. Oh well, I opened my eyes to find that I had crashed on my front lawn and the sprinkler system was doing its nightly routine all over me. I picked myself up out of the mud and went into the house, straight into the spare bedroom on the ground floor so as not to disturb anyone. So, the next day, I spent my time cleaning the spare room while enduring some frosty glares from my wife and disappointed looks from my daughter. Apparently, some sort of filthy swamp monster had shed its clothes in the spare room and then obviously waved them all over the place in some ancient ritual, covering the room and bedding in mud. Not my finest hour, but I had done worse in the past, so this was a step up, I guess? Maybe maturity was kicking in at last?

I was flying my ass off at this point. Being one of only two guys on the squadron every day, I could schedule myself for as much or as little as I wanted. Aware that my clock was ticking, and all told, I would have spent six months of my tour on the ground, I was desperate to go home with at least 500 hours on the Hornet. Hours are not everything, and there was no way I could get a coveted 1,000-hour badge, but I loved the Hornet so much, I couldn't get enough of it. I flew 40 hours in January

'97 alone. I had never flown that much before, even during summer at RAF Valley, when we banged the trips in like you read about. I could have got many more hours by going on the road every weekend, but why would I do that? I was loving going to the beach with my family, maybe over to Coronado Island, and then going for Sunday brunch at the Navy North Island O-Club where some of the *Top Gun* scenes had been filmed. No, I would just make sure I packed every weekday with as much flying as I could. And like I said, it was so varied, but also so relaxed on 134.

About this time, I received some bad news. Indy called me to say he had just heard at HQ that a Hornet from 121 had crashed into the Yellow Sea, and the crew were missing, presumed dead. It was Puke and Bluto. They had been doing some intercepts into combat and it was believed that they had both G-LOC'd before crashing into the sea. Although I had only served with them for less than a year, they were both great guys and great Marines. I had flown with Bluto more times than with any other WSO on 121, and we had shared some dramas, but a whole lot of joy and success as well. As with all aviators who die in aeroplanes, they were gone way too soon. Aviation may have finished with them, but I am sure life had not. Fast jet flying is terribly unforgiving, and only a couple of years earlier, my stupidity had led me to G-LOC in a Hawk, and it had almost killed me. There but for the grace of God? Puke and Bluto were not so lucky. 'Semper Fi until you die.' RIP, you Devil Dogs.

Two announcements followed shortly afterwards. The first was that 134 was going to deploy to Key West in Florida for an air-to-air gun shoot. I was excited, but equally sick to my stomach, remembering my last experience on the flag with Slop. I will come back to that in a minute. The most amazing news though, was that my wife was pregnant again and due before our return to the UK. So, we were expecting a California baby—baby! Holly had been a model child and we loved her more than words could say. If we could have another one like her, life would be just peachy. In my experience, it seemed that success in procreation in the States consisted of having a son to carry on the family name. The Marines who had baby sons would come into the squadron with a box of cigars and would name their sons Junior or Champ or name them after themselves and put 'The Second' or 'The Third' on the end of it. This had not rubbed off on me. I was desperate to have another daughter. I mean, underneath that, I would be happy with just a healthy baby no matter the gender, but if we could have another daughter, I would be in heaven.

Putting that great news to one side, I had to shoot on another bloody flag to prep for Key West. I was still having sleepless nights about the many near mid-air collisions I had had on the last flag, trying to follow

Slop's random pattern of speeds and manoeuvres, and things weren't shaping up too nicely this time either, as leading the mission was Postal. 'Going Postal' was a phrase they attributed to the lone gunmen (usually disgruntled postal workers by all accounts) who went mad and started shooting up shopping malls and the like. It wasn't a complimentary callsign, but all in all, he was a bit out there. Not surprising though. Before becoming a very experienced aviator, Postal had led a Force Recon unit so, special forces, behind enemy lines—all that stuff. No wonder he was different. Don't get me wrong, I thought he was brilliant, and an outstanding aviator, but if I could choose somebody to lead a gunshoot, I would probably choose Slop over Postal. No—scratch that. No way I would choose Slop! I would claim my aircraft had broken on start-up rather than go through that again. I had to eat my words. The trip went like a dream with Postal setting up the most stable pattern I had ever seen, and the four of us slotting in and out with seamless precision. We weren't firing live, so the tow set up over the Salton Sea which was a highly salted inland lake near R-2507. It was a beautiful hot Southern California day, and not a cloud in the sky, as our Hornets danced with each other, never once getting into a tizz. When we checked the tapes afterwards, Postal was on the numbers, and had we been shooting live, there wouldn't have been a scrap of flag left. I was so happy we had buried that ghost and looked forwards to the Key West deployment.

We had three new guys join the squadron prior to that. Burn and Fox had retired from active service directly from TOPGUN! They had been instructors on the school for the past three years and were shit hot. They were very junior in their new jobs at the airlines, so had lots of spare time to spend on 134. I think they were horrified at some of the relaxed attitudes, but took it in different ways. Burn was a cool, almost horizontally laid-back guy, but Fox was brimming with desire and zeal to make 134 the best and most professional fighter squadron ever. He would run out of heartbeats before that happened mind you, but by God he tried. To be honest, his attitude whipped me into shape as well. I had come from my feral period, straight into the reserve mentality, and had probably gone off the rails a little when it came to ultimate professionalism. I wasn't completely *mañana* but I was well on the way before Fox pitched up. The third of our new Marine reserves was Solo. He had been a youngish instructor on the RAG when I went through, and was a really nice guy. He had a brilliant claim to fame though. One of his best mates from college was a film producer who worked on the Will Smith film, *Independence Day*, which had lots of F-18 sequences in it. He tapped up Solo to be an official advisor and a fair bit of the film was shot in VMFAT-101's spaces at El Toro. The briefing scenes near the beginning have loads of genuine Marine and Navy F-18 pilots in them. Solo even got a bit of a starring role towards the end, although he told us his one line ended up on the cutting room floor. He's right there in the film though!

Yep. Good shoot

So, the day came and we launched off as three separate 4-ships separated by about 30 minutes, across the country for a turn through Dallas Fort Worth. I seem to remember that there was another Marine Reserve Hornet squadron based there that were nicknamed 'The Cowboys' of VMFA-112, so we used their ground crew to turn us. The Cowboys had been through a bit of a to-do and had a reputation for being bad boys. They were definitely in the dog house for some reason so had taken the heat off 134. We were welcomed like long-lost friends—partners in crime, I guess? Another couple of hours airborne out of Dallas, and we were breaking into the circuit at NAS Key West. Oh wow! It looked glorious from the air. The Florida Keys extended out like the Devil's bony finger with the long nail at the end being Key West.

Key West was an absolute party town, and once I stowed my gear in my room, we headed into the O-Club bar for a couple of sharpeners before hitting the town. Alf had started a tradition that the Queen bought the first round of beers, as our RAF allowances were much more generous than the Marine Corps per diem (as their allowances were called), so I got them in. Towards the end of that beer, one of our number called Baller got out a set of dice and gathered everyone around. He got me involved too, and I found out that whoever lost the dice game would buy the next round. Not knowing any of the rules, I lost, so the Queen bought the next round too. I could tell that a couple of guys were uncomfortable and offered to buy the third, but Baller insisted on the dice. This was a man who had been a captain in the airlines for some time so was paid a fortune, claimed a reservist's wage, and was getting per diem but wouldn't buy a round of drinks. Baller was the most unpopular guy on the squadron and his pure human reputation in the Marine Corps was dire. I eased away from the game with Hannibal, Salsa, and Hedge, and they beered me up before heading into town.

I fell in love with Key West. It was relaxed, bohemian and a little bit subversive, just like 134, or how I felt 134 was. I managed to do the museum visits to Hemingway's house and President Truman's house, but all in all, I hung out in amazing restaurants and bars with a band of brothers who acted like they were on spring break despite some of them having kids old enough for them to be worried about them going on spring break. Hannibal was like a child. A big fat loveable child, and he regaled me with stories of outrageous partying from when he and

Salsa had been together on the Phantom. I thought I had some shocking tales from the F-4, but these guys were something else. Underneath it all though, they shared that unbending brotherhood, even with me, that told you that if the shit hit the fan, the USMC would wade in on your behalf.

First flight was a guns shoot with Thud towing the flag. Thud was another full time Marine who worked over in Group HQ, but flew a lot with us, as well as the F-5 aggressors in Yuma (who were also in MAG-46). He was called Thud because he was a little dull. I think it was also the sound you hoped he would make hitting the floor after you punched him in the face. Not a likeable character. Anyway, maybe that was why he was towing the flag. As we walked for the jets, I noticed that there was no indication as to what colour my bullets were. I asked Gunny Tinker and he just grinned and called over Gunny Peterson. Gunny Peterson was from the deep South and about as Marines as you could get.

'What can ah do for you Flaaht Lootenant Wilson?' he asked in his Southern accent.

'Just wondering what colour my bullets are, Gunny.'

He looked at me quizzically, but way too dramatically.

'Why, Flaaht Lootenant Wilson. They are silvah like everybody else's Suh,' he replied completely straight-faced. Gunny Tinker was pissing himself laughing.

'I meant the tips, Gunny.'

'Oh, we weren't asked to paint the tips, Suh.'

So, four of us walked to shoot holes in a flag that would all look the same afterwards. We wouldn't be able to tell who had hit and who hadn't. Off we went then, and I had to concentrate on the pattern and not get distracted by how achingly beautiful it all looked, with so many shades of blue in the sea, and golden sands, and …

VVVVVFFRRRRR!!!! Went my hard as nails gun as I lobbed eighty rounds or so at Thud … er, the flag. And then lots of G to climb up to the perch for yet another set of weapons checks before tipping in again, calling 'in hot' and loosing off another eighty in a relentless orgy of rock 'n' roll gunnery in my rock star space ship. I was bloody buzzing when I landed and even the old hands had big grins after the shoot. Despite Thud making it back in one piece a little while later, nothing could dampen our spirits as we wandered out to the front of the hangar to have a look at the flag. Now I was used to debriefing the sortie first, then checking the film, and then checking the flag. Chilli, who was leading, waited for the flag first and led us all out to have a look. It was frayed to buggery with holes all over the place. How it was still attached to the spreader bar, I will never know. Chilli walked around it twice then looked up and simply said 'Good shoot,' and nodded his head. The other two reserves said, 'Yep. Good shoot,' and wandered off. No debrief! No films! No idea who had hit the flag! No idea if I had actually been any good, so I collared Fox and asked if he would run his eyes over my film. He said I had definitely hit the flag and then gave me a couple of pointers for next time which I was grateful for. However, even Fox and his unswerving professionalism couldn't swim against this tide, and very quickly, we all relaxed into Key West mind-set and 'Good shoot,' and a nod became the standard debrief for the gun sorties. It would have made a RAF QWI apoplectic.

We also had time to fight against a random F-16 unit that happened to turn up, as well as doing lots of in-house 2 vs 2s. It rapidly turned into one of my favourite dets of all time. The social life down town was amazing. Being the new boy on the squadron, I was subjected to a few pranks and spoofs, with Hannibal leading the way. Hedge was retiring from the reserves, so Hannibal and Salsa were arranging a social event for him and he had asked a small select group of his closest friends to accompany him to his favourite Key West restaurant. I was very honoured to be asked along and was happy beyond belief to be accepted by what I saw as the 'fun group' on the squadron in such a short time. We arrived en masse at the restaurant to find that it was Cuban. I had not eaten Cuban food before so this would be a new experience for me. It was even more novel, as we realised that Hedge's favourite restaurant was a gay Cuban place with the most outrageously camp waiting staff. Key West was a haven for free living and what was then described as alternative lifestyles. However, here I was with a bunch of older Marines who were about as far from alternative as you could get, in a gay Cuban restaurant, having a whale of a time bantering with the staff. What an absolute hoot we had in there. It was a brilliant place.

They brought out bread rolls and small plates with butter on them. Hannibal immediately asked if it was hot in there and got Salsa to put his hand on his forehead to check the temperature.

'No man. You feel fine,' said Salsa.

'Are you hot, Tug?' asked Hannibal.

'A bit, I guess. Yeah, it is hot.'

'I am so hot now, I bet I could melt that butter just by holding my hand over it. Hey! Tell you what, Tug. Let's have a race to see who can melt the butter first.'

'Huh?'

'Just hold your hand over the butter like this.' Like an idiot, I did and he just slapped my hand down into the butter, and howled with laughter.

'GOOD GOD, TUG!' he shouted as the rest of them laughed along, 'What is wrong with you, man?'

'How old are you, Hannibal?' I asked while wiping my hand on a napkin. I swear to God, the big oaf was crying with laughter.

After we finished eating (I left my bread roll—couldn't eat it without butter), we wandered out onto Duval Street to find a bar. That wasn't difficult given how many of them there were. The guys walked past all of them with some purpose, saying we had to get to the pier to see the green flash. Hannibal started telling me the story of the green flash, but I cut him dead. My palm still stank of butter so I wasn't going to fall for another one of his tricks that night. Apparently, when the sun disappears below the horizon, if the atmospherics are right, there is a green flash in the sky. Pirates believed it signified the return of a soul from the world of the dead. It's bullshit of course, and I told Hannibal so. I had been spoofed with stories of orange llamas in the Falkland Islands so I was a pro at sniffing these things out. Jesus, they were all in on it, even Harry O. Still, they wouldn't catch me out this time. I waited at the end of the pier sipping an ice-cold beer with a bunch of real mates, watching the amazing natural spectacle of the Earth turning away from the sun, giving the impression that the sun was moving down below the horizon. And wouldn't you know it? There was a stinking big green flash, followed by everyone cheering and a big meaty hand slapping me on the back.

'GOOD GOD, TUG! DID YOU SEE THAT? DID YOU SEE IT?!!!' Oh, and the orange llamas in the Falklands are real too.

He had senior officer written all over him!

On the way back to base that night we passed by Sloppy Joe's, the most famous bar in Key West, where Hemingway used to hang out, and we heard lots of good-natured shouting and abuse. Looking across the road, we could see Gunny Peterson and some of our Marines sitting just inside the bar having a beer. We threw some banter back and I started across the road when one of the guys stopped me.

'What are you doing, Tug?' he asked.

'I thought we were having a beer with the troops?'

'Er, no. We don't do that,' he said and they walked on. This was a bit alien to me so I continued across the road thinking that at least one of us would have the courtesy to drink with them. The looks on the troops' faces as I approached them told me I had broken some sort of etiquette rule by going to drink with them. I was committed by then though, so tried to style it out.

They all scrambled to attention and I tried to calm things down by offering to get a round in.

'No, Flaaht Lootenant Wilson. We shall get you a drink, now please sit down, Suh,' said Gunny Peterson. They hastily got me a stool and put it in place of honour next to Gunny who nodded to one of the guys. That guy rushed off to secure me a beer as I sat down. My attempts to relieve the tension were clumsy at best.

'Hey, Gunny, if it's OK with you, please just call me Tug while we are in the bar. What's your first name? I can't keep calling you Gunny.'

'No, Suh. You are Flaaht Lootenant Wilson to us, Suh. And mah name is Gunny.'

I looked completely perplexed, and he sighed and explained it to me.

'The Corps is mah life, Suh, and I have worked hard to make the rank of gunnery sergeant. Therefore, I want to be called Gunny as it is a mark of respect among mah fellow Marines.' They were all nodding at this point. 'You Suh, deserve the respect due to your rank Flaaht Lootenant Wilson.' And there it was. The Corps was everything to these guys and girls and that one awkward conversation crystalized it for me and cemented my love for them, the Corps, and the colours on my squadron badges.

'Gunny it is then,' I said, and he broke into a smile and clinked my bottle with his. I was aware of a collective sigh of relief from the troops who were sitting around watching us. I finished my beer in double-quick time, said my goodnights, and left them to it. I didn't realise it at the time, but I became the talk of the squadron. Watt was furious when he heard I had broken protocol, but the ranks closed around me and I had grinning faces greeting me at the aeroplane each day, and some of them even attempted an idiotic British style wave as they saw me off, putting a smile on my face.

As we were all the way over on the East Coast, I was only a couple of hours away from Beaufort, so I belled up Zulu and asked if he and Lizzie wanted a visitor for the weekend. In all honesty, it would do me good to dry out that weekend after a lot of partying. So, Friday afternoon, I fired up a jet and scorched out of Key West, north up to the Carolinas, passing Cape Canaveral on the way. I could see all the launch pads of the complex. These were the very launch pads that I watched the Apollo missions blast off from on TV when I was a young boy. My earliest memory was watching Neil Armstrong walk on the moon, and here I was, in a single-seat Hornet, flying over the historic site of my childhood dreams. Sometimes, life just throws you the most magical of moments. I had spent most of my flying career thinking I wasn't very good, yet here was the world's most powerful military, trusting me to fly one of their war machines through their airspace, on my own. I mean—come on! Holy hell, I hope I don't screw this up, was all I could think. Thankfully, I didn't (this time) and I landed in a hot and humid Beaufort where Zulu picked me up in his Mustang again and I spent a very pleasant weekend with him and Lizzie.

It appeared I had gate crashed a fancy dinner though. They were hosting Zulu's boss and the group boss and their wives for dinner on the Saturday night. I felt a bit of a knob imposing myself on them, but they were very gracious and roped me in to help out a bit. Lizzie was a very accomplished cook, as I have already said, and her and Zulu had been on a wine-tasting course, so he was able to pair up the wines to match the food. He had senior officer written all over him! The last proper dinner I had enjoyed had me sitting in a gay Cuban restaurant, wiping butter off my hand. It was obvious this was going to be a bit more up market. Zulu's group boss was Hammer, who had been my CO on 101 at El-Toro for a little while. I hadn't spoken to him much before, but this more intimate setting gave us an opportunity to chat a bit. He was retiring from active service and at the end of the food, Zulu proposed a toast to him leaving. I asked him what his plans were and he casually announced that he was joining the reserves and was going to be the CO of MAG-46! My group boss! I hastily rewound everything I had said at dinner in my mind, but nothing stood out as me shooting myself in the foot, so I relaxed a bit. He was a great guy with an outstanding reputation so we should be OK.

After a great weekend, I carried out the most professional start-up and take-off from Beaufort, just in case Hammer was watching, and broke into the Key West circuit 2 hours later like a complete hooligan. We were ramping up the trips with the F-16s and had a week's worth of 4 vs 4s against them coming up. As I was scheduling, it was down to me to arrange things with the Vipers. Their scheduler wanted a quiet word with me on the side. Apparently, of all of the trips we had done against them so far that det, we had mostly turned up late in the airspace and delayed the start of the missions and it was starting to piss them off. I know I said I was enjoying the fast and loose nature of 134, as it allowed me to be a gash fighter pilot—well, internally on the squadron that seemed to work. However, when it started to impact other units, it just reflected badly on us, and it was now time for a reset. I told Chilli what had been said and he relayed it to everyone at met brief with a sharpen up sort of chat. There were a few grumblings about the USAF being anal, but all told, we were a little bit stung about our professionalism being called into question.

Hey! Let's just roll the dice

I was on the 4-ship that afternoon and it was being led by Total. He had been one of my sim instructors on the RAG and was a cool guy and well liked. Number 2 was an old and bold guy called Louis, and Burn was my element lead with me being tail end Charlie again. I figured with Total leading, and me and Burn being along on the sortie, we should be OK. I was a full-time military aviator and Burn was fresh out of TOPGUN. I figured wrong of course, didn't I? Total's brief was, well ... a total mess. He rambled on for what felt like an eternity. Whenever we went off to do air combat on a trip, we had to brief up the official rules of air combat, and the recovery actions should we lose control of the aeroplane. For some reason, Total went completely off track and started talking about when he flew the T2 Buckeye way back in flying training and what the spin recovery actions were, and did we all remember when we were taught ACM for the first time, and what a blast that was etc. etc. I was getting more and more agitated as our walk time came and went and Total was going further down memory lane. Burn and Louis didn't seem phased at all, and eventually we finished the brief almost 30 minutes late. We actually watched the F-16s getting airborne before we even walked out to our own jets. This was going to be embarrassing.

I had never started the jet up so quickly, but it made no difference. We shambled out to the runway and eventually checked in about 20 minutes late. The F-16s were a bit chippy on the radio (understandably) and we only managed one split before they had to go home. Now, it might have been politic for us to return with them so we didn't keep them waiting to debrief, but instead, we did some in-house intercepts to burn off our own gas before going back. Their leader was seething, and made some not-so-subtle comments in the mass debrief. The USAF already saw the USMC as lower beings in military aviation, and being reservists, we were almost expected to be a bit gash. We wanted to be taken seriously, but we delivered all of the evidence these USAF pilots needed to prove their point about us, on a silver platter. I was embarrassed, but I had to suck it up with the rest of the guys. I knew I was going to get some more shit from their scheduler, but we deserved it. So be it. However, when we got to our own 4-ship debrief, it was like it was no big deal! Total shook his head and just said, 'Man. I have no idea how we ended up so late, have you?' Burn and Louis shook their heads wistfully. I wasn't surprised at Louis, but Burn? TOPGUN instructor? Nothing. I guess over the weekend, he had mellowed out so much on the beach, he wasn't registering what had just happened? Knowing it was me that was going to have to deal with the fallout, I couldn't stand it any longer.

'It was the brief, Total.'

'How do you mean?'

'Well, it wasn't brief. You over ran by thirty minutes.'

'Huh?'

I told him about all the time he had wasted telling us about the T2 and other irrelevant stuff, and then instantly wished I hadn't. Oh no. It was like I had shat in the fingerbowl! He looked really hurt. Louis and Burn gasped like I had broken some unwritten rule on not criticising each other. Come on guys. We just had our asses handed to us regarding our lack of discipline and you are too sensitive to lift up the stone and sort it out? Was I the only one who was pissed that they were dissing the Marine Corps? Shit! Why did I listen to Fox? I could have just stayed in my euphoric feral reservist haze and not got involved.

The debrief was wrapped up quickly after that and we drove back to the bar in silence. I really felt like I had killed the best thing that had happened to me recently, so I went to get a beer to drown my sorrows. If I had seen Baller's dice at that moment, I would have shoved them up his ass. A couple more beers and it seemed that everyone was over it, but I made a mental note about managing these situations in the future. Silently seethe maybe, but concentrate on my own reputation and just try to enjoy flying with these great guys, in this great place and on this great jet. If I was leading, we would be on time. If I wasn't? Hey! Let's just roll the dice and see what happens! Once I had come to that accord with myself, I mellowed out even more, and if it was even possible, the flying got more enjoyable. Early that second week, I got a random call on the ops phone from a Brit called Daffy. He had been one of the brilliant Tornado GR1 pilots I had met in Eglin with Indy. Daffy had left the RAF and was training up with Virgin Atlantic. He had flown into Miami and was staying a couple of nights so wanted to see the Keys. Indy had told him that I was in Key West and he called up to see if I fancied a beer as he was staying in town. I scheduled myself for a day off the following day and arranged to meet him at Sloppy Joe's.

Daffy was just one of those guys who could connect with anybody, and although I barely knew him, we had a great night swapping stories while we beered ourselves up. I took him for dinner at the Hog's Breath Saloon and insisted he order conch fritters. This was the signature dish in Key West and it was almost the law that you had to eat them. As we drunkenly said goodnight, he told me how lucky I was to be flying the Hornet and how he and most other RAF pilots would dream of doing it. Of course, I knew how lucky I was, but to hear it said by an experienced RAF pilot really brought it home to me. All I had to do for my last year was strap in and hold on for the ride. And what a ride it would be.

Flying was pretty much done for this det, so we had a big night planned before prepping the jets for the long haul back to Miramar. 134 had put on some beers and food at the O-Club and our SNCOs were invited too. Gunny Peterson was on night shift prepping the jets, so Gunny Tinker joined us for a drink or two. It got a bit raucous and Burn asked me what sort of things we got up to in the RAF. There were some common themes like carrier deck landings, where aircrew would launch themselves head first along the mess tables as if they were landing on a carrier. There would be a small gap between the tables that you tried to hook your toes in, to 'catch the cable' with your hook before you flew off the end in a clatter of bits. The tables would then be soaked in beer as if it was a wet deck, and people would rock the tables to signify a rough sea. All very childish, but excellent fun, despite the injuries. I also told Burn that we sang a lot of bar songs, some of which were flying related, and others that were just downright disgusting. The guys asked for a bit of a rendition, so I sang a couple of flying songs, mainly about the Phantom and the RAF, and some generic fighter pilot stuff. A bit of a crowd gathered and I ended up singing for about an hour. Since the Tailhook Scandal, stuff like that just didn't seem to happen in the US Navy and Marine Corps. I was a Brit and therefore uncouth, so could get away with it. I didn't notice Gunny Tinker smiling and obviously plotting something for the future though. More of that later.

I was living life at 700 knots

We flew the jets back in a one-er behind a couple of KC-10 tankers. The KC-10 would usually use a boom to plug into a fighter such as an F-16 or F-15, but it could also refuel aircraft with refuelling probes. I had heard nightmare stories of Phantoms and Hornets refuelling from the bastardised system on the KC-135 and KC-10 where they put about 12 feet of hose out of the end of the boom, and you refuelled from that. You had to connect with the basket with about 1–2 knots of overtake only. Any faster and it was like hitting a brick wall and could rip your probe off. Any slower and it wouldn't connect properly (that was called soft contact). Once you did connect, you then had to push an S-bend kink in the hose or fuel wouldn't flow and then you had to maintain a really tight position throughout. For a pilot of limited ability like me, that was a nightmare. Fortunately, our KC-10s had the traditional long hose and basket configuration, so that's what we used. The tanking position for that is much more relaxed and flexible, as the long hose takes up some of the slack from your ropey flying. As there was only one hose, the other three guys in your formation had a grandstand view of your attempts to tank so the pressure was on. The banter on the back radio didn't help either. For once, I got in first time, without jousting, on all the tanking brackets, and five long hours later, we plonked them on the ground at Miramar. I didn't care how many people told me how lucky I was to fly the Hornet—5 hours behind the tanker in any fast jet is cosmically boring. You have hours and hours of grind interspersed with 15-minute periods of hyperventilating and sweating as you crash your aeroplane into a tube that pours volatile liquid into you.

I hadn't been back in San Diego long when news broke that thirty-nine members of a religious cult called 'Heaven's Gate' had committed ritual suicide in a house up in Rancho Santa Fe, which was a suburb in the San Diego area. By all accounts, they believed that there was a spaceship behind the Hale-Bopp comet that had come to take their souls to Heaven (or something like that). All they had to do was free their souls from their Earthly bodies and that punched their ticket for the ride. I knew this stuff happened in places other than California, but … only in California huh? Holy hell, my life on the squadron just exploded into an absolute melee of flying. I could barely keep up; I was flying so often. And once again, the variety of the trips blew me away. I was buzzed on the adrenaline all day every day, and it's a wonder I didn't burn out with it. I guess the bottom line was that I didn't have time to burn out. We did a whole week of 4 vs 4 full-up combat against another random F-16 unit that deployed to Miramar specifically to fight against us. Those trips were absolutely brutal. We were pretty even against them, but I got my tail shot off more times than I can remember, or was comfortable with. The G was relentless, and not for the first time did I wish I could pull 9G like them, and then instantly thanked my lucky stars that we weren't stressed to 9G after all. 7.5G was more than enough for me, thank you.

We went straight from that into a week of flying combat against the F-5s out of Yuma. That whole week consisted of flying out of Miramar to meet them in R-2507; fight them; land at Yuma; fight them again on the return trip to base. I had done that gig before and it was exhausting. In the middle of all of that, we did an utterly ludicrous 1 vs 1 vs 1 vs 1 trip, so four aeroplanes fighting each other individually. Absolutely mad rabid crazy, and I loved it. No idea what was going on, mind you, but what a blast. Cheating, ganging up on Baller, pretending to ally with someone and then shooting them in the back—boy's own stuff. The pace was relentless and I just opened wide and kept on eating it up. My body must have been toughening up to the G as it just kept on going. I was living life at 700 knots, and our social life kept pace with it. We were very active with the expat community and it was the season for non-stop visitors from the UK. We had some of my wife's family out first and then Annie and her husband, Bonk, dropped in as part of their western US tour. They bookended an epic driving tour by staying with us a couple of nights, and coming back to us afterwards. A couple of nights prior to their flight back, I picked up our next set of freeloaders/visitors from the airport—Dickie Duke and his partner Pat.

Dickie had been my first ever QFI on the Chipmunk, and I owed my whole flying career to him. Basically, I was a bit shit at flying at the start, but he obviously saw something in me that was worth the effort, and he moved heaven and earth to instil confidence in me and teach me the basics of flying. He was old when I first met him, and the pace of flying three times a day took its toll. He would regularly fall asleep in debriefs, even when it was him that was talking! That absolutely sounds like I am spinning a line, but trust me, it was true. I loved him as you would your grandfather, and I was thrilled that he was coming out to stay with us in California, and more importantly, I would get to show him my jet. I made sure that everyone who came to stay with us had as much experience of Americana as they could. The next night after their arrival, I took Dickie, Pat, Annie, and Bonk to a baseball game. I felt like a true American as I explained the game to them and all the intricacies of the play. Dickie fell asleep, but I was putting that down to the jet lag and not me droning on about the game. The following day, we spent on the beach bodyboarding and coaxing Holly into the waves. I remember vividly driving Annie and Bonk to the airport the next day to see them off back to the UK. They were flying up to LAX and connecting through there. Annie was horrified by the tiny size of the city hopper aircraft that she was expected to get on for the short hop up to LAX. I assured her that she wouldn't need to pedal her way up there and off they went. Every flight since then, she has had to take Valium before getting on an aircraft.

Dickie was completely enamoured with Holly, and asked if he could read her bedtime story one night just as he had with his own children and grandchildren. We gave him a selection of her favourite books and he sat down beside her bed to read. I listened by the door to make sure Holly was settling, to hear Dickie say if it was OK with her, he was going to tell her a different story. He then went on to make up a story on the spot about a princess called Holly who lived near the beach in California. He kept it going for 20 minutes and, of course, Holly loved it. No chance of her going to sleep as she wanted to know all about what would happen in the story. She asked him questions throughout and I found myself sitting on the floor outside her room listening to that magical moment, almost bringing tears to my eyes. I was waiting for Dickie to fall asleep if I am being honest. He did have previous.

Dickie had just passed 65 and had retired from RAF reserve service. To celebrate, we took him and Pat to the Navy North Island Sunday brunch in the O-Club. This was an eat-athon extravaganza. If there is one thing the Americans excelled at, it was stuffing immense amounts of food down their throats. Being on the coast, the seafood bar was superb and fresh as you like. I had had a plaque made up with the RAF crest on it and Dickie's service dates, and presented it to him at the brunch to mark his retirement.

The look on his face and the fact that he started crying will stay with me forever. Here was a man who the RAF thought was nothing special. He had been in the mix with everyone else in the huge air force of the postwar period. But, to students like me, who he taught and nurtured through those difficult early days of flying training, he was everything and more. I know I have just said it, but it is worth reiterating—I owe my whole flying career to Dickie Duke. Once we were bursting with grub, I drove us up to Miramar and opened up one of the jets on the line so Dickie, and then Holly, could have a sit in. Dickie had been a fighter pilot on Vampires (look it up—proper fighter pilot stuff!) and then had flown Canberras for a long time. I sat him on the ejection seat and he looked in amazement at the cockpit I was living in. He turned to me and said, 'I am so proud of you. I knew you had it in you.'

'Even if I didn't, Dickie?'

'Yes. And now look at you. Wonderful!'

Is everyone in Chicago called Jimmy?

Even though we had visitors almost non-stop, I was still working hard on the squadron during the week. Muster weekend saw us doing surge ops, so flying as many aircraft as much as possible to prove we could do it from both an ops and a maintenance point of view. On one sortie, we launched ten aircraft and conducted a 6 vs 4. Bloody Hell! That was a mad, mad trip. There were airframes everywhere in the sky and God only knows what happened up there. It was real Battle of Britain stuff, as everywhere you looked there was an aeroplane. There was a rule of air combat that you weren't allowed more than four aircraft in a single visual engagement, for safety reasons. Yeah? That got blown off as I flashed around the windscreens of nine other jets, and vice-versa. You could barely tell who was who, but it didn't matter. My jet was turning itself inside out and inside in again as it responded to the ultra-violent inputs I was giving the controls. It just wouldn't quit and neither would I. My grin was enormous after that one mad bastard trip. It was soon wiped off me though as we then launched to do a 4 vs 4 at night. The two trips could not have been more different. Whereas the day trip was a 'fling yourself around and try not to hit anyone' kind of thing, the night trip demanded discipline, accuracy, and cool heads. Eight Hornets with nothing but their own radars (no data-link on these old F-18s—not one that was any good anyway) trying to coordinate safely in the pitch black. Nobody was smiling after that one.

Our next visitors were Von and his wife. Von had been a navigator on my first Phantom squadron and we had shared many experiences.

Most notable would be a big engine surge one night when we were new boys on 92 Squadron. We thought we handled it well, only to find we (and by that, I mean, I) had destroyed the engine by trying to relight it afterwards. Everyone knew you didn't relight an engine after it had been through a major surge like that. That is everyone except Flying Officer Knobhead Wilson and his equally clueless navigator. Anyway, we both survived that incident and it was joyous to welcome them out to San Diego. I missed the weekend of Von's trip, just before they went off on their own road trip. Harry O had asked me if I fancied taking a couple of jets on the road with him. He was going home to see his family in Indianapolis and wanted to take a pair of aircraft. As much as I liked Harry O (we had become quite tight working together every day and being the only full-timers) I wasn't sure Indianapolis was really on my 'must see' list. And then he came up with the deal breaker.

'Yeah. My family has tickets to the Indy 500 every year and I wondered if you wanted to go.'

'The Indy 500?!' I asked.

'Yeah. You heard of it?'

Of course I had heard of it. I was a huge motor racing fan and the chance to see one of the most famous races in history, and one of the triple crown events (along with the Monaco Grand Prix and Le Mans), was too good an opportunity to miss. I was beside myself! Miramar was going to be closed on the Friday so we would need to find a base for Thursday night before dropping into Indy on the Friday. We got the maps out and I had a look at where Indianapolis was. Just up and to the left I saw Chicago.

'I've never been to Chicago, Harry,' I said.

'OK. My cousin Jimmy works for the mayor of Chicago. I'll get him to book us into Midway Airport.'

'Great!'

'And my best buddy from college, Jimmy will put us up for the night.'

'OK. Is everyone in Chicago called Jimmy?'

'Yep. Pretty much.'

And so that was settled. A night in Chicago followed by a race weekend at Indy. It was shaping up to be an amazing weekend. I had no idea how amazing though.

A couple of days before our epic trip, I was flying as number 4 of a 4-ship strike mission, with all of us carrying 8 x 500-pound bombs. Burn was leading and briefed up a low-level ingress into a high-pop for a 45-degree dive attack onto one of the airfields in R-2507. The dummy airfield had criss-crossing runways and each of us was assigned one of the thresholds as our target. 4,000 pounds of stores was quite a load, and the jet moaned as it trudged the bombs down the runway and sloped off airborne like a surly teenager. Once the gear and flaps were up, it was like the fug was lifted, and our Hornets suddenly looked eager to get on with it and blow the living shit out of something, even if it was only an arbitrary bit of desert. On entering R-2507, we slipped down to low-level and skimmed across the ground looking dead hard. There were a couple of F-5s in there simulating enemy fighters and we fought our way through them to the target. This self-escort fighter-bomber role was what the F-18 was made for, and once again, I marvelled at how totally and utterly brilliant it was and how lucky I was to be flying it. Eventually, we got to the pop point and I slammed the throttles into full burner and hauled the nose up to climb up to about 12,000 feet and then snapped the nose over to drop my designation on my bit of the airfield. Burn and his wingman's bombs had already hit and the black and orange explosions were billowing up to about 3,000 feet (a bit less for a 500-pounder). As I refined my designation, and mashed down on the pickle button, I heard Burn shout 'PULL UP SPIDER!' Spider was the number 3 and my section leader. He was a reservist who predominantly worked over in the Group HQ and flew with us sparingly to keep current. Nice guy and an ex-A-4 Skyhawk pilot, but not so sharp due to his lack of flying currency. Burn had recovered from his dive attack and was circling overhead watching the proceedings, when he saw Spider fly right into the debris plume from his bombs.

Bft, bft, bft, bft went my eight bombs off in pairs, and I hauled to 4G to recover from my own dive. The Z diagram had a minimum height after recovery of 5,000 feet and ordinarily, that would have been more than easy to achieve. Spider had become so fixated on seeing his own bombs hit the target, that he forgot to pull, and ended up recovering below 3,000 feet, and he collected a load of crap from Burn's explosions.

'I need a visual inspection!' he shouted, once he made sure he was still alive. As formation leader, Burn joined on him to check him out. His nose cone and canopy were badly pitted; the seeker heads from the Sidewinders had been ripped off and the front of his LAUs were gone; there was major damage to the leading edge of his wings; and I have no doubt his pants were scorched and full of organic shrapnel. We recovered back to Miramar, slow speed, staying together as a 4-ship, and Burn made sure that Spider was safely on deck before the three of us landed on the other runway. We taxied past Spider and the hundreds of safety and fire vehicles surrounding him, dobbed through the hot pits, and shut down for the day. Spider was as white as a sheet and rightly so. When we saw his film, it was an absolute horror story, and I think it dawned on him how close he came to either hitting the ground, or being killed by the frag pattern. There was no need to debrief it any further—the film said it all, and no doubt the subsequent unit inquiry would publicise the dangers of target fixation.

Speaking of fixation, Holly was at the age where Disney films were basically her whole life. She had fallen in love with *The Lion King* and she had danced along at Disneyland to the huge Lion King parade. Being no slouch when it came to merchandise, Disney had produced Lion King stuff by the truckload, and I think I must have bought most of it for her. Her prized possession was a cuddly toy of Simba the lion cub, and she took it everywhere, and slept with it every night. The playgroup that she went to held 'show and tell' sessions each week, where every child would take something in and tell the other kids what it was and why they had chosen it. Show and tell was a great way to build confidence in them, especially the shy kids like Holly. Every week without fail, Holly would take Simba. Every week! The other kids must have been sick of the sight of that bloody lion, and no doubt went home and told their parents about the poor British urchin who only had one toy. I watched through the classroom door once to see her teacher ask her, with a big smile on her face, what Holly had brought in that week.

'Is it Simba, Holly?' Holly nodded.

'OK. Tell us about Simba,' and Holly would tell them another story from the film. She was so animated as she explained things—it was lovely to see. If I am being completely honest, I was only watching to see what the swingers' kid had brought in for show and tell from Daddy's secret drawer. I could almost see the headlines in the papers.

'Pre-schoolers traumatised at X-rated show and tell!'

Wiping chimney soot off my ass

A couple of days after witnessing Spider's near demise, I sat on Harry O's wing as we launched off for our race weekend to Indianapolis. There was a fair amount of wind in our faces, and it took us 2.5 hours to fly to Tinker AFB in Oklahoma, by which time I was sucking on fumes. We spent a little time on the ground while we refuelled and got the LOX (liquid oxygen) pots filled up. In the F-18D on 121 squadron, we had an on-board oxygen generation system (OBOGS) meaning we didn't have to carry our own oxygen. The A model I was now flying carried a LOX pot like my old Phantom, and the Hawk. Not everywhere had a LOX bay, so we filled up wherever we could. The problem with LOX was that the pots leaked a bit, and overnight they would empty out.

Before getting off to Chicago, Harry O and I had a look at the published approach procedure and noted there was a warning about an old stone chimney on finals that we would need to be aware of. It would mean a slightly steeper approach as far as I recall which would lead to us being a bit faster on landing. As it was a very busy civilian airport, we would stick together as a pair as long as we could so that we were a single speaking element, and then I would slow down and separate on finals so we could do individual landings. The runway was only 6,500 feet so we didn't fancy the added mare of a pairs landing from a steeper approach, so the sensible or safer thing would be two individual landings. Safer? Yeah … let's see what actually happened.

Nothing at all happened for about an hour and a half as we trudged across country towards the Windy City. And then our workload went through the roof. While Harry O negotiated the complicated approach procedure and spoke to Air Traffic Control, I welded myself to his wing as the area got more and more built up. We got onto a 10-mile final and Harry started requesting separation into two separate elements, but we were asked to stay together for a little while longer. As we got closer, Harry O had to slow and then signalled for gear and flaps. I held on in there as they came down, but it was going to be tricky separating from him as slowing down would put me near the stall. Midway looked like a bloody postage stamp so Harry O couldn't go any faster. Eventually, I was cleared to separate and I weaved out away from Harry O, and did some violent S-turns on the alpha limit behind him to put some distance between us.

I hadn't really achieved a whole lot of separation, but what I had done was dropped low while doing it. All of a sudden, I saw Harry O pull up sharply and I ended up with a face full of chimney. I hauled myself up with a load of power and was left too high and too fast. That's better than too low and too slow any day of the week, but landing on Midway's micro-runway was going to be an issue. I should have gone around and tried again, but doing a go-around at Midway and trying to get sequenced in again would have been a nightmare, so I tried to tough it out. I side-slipped to lose height (full aileron and full opposite rudder will sink the aeroplane), but that only added to my airspeed woes. Harry O had landed on the right-hand side of the runway, knowing I was very close behind, and so giving me a clear lane on the left. I mullered it down onto the concrete and jammed on the brakes. The poor jet must have thought it was back on the carrier. Halfway down the runway, I overtook Harry O, which was a bit concerning, but not half as concerning as the end of the runway and the highway beyond it which was rapidly approaching. I pushed the toe brake pedals through the radome and my jet eventually came to a halt with my nose just pointing over the end of the runway. This is not embellished for dramatic effect. I still have sleepless nights over that one. Almost another diplomatic incident.

The F-18's nosewheel castered sideways thank God, and I was able to gently power my way around and taxi into the visiting aircraft section, with my heart pounding in my chest. It was interesting to think that here I was, a third tourist, and experienced aviator and instructor, still managing to get myself into scrapes due to my pride and incompetence—each one of them in competition to see who could screw me up first. If I had to bet right then? Incompetence took it hands down. We were being handled by a VIP aircraft company that Harry O's cousin had arranged through the Mayor's office. I shut down on the chocks and heaved a huge sigh of relief. The civilian ground crew shook my hand and said, 'Hey! Cool landing!' He should have been sitting in my bloody seat 5 minutes prior.

'Er, thanks,' I replied.

'Yeah, we just saw your boss off and then watched you land.'

'My boss?'

'The secretary of defence is in that Falcon 900 just taking off.'

My knees wobbled a bit thinking that one of the president's right-hand men had just seen two of his Hornets guff their way through a dodgy landing with one of them almost collecting a load of commuter traffic on the way. Hopefully, he was too busy studying plans for whatever country was next to feel the military wrath of the US to notice me cooking my brakes and wiping chimney soot off my ass.

The moment was rapturous

Harry O's Jimmys were both there to greet us and after introductions, a plan was made to drive into the city to grab a beer. I was about to go and change when Cousin Jimmy said we would be OK in our flying suits. This was a complete no-no for me previously in the UK with the IRA threat, but I suppose if I could throw down a margarita and then throw it up again in a Florida roadhouse in my flying suit, then I could probably tough out a beer in Chicago. Harry O jumped into College Jimmy's huge BMW (he was a self-made millionaire, or near as damn it, by the age of 30), and I shot-gunned Cousin Jimmy's official assistant to the mayor of Chicago's car. As we drove out of the airport, I saw a Boeing 727 with the Miami Heat's logo on the tail. I pointed it out to Jimmy saying I forgot the Heat were playing the Bulls in the playoffs, and we got chatting about basketball. He was amazed at how big a fan I was, and then he said, 'Do you wanna go to the game tonight?'

'I would kill for it, Jimmy, but Bulls tickets are always sold out so no chance on the night.'

'I'll call the mayor, Tug. He'll get us tickets.'

'No way!'

And that is exactly what he did when we got to the bar.

We went to a bar under the L (elevated train) and the place went quiet as we walked in dressed in flying suits. Cousin Jimmy was known in the bar and he said rather loudly to the barman, 'Hey Frank. This is my cousin and his buddy. They are Marines and just flew two F-18s into Midway. Can I get them a beer?'

'On the house,' said Frank and beered us up. Then it seemed that everyone wanted to talk to us. After lots of back slapping, free beer, and 'thank you for your service' comments, I was pretty well shitfaced and in need of food to soak up the drink. Food arrived from somewhere (on the house again) with more drinks, and Cousin Jimmy came back from his phone call to announce that we had tickets to the Bulls game that night! I full on hugged him. I couldn't believe my luck. Harry O and I nipped into the loo to change into civvies, as we thought flying suits might be a bit gauche for the game. As we left the bar, we got a round of applause from the punters and I staggered to the car for the drive to the United Centre, where the Bulls played. Cousin Jimmy's official car got us through the roadblocks right into the VIP car park, and I found myself looking up at the iconic statue of Michael Jordan flying through the air, holding a basketball one-handed above his head (it's the logo on your Nike Air Jordans, kids). By the way, it looked nothing like my attempts in my back garden with my kid's size ball.

We were met at the door by the United Centre's head of security, who had been a US Marine Huey helicopter door-gunner in Vietnam. The first thing he did was apologise as he had only been able to get us nose bleed seats in the upper level. He was kidding right? Apologising for getting us the most sought-after tickets in world sport? Or at least in the US.

'Before you go to your seats though guys, just follow me.' He led us through some service corridors and then held us at a door before talking into his radio. When we got through the door, we were at courtside! I could see the court with the giant Bull's head in the centre. Holy shit, I had seen this place on TV and here I was! A booming voice came over the tannoy.

'Ladies and gentlemen. Coming onto the floor, we present your United States Marine Corps fighter pilots!' The four of us were led onto the floor and about 18,000 people cheered and gave us a standing ovation. I felt a bit of a fraud not being a Marine, but Jimmy and Jimmy were lapping it up, so I smiled and waved as we stood on the Bull's head and had our photo taken. This trip could not have been any better. And then it was. We were held just off the court and told not to move. The intro for the Bulls began and then the lights went down and the Bulls cheerleaders ran out and stood in line right in front of us, as close as if we were in a bus queue. As the lights came up, the announcer called out the arrival of my sporting heroes.

Luc Longley, Steve Kerr, and Tony Kukoc were announced, and ran out close enough for me to touch them (I didn't, by the way). And then I almost fainted with joy as Dennis Rodman, Scottie Pippen and then the legend himself, Michael Jordan, jogged out onto the court. They had no idea I was there. Just another face in the crowd, but to me, the moment was rapturous. We went up to our seats in a daze, not even noticing how high we were. Who cared? I was light headed. Either it was the booze or the feeling of euphoria. Or maybe the fact that we were short of oxygen being so far up. The Bulls beat the Heat and won the Conference Finals, buying them another place in the NBA Finals, in which they would go on to beat the Utah Jazz and set up for another threepeat the following year.

I was still in a state of shock as we filed out to College Jimmy's BMW for the drive out to his mansion in the suburbs. I can't remember how many times I thanked Cousin Jimmy, but it was a lot. It was about 0200 by the time we said a quick hello to Mrs College Jimmy and flopped into bed completely exhausted, but totally buzzed. I was a little more polite in the morning chatting to College Jimmy and his wife (I might as well just call him Jimmy now), and thanked them profusely for putting me up in their frankly gobsmacking home. Jimmy apologised that he couldn't take us back to Midway as he had work meetings, but he had arranged a lift for us. We said our goodbyes and Harry O and I walked outside and into a stretch limo, which was a final present from Jimmy. If we hadn't been in flying suits, I would have felt like a film star. We certainly looked like film stars as we drew up in the VIP area at Midway in front of our two Hornets. Yeah—that 727 might have had the Heat's logo on the tail, but it didn't have MARINES written on the side of it, which my jet did. Bloody Hell! I was loving myself right then.

As payback for the tickets to the game, we had arranged to show a few of the security guys from the United Centre around our Hornets. I loved doing stuff like that and about half a dozen of them turned up, with a few in police uniform. Turned out that most of the security staff were Chicago PD who moonlighted at the Centre. We sat them in the cockpits and took some pictures with them, but all too soon it was time to launch for Indianapolis. As a parting gift, they presented us with Chicago Bulls ball caps, apologising for not being able to nick the Conference champions hats that had just been released the previous night. They watched us rage off from Midway in a fury of afterburner. We probably could have done a dry power take-off, but I was having the heebie-jeebies about my landing the day before, and wanted to take no chances on the short runway. And besides—it looked bloody cool! It's a shame that only an hour and thirty later, I had forgotten about my near diplomatic incident at Midway, and flew headlong into another.

Having cheated a balloon-filled death

Harry O's family were going to be on the ground at the airport so it was only fair that we did a couple of 'circuits' for them. I can't imagine how proud they must have been to see him raging around in a Hornet. We came up with a plan that we would separate into singletons once we saw the airport and then do a couple of run-in and breaks each, before gracefully smoothing our war machines onto the runway. Best laid plans and all that. Usual break height would be 500 feet and speed of 350 knots, climbing up to 1,000 in the break turn to downwind. Harry O ran in about 200 feet, so I had to be lower than that, yeah? It was the law of the fighter pilot jungle that number 2 had to be lower than number 1. And, I was. I broke level at about 100 feet and 7G to ditch the extra speed I had added by mistake (honest). I intercepted a rough finals picture and did an acceptable landing before slamming the throttles into full burner to scorch airborne into an immediate climbing turn downwind as the gear clumped up into the belly of my jet. I knew that there would have been a raging howl from the engines as I slammed straight from idle to burner.

'Coooool!!!!!' somebody said over the radio. I figured it was the Tower controller, but it wasn't. I was dimly aware of an airship on the grass between the runway and the downwind leg. It was the famous Goodyear Blimp which did aerial shots of the Indy 500 and all sorts of other major sporting events. The pilot was obviously impressed with my opening verse, so that spurred me on for the chorus. Jesus—Harry O was low on his next run. I got to initials at about 500 feet and watched him pass underneath me on his way in. I was going to be subterranean if I wanted to top that. We were separated by about twenty seconds, and I saw him absolutely shag the airfield ahead of me. My turn. In between Harry O's break and my upcoming showstopper, ATC gave the blimp permission to lift into the air. I was so maxed out trying not to hit the ground, I didn't hear that call, and subsequently broke directly into a face full of giant balloon that hadn't been there the last time I raged across the airfield. Having told me I was cool on the previous run, the blimp pilot now had eyes the size of dinner plates, as his new hero almost joined him in the cockpit.

'Shit!' I shouted and violently barrelled over the top of him vaguely in the direction of downwind. My heart was pumping overtime as I wrestled the jet into some semblance of order before semi-crashing it in a carrier landing, onto the runway. Good God, I could see the headlines—'British hooligan destroys national treasure. In other news, British father arrested after second show and tell scandal at playgroup.' Two almost diplomatic incidents in two days were not going to look good on my CV. How the hell did a buffoon like me luck into an exchange like this?

Harry O's family were beaming at him, and he was already out of his jet as I taxied in and shut down. What a perfect moment for him. He had a big family (three brothers and a sister) and his parents and step parents as well as his grandparents and in-laws were there. They had all gathered for the race so it took a long time to introduce me around the clan. We were spending two nights with his mum and then two more with his dad. His siblings were an eclectic mix, with his eldest brother having been a Marine Corps grunt who ended up on the embassy guard detail; then his next brother was a film producer; I don't recall what his sister did, but the youngest brother was a struggling actor waiting for his big shot. They had a lot of catching up to do so the first night descended into a beer filled frenzy, which I threw myself into, having cheated a balloon-filled death. I fessed up to Harry O about my incident with the blimp, and he just shrugged and clinked my beer bottle and that was that. There was a local shop that sold fresh underpants, so all was good. He showed me around Indianapolis the next day. I have to say that it looked beautiful and it was definitely all-in with Indy 500 fever. He showed me the frat house that he lived in while at college and the sorority house his future wife had lived in. They had been childhood sweethearts, so with going to college together, it was inevitable that they would end up marrying.

Thank God it was a quieter night, as we were up early on the Sunday to get to the track. Everything is bigger in America, so they say. The Indianapolis Motor Speedway is colossal. A 2.5-mile oval track set in about 600 acres and capacity for 400,000 people. It truly was the biggest single day sporting event in the world. I was awestruck, especially when I saw that our tickets were for seats at the first corner. We had a full view of the main straight. The only downer was that it had been pissing down with rain and the track was soaked. Not an issue for the Americans though. Why not just strap a jet engine vertically to a big truck and use the jet pipe as a sort of hair dryer for the tarmac? By the time the cars were on the grid, the track was dry enough for the ceremonies to begin.

'Gentlemen. Start your engines!' boomed out of the tannoy, followed by an unholy sound as what appeared to be a thousand race cars fired up and set off round the track for a few parade laps. They looked like flat hot wheels toy cars glued to the track, but the noise? It was ear-splitting. I looked around me at Harry O's family, and even though they went every year, they still had a look of absolute wonder on their faces. They were in good company, because I was beside myself with joy. And then, about twenty laps in, the heavens opened and the race was delayed and then subsequently cancelled until the next day. Despite the disappointment, I had seen a bit of the Indy 500 and had the rest of the race to look forward to the following day. It didn't even get started on the Monday, so we drowned our sorrows together and got ready for the long trek back to Miramar on the Tuesday.

It was time to pit myself against the best

They ran the full race on the Tuesday and just before the cars lined up on the grid, two F-18s blasted over the Speedway and pulled up vertically in burner, before rolling away from each other to make the top of a heart shape. I joined back on Harry O's wing and we headed back to Tinker. According to his family, we looked brilliant and the noise was tremendous. Over the weekend, the LOX pots had discharged and there was no LOX at Indy, so we had to transit to Tinker below 10,000 feet. This meant we would have to fly slower to save gas and make sure we could get there. After a heavy weekend, that was tedious, I can tell you. Fuel and LOX replenished, I took the lead out of Tinker (I think Harry O was sick of leading and having me freeloading on his wing), but he quickly saw that the ATC agencies were ignoring my British accent and then my nav kit wandered off to Hawaii so he had to do the navigation anyway.

It became obvious that we would need to do another stop, and rather than eek out the fuel to get to Yuma or El Centro for a quick splash and dash, I put us down about half way home into Holloman with no pressure on us other than having to do a TACAN approach on the instruments, through some thick cloud. Harry O split off for his own approach and after a quick burger and more fuel, we were off for our third trip of the day and another 90 minutes in the logbook to get us on deck at Miramar. Although we were weary, I just couldn't stop jabbering to Harry O about how great the trip was and how grateful I was to him, his family, Jimmy, Jimmy and any other Jimmys I might have missed. It was the best weekend I had ever spent in a flying suit. And the next day? 1 vs 1 intercepts and 1 vs 1 ACM as usual, as if the greatest weekend ever had never happened. I would say it was back to the grind, but this tour was never the grind. It was always a pure joy to climb into the Hornet, even for the most mundane of trips. I was banging in around 30 hours per month, flying twice a day most days. As the temperatures rose into summer, we did either one trip, through the pits, then out for another, or we flew into the sauna of Yuma to turn and fly again back to base (doing air combat on almost every trip).

Chilli briefed up that we were to schedule guys for a maximum of two trips a day only, due to the heat. I really liked Chilli. He wasn't your typical bullish Marine. He was quiet and soft spoken, non-antagonistic and happy to let things ride without taking sides. Just what the squadron needed after its recent history of turmoil and conflict—a steady hand. I asked him one day what it was like flying the 747 and then getting his hands on a Hornet.

'Oh, I don't fly the 747, Tug. I'm a flight engineer,' he said.

'What?'

'Yeah. I push a bit of fuel around the jet mostly.'

I couldn't believe it. In those days, a lot of ex-military pilots would join the airlines as flight engineers on aircraft like the 727 or 747. They would do a year or so on minimum wages (hence the need to join the reserves) then get a co-pilot's course. Chilli had been caught in a bit of a downturn so stayed as a flight engineer for a while. In that time, he had risen to number 3 in seniority of flight engineers in Northwest Airlines so it meant that whatever trips he bid for in the scheduling process, he always got. Therefore, every month, he flew for ten days to/from Japan, and spent the rest of his time either relaxing at home or flying Hornets. What a life. They had offered him straight conversion to a captain's seat several times, but he had always turned it down as he would have lost his seniority and been at the mercy of the schedulers.

In the meantime, my successor from the RAF had been named and was due to arrive with his family in a couple of months. Whilst I always knew this was a three-year deal, it felt like a punch in the guts that the RAF had plotted to replace me with somebody else. How dare they?! Did they not know about all the good stuff I was doing? Obviously not, as another promotion board came and went, and there was no visit from the air attaché at the embassy to shake me warmly by the hand and say 'congratulations on your promotion, Squadron Leader Wilson.' So, that was settled then. I would be returning to my beloved RAF as a bog-standard flight lieutenant—almost unheard of from an exchange. I didn't really know my replacement, but I had heard of him. Blower was ex-Phantom and then Tornado F3. He had been UK Phantoms at Leuchars, so apart from seeing him a couple of times in the bar when I had been a student on the Phantom OCU, I knew nothing about him. However, as soon as he got in touch, I tried my best to help him as much as Alf had helped me a couple of years prior. I tried to make sure the Marines would keep the exchange on 134 as that was where I had had the best time, and MAG-46 started the process of keeping the funding going for Blower.

According to my annual reports from the Marines, I was performing so well, I must have been the son of God in a flying suit. We all knew American reports were vastly inflated, but I had done all the right things before coming to the US to get promoted. I had even passed the service writing course (with a C grade and a 'must do better comment') so it was a bit of a slap in the face. To drown my sorrows, I would fling myself into a last torrid affair with my F-18 for the next seven or eight months and lose myself in the unadulterated joy of being a fighter pilot in a proper fighter jet. That started badly though. I had programmed myself for an in and out to Yuma, flying 1 vs 1 combat against Fox. I figured that although I thought of myself as pretty handy, it was time to pit myself against the best. What could be better than an ex-TOPGUN instructor?

I briefed up the trip and led us out to R-2507 to set up for the first fight. As I was leading, I had all the advantage of setting up so that I could use the sun where I wanted it—the plan was to put the sun behind Fox, which would be unusual, but once we merged, I would climb up into it and hopefully go unseen. I would also turn in early so as not to lose him pre-merge, and to dictate the way he would need to turn across my tail and therefore be looking directly into the sun after the merge. Great plan. Didn't work. He was all over me like a rash. I had never been more humbled in air combat than on that trip. OK, I had been shot down plenty of times before, but nothing compared to how easy it seemed to be for him. No matter what I tried, he just swatted me like a fly, er … a Hornet. And the worst thing? He didn't even cheat. He didn't have to. He was that good. I might even have applauded him in the air had I not been so damn busy getting my ass shot off. It was a beautiful and a horrible thing to watch a true professional at work. It was obvious that Fox had spent every single minute of his 2,000 hours Hornet time honing his trade and being the best he could be. I had spent my 400 hours Hornet, learning a bit, relying on a bit of previous experience, and generally just gashing about having a good time. Before you think I am making a big deal about the hours, I am convinced that even if I had 4,000 hours on the jet instead of 400, he still could have beaten me with a blindfold on.

Mercifully, the gas ran out and we headed towards Yuma. Well, the debrief was going to be uncomfortable for me, but maybe I would learn some useful stuff from this Grand Master of air combat. That's what I hoped anyway. I had always been aware of my shortcomings so would suck as much training value out of every pilot that was better than me, if I could—and there seemed to be a hell of a lot of them about! I raged us into the circuit and we broke downwind. I was in a bit of a fug not really knowing what had gone wrong on the trip, but tried to put it behind me and get on with landing. There were a few AV8Bs from the resident squadron flashing around, so the circuit was busy. The Harrier ahead of me decided to do some sort of short landing, semi-hover thing, so by the time I was on short finals, he was still faffing about on the runway and I had to go around. I eased myself across to the dead side and started to climb up to circuit height. I heard Fox land behind me and waited for the Harrier that was downwind to pass me before I could turn. For no reason whatsoever, I looked out to the right before turning left downwind, and was staring into a face full of planform AV8B that was breaking into me. 'Holy shit!' I shouted and slammed the stick forwards as hard as I could. There was a bit of a bang as my engines complained at my gross mishandling, quickly followed by an enormous roar as the Harrier flashed over my head, missing me by God only knows how much. I guess some days you are the fast jet, and some days, you are the blimp?

I bottomed out at about 500 feet and climbed back up to turn downwind. I got my shit together (which was spattered all over the cockpit), took note of the Harrier's callsign when he called finals, and then blanked out everything else other than putting my abused Hornet back down on deck. I think I was actually in shock as I taxied in. I know I forgot to put the canopy up to taxi back, which is a cardinal sin for a fighter pilot. My hands were shaking as I shut down the nav system and I slowly extricated myself from the cockpit to see Fox's happy smiling face next to his jet. He saw that I was white as a sheet and probably thought it was a reaction to the spanking he had just given me. I told him the tale and said I needed to go to the AV8B squadron and track down the pilot who had almost killed me.

This was my shot at stardom

When I found him, he was just a young lad fresh out of the RAG. He hadn't even known I was there so there wasn't much discussion to be had. You can't debate with someone when they have no idea what you are talking about. I needed to bury the ghost by talking it through, but he just had a confused look on his face so there was no point. It would have been so much easier if he had argued that it was my fault. At least we could have had it out with each other. Without that closure, I think it shook me up even more. Fox and I were supposed to do another 1 vs 1 ACM on the way back to Miramar, but I told him I thought I had used up all my luck for the day and wanted to just press back to base without taxing myself. He was gracious enough to agree, and it was a very relieved Mr Tug that touched down at home and sat in the hot pits contemplating life and nothing else for 20 minutes while they pumped my tanks full. My emotional tanks were shot to bits and it struck me that since I had started flying eleven years previously in 1986, I could pinpoint seven other times where sheer luck had saved my bacon in dodgy situations in aeroplanes (I am sure there are some other 'Confessions' books out there that have those stories in them).

If I had been a cat, I would have been wrapping myself up in cotton wool and given up flying altogether. That's not what we do though, and as I drove back to OB in the blistering sun with my roof down and my Wayfarers on, I thanked my lucky stars that I had looked right before turning downwind. On reflection, maybe I had heard the Harrier call that he was joining the circuit and being a professional aviator, I was actually looking for him by looking right. Or maybe I was just lucky. The old fighter pilot adage of 'I'd rather be lucky than good' sprang to mind. Whichever it was, it worked. And the debrief? Turned out there was no secret formula to Fox's dominance on the trip. Turned out it was just as I feared—he was brilliant and, relatively speaking, I was shit. He was by far and away the best fighter pilot I had ever seen.

Baby Wilson Mark Two was growing apace and we needed to make plans for where the birth was going to be. My wife had attended her first appointment at the US Navy hospital in San Diego, and had vowed never to go there again. The only other option the embassy would fund outside of military medicine was a Birthing Centre. I think they were a relatively new concept, at least for the embassy to grasp, but they were nice relaxed environments run by new-age hippy midwives. They believed in natural childbirth so zero pain relief, which was a bit worrying for my wife. However, it looked a lot better than the 'do it by numbers' approach of the military hospital. It was decided then. Wilson Junior would enter the world amid a shitload of agonised screaming, the pungent smell of joss sticks and a bit of Buddhist ohm-ing no doubt.

My wife had to undergo some tests that, once the results were in, would definitely prove the gender of our baby. We chose to find out rather than have the surprise. We had done that with Holly so were happy to be better prepared this time around. We got the phone call one afternoon and after telling us the tests had come back OK, we were asked if we wanted to know what we were expecting. The doctor then told us we were having another girl. I was upstairs on my own on the other telephone extension with my wife downstairs. I swear to God, I was crying my eyes out, I was so happy.

News came through at work that Harry O had been selected to go on the next TOPGUN course. I was really pleased for him as he was a brilliant guy. Chilli came in the office for a quick chat and basically told me that to all intents and purposes, I would be the ops officer while Harry O was away. In turn, this would sort of make me the de facto acting boss when Chilli wasn't around! Me! Flight Lieutenant Wilson. Acting CO of twelve Hornets and 150 Marines. Well, the RAF could go fuck itself—not promoting me. This was my shot at stardom. In reality, nothing much would change, but for six months or so, I could at least pretend I was leadership material. I came up against my first issue with Thud. We were still banging in the trips to Yuma and back, fighting the F-5s. As Thud was the group safety officer, he had to have visibility on the F-5 squadron and as such, was qualified to fly the aircraft. Chilli had decreed only two trips per day through summer, but Thud was flying to Yuma in a Hornet, then conducting two trips in an F-5, then flying back to Miramar in his Hornet. It set a bit of a bad example with him being the safety officer and all, so I needed to keep an eye on it. The whole thing came to a head just before muster weekend, when I flew back late from Yuma. As I taxied in, knowing I was the last trip on the schedule, I passed one of our jets taxying out, which was a bit strange. I asked Gunny Tinker what was going on as I signed my jet in. We needed an air test on one of the jets and it had been slated for the following day on the Saturday of the muster. Thud had decided to do it that afternoon, which all things being equal, was sort of illegal as it wasn't on the schedule so not part of official orders. As I was the ops officer (and airborne at the time) and neither Chilli nor the XO were around, there was no-one to authorise the trip. Thud had taken it upon himself to rewrite the orders and go flying.

OK, I wasn't a Marine so I shouldn't have been that bothered about it, as I found the whole 'schedule as orders' thing a bit inflexible. But I was bothered. Chilli had discharged responsibility down to me and not Thud, and that trip was his fifth of the day in scorching temperatures. I needed to head this off. I wrote the schedule for Saturday and Sunday and put Thud on the desk for both days. This was not unusual for Harry O and me not to fly on the weekend as we had to maximise flying for the reserves who weren't there all the time. Thud was semi-full time with us, being based over at Group HQ. He was incandescent with rage and blew up at me in the ready room in front of everyone.

'Shall we take this into a briefing room, Thud?' I asked him calmly.

'Damn right!' he shouted and stormed off. I looked at all of the guys and shrugged, and then saw Chilli grinning like a Cheshire cat. I had already briefed him on the situation and he winked as I went off for my meeting with what seemed to be NATO's angriest man. It went as expected. Thud exploded into an incoherent babble of shouting about how unfair it was that I had put him on the desk, and how he wasn't getting enough flying etc. etc. I let him blow himself out and then asked him to sit down so I could speak. He didn't, so I told him to sit down and pin his ears back, leaving him in no doubt as to who was in charge. Ballsy move as he was huge and I was a sickly looking streak of piss compared to him. He was a classic bully though and acquiesced immediately.

'OK, Thud. Here's what I am seeing. You say you aren't flying enough? Three days this week you have flown four trips, and one of those days, you flew five times. This was despite Chilli stating that two trips per day was the maximum. The fifth trip you flew yesterday was illegal, but I saved your sorry ass by rewriting the schedule for you while you were airborne. Despite that, you are the safety officer for fuck's sake, so act like it! What impression do you think that gives? Safety is important to everyone apart from the actual safety officer? How long have you been flying, Thud?'

'Eleven years.'

'Not how long have you been a Marine. How long have you been flying aeroplanes?' I knew he had been a FAC grunt at the start of his career.

'Six years,' he said quietly.

'OK, six years. Well, when you have been flying as long as me, you will realise that the world of aviation doesn't revolve around you OK?' God, I sounded like I was Winkle Brown or someone like that.

'And the other thing is that Chilli made me the Opso and not you, so if you have an issue with how I am running the show, take it up with him. Are we clear?' He flounced out and went immediately to see Chilli. A very quick conversation later, and Thud was on the desk and no longer a problem.

This loud shouty stuff was something else

There were two much more pressing issues on the horizon for me to deal with on 134. Firstly, we had told the Marine Corps that we weren't able to use all of our allotted weapons and so we were in the process of 'handing them back'. Each squadron was allocated an annual allowance of weapons to use in training, but we had not managed to use all of ours. We were quickly told by the USMC that we had to use them all up as some of them were almost out of date and decommissioning them was harder than dropping them. All told, I think we had nearly 240,000 pounds of bombs to drop; a shitload of gun ammo; and a boxful of missiles to loose off. We would need to do a couple of weeks of surge ops to get rid of it all. We came up with a plan to go weapons mad in August, as in the meantime we had a big deployment to Alaska to fit in. The plan for that was to fly up to Elmendorf Air Base near Anchorage and fight against the two resident F-15 squadrons based there for two whole weeks. I was over the moon that I would get to see Alaska, but the reservists were moaning like hell about it. And then I heard the story of why.

VMFA 134 had done the same deployment a year before and it hadn't gone well. The F-15s had played the Blue Air (friendly) side of the house meaning 134 had to pretend to be Red Air (enemy) fighters. As I have already said, when you are Red Air, you cannot use the full performance of your aircraft, radar, or weapons, and are severely restricted in manoeuvres, to help give Blue Air an advantage. In essence, you are sent up there to do prescribed moves and die bravely in the process. I have no problem doing that so long as we swap roles during the deployment. The F-15s had obviously seen that 134 was a reserve unit, so played Blue Air on every trip, treating our guys as if they were just there to provide a service, and to build the already over-inflated egos of the Eagle drivers. Worse still, they showed no class or grace in the debriefs, even high-fiving each other when they got kills. All very distasteful, but very USAF F-15. At the end of the two weeks, there had been a beer call and presentation. The Eagles gave our guys a big picture of an F-15 (like we gave a shit about their jet!), but the Marines had come up with something special as their present to the F-15s. Apparently, it was a fake plastic dog poo, nailed to a bit of wood, and a plaque that said, 'Thanks for nothing. It was shit!' or words to that effect. The USAF had no sense of humour, and their complaints winged their way up to the Head of the US Air Force, who then strode across the Pentagon to shout at the Commandant of the Marine Corps. He then sent his shit downhill to land on 134's collective head. The solution then? Let's send the bad boys back to Elmendorf where everyone could work hard on being friends again. I know. What the hell were they thinking? At least I would get to see Alaska.

Just before deploying, I took a drive up to John Wayne airport to welcome Blower and his family to California. It was decidedly odd to stand there and watch his family explode into the arrivals hall, much as we had done two and a half years earlier, knowing that I was coming to the end of my tour whereas he was just starting. I had fitted a lot into my tour so far, but now I really could hear the tick-tock of the inevitable passage of time. It was almost over for me and my mind was turning to the future. The poster had told me I was going to be on the Tornado F3, and I would be posted to RAF Leeming in North Yorkshire. It would be my third fast jet in my logbook so that would be cool. However, with no promotion to squadron leader, it would be as a bog-standard squadron pilot rather than as a flight commander. I was a bit stung by that as everyone would have expected me to have been picked up, so I am sure they would be wondering where I had screwed up. Chicago Midway, Indianapolis airport and somewhere arbitrary off the coast of San Diego if this book is anything to go by of course, but they were not things the RAF would have known about. No—I just had to face facts. It was going to be a little while longer before I became chief of the air staff.

I secured Blower and his clan into the same hotel we had stayed in on arrival in California, and then just regurgitated the tried and tested 'Alf plan' to get him squared away with real estate agent, car dealers, Marine security, ground school and the rest of it. I then had to leave them to it, much as Alf had done with us, and get back to flying. I was banging the trips in and still averaging about 30 hours a month, with the usual variety of missions. Some of the big bombs filtered through to us earlier than we planned. so off we went and slung them into the desert, destroying whatever we could find out there.

I dropped 4 x 1,000 pounders in one go onto an aircraft hulk on a dummy airfield. I would love to tell you that I saw the aircraft blown into the air, but I didn't. I heard the dft dft as they blew off the carriers in pairs, recovered from the dive (Spider take note!), and dropped my right wing to fix my eyes on the aircraft hulk. One second it was there, and a moment later, there was just a huge cloud of black smoke and gouts of orange flame as the mad angry bombs did their thing and just obliterated the whole area. Holy hell! I don't know if I was more surprised at the carnage, or the fact that I was actually enjoying this air-to-ground lark. The fighter pilot in me still loathed academic practice bombing at the range, but this loud shouty stuff was something else. I was really going to miss it. I was going to miss the Marines too. In the time I had spent with them, there had been many frustrations with how they operated. This will always happen when you have to adjust to a different system, but it was exacerbated by the fact that I was a pure aviator whereas they were Marines first and aviators afterwards. Over time, though, the USMC had got under my skin, and the ethos and camaraderie had become a part of me. Semper Fi until I die? Not quite yet, but I was on that path, and I was willing to fight for my squadron mates, my colours, and the Corps against anyone and everyone that fronted up to us.

Good job I was, because the F-15s at Elmendorf hadn't really changed their view of 134. I was in the back of one of the KC-10 tankers that deployed us to Alaska. We took eight jets and the whole squadron up there, and for once it was nice to be relaxing in the freighter rather than hyperventilating and sweating while trying to refuel a few times, interspersed with long tedious periods complaining of a sore arse, sitting on an ejection seat. I spent a bit of time up in the cockpit and down at the refuelling station watching our guys plug in and tank. On arrival, the USAF bundled us into a large auditorium for some in-briefings. These included the course rules for Elmendorf, which looked incredibly complicated to say that the airfield was in the middle of stinking nowhere, or so it seemed. We were then allocated our accommodation and that's when things went a bit south. The admin officer told us in a quiet voice what building we were in.

'Where are we?' asked one of our guys. He repeated the number in an even quieter voice.

'Shit! Is that the Crack House?'

'Er, well we don't like to call it that.'

'They've put us in the fucking Crack House again!' came the shout, followed by lots of moaning and grumbling. I leaned across to Salsa.

'What's the Crack House?' I asked.
'Worst accommodation you have ever seen, Tug,' he replied.
'It can't be that bad, surely?'
It was.

Obviously, our Hornets were the best-looking

We were bussed to the Crack House with our kit. It was two Portakabins, end on end, built in a swamp. The Portakabins had subsided into the swamp and were at an alarming angle. We cut our way through a curtain of mosquitos and got in through the screen door. I staggered to my room trying to deal with the slope in the corridor, and dumped my bags. My room had a bed, a sink, and a wardrobe. What more did you need for two weeks? We had more in-briefings the next day so it was time to hit the town. Anchorage was something else. In those days, that city was the final frontier of human decency. I saw things in the bars there that turned my hair white, and then turned it back brown again. My Marine buddies were laughing their heads off at the look of pure shock on my face, as I no doubt looked like the last virgin at the orgy. The only thing to do was to drink myself blind to blot out the bizarre things that I was seeing. So that's exactly what I did.

We finally spilled out of the last bar at about 11.30pm to find bright sunshine hitting us in the face! We were at such a high latitude that darkness rarely made an appearance in summer. It was gobsmacking to see. We got cabs back to base and as I settled down for my first night in the fabled Crack House, I pulled my curtains closed to find that they didn't meet in the middle. There was an 18-inch gap between them and bright sunshine streaming through the window. Even the immense amount of alcohol I had forced down could not fight the brightness and I got about 2 hours of decent kip before it was time to get up again. I have no idea what the in-briefs were about as I semi-slept through most of them, as did nearly all of the Marines. However, I think we got the gist and I set to writing the schedule for the following day. Everyone grumbled that it was business as usual as the F-15s programmed straight into 4 vs 4s with us as Red Air. The same template was applied where our guys were severely limited in what they could do, and were shot down repeatedly as we supported the Eagle benefit concert.

My first two trips were complicated to say the least. Straight into the low-flying area (which was enormous) as part of a 4-ship, escorting and sweeping for four F-16s who had randomly pitched up from somewhere. Actually, they had flown in from Eielson Air base which was about three hundred miles from us. We had to clear them through a 4-ship combat air patrol (CAP) of the Golden Gods and then land at Eielson to refuel and do it all again on the way back. We were carrying live chaff and flares on our missions, but there were strict rules about minimum heights for popping flares. If we did it at low-level, there was a good chance it could cause a catastrophic forest fire in the play area. This was hammered home to us during the in-briefs and was one thing I was awake for. Twelve awesome looking fast jets launched out of Elmendorf in a cacophony of shock and awe. Obviously, our Hornets were the best-looking, but after that? Who gives a shit? The F-16 and F-15 were not the F-18 so I didn't care. The Eagles split to one end of the range and we marshalled with the F-16s at the other. The F-16s were just as pissed as us about having to play dumb bandits, so it seemed the Eagles treated everyone else equally badly.

The scenery of the play area left me breathless. It was achingly beautiful up there, and I was raging over it at about 250 feet (minus a bit) and 420 knots (plus a bit). Running the radar down there while trying to maintain tactical formation and process what we were hearing from our GCI controller was a feat in itself. I was working harder in the cockpit than I had ever worked before, but what a buzz! I kept getting a tickle on the radar warning receiver (RWR) which told me the Eagles had picked me up in search mode. That could well mean an AMRAAM was on its way to spoil my day. Not sticking strictly to our brief to play dumb, Hannibal who was leading our 4-ship had planned for us to bomb-burst into four singletons to defeat the first AMRAAM shots. We would then all face up from different directions to try and overload the Eagles so the F-16s could slip through. I can just imagine what the radar picture would have looked like in the F-15. Four lambs to the slaughter in a neat formation. Take that initial AMRAAM shot and watch it countdown, ready to call the kill, and then? Shit! What are these guys doing? This isn't supposed to happen. They are supposed to walk into our missiles. Four blips going crazy on the scope and disappearing down into the weeds and then off the screen altogether as the ground masked their radar.

The Eagles should have reset back to CAP, but then once a single blip lit up their scopes, they lost all discipline and bit off on the first thing they saw. I was alone and unafraid somewhere in Alaska (no idea where at that point) and decided the time was right to turn hot and stick my nose back into whatever punch up I could find. From what I could hear on the radio, Salsa was being attacked by at least two of the F-15s, but it seemed that the F-16s were in the clear. My radar painted a target that was scorching in my general direction at about 1.2 Mach. There was nothing on my RWR so he hadn't seen me. Instead of locking him up to alert him, I selected Sidewinder and planned to go eyes on and shoot him in the face before he saw me. I would describe it as if it happened in slow motion, but it bloody didn't. He closed on me so quickly, it was going to be over in a heartbeat. I hugged the ground to skyline him, and there he was, scything through the crystal-clear air towards me at low-level. I couldn't get the Sidewinder to take visually, so bore-sighted the radar and put him in the circle in the HUD. That wonderful radar locked him up and the Sidewinder head immediately growled. I hit the lock button for the Sidewinder, got the tone and called 'Fox 2' as I pulled the trigger. He was a dead man. The radar lock obviously warned him that I was there, and then the cheeky bastard popped four flares out! The rules we worked to with flares negated the kill, so I pulled hard towards him and selected the gun.

After a bit of manoeuvring, I got right in behind and called a guns kill with him continuing to pop flares out even as I got in close to gun him. As I broke off to head roughly towards Eielson, I was called dead over the radio so I guessed someone else had come in and shot me down. Nothing on the RWR mind you, but it is always the one you don't see that kills you. We tried to join up for recovery to Eielson, but gas was low so we ended up arriving in dribs and drabs like stray dogs. However, we had shaken the Eagles up and given them a bloody nose, so not bad for dead men walking. There was lots of adrenaline-fuelled chat and banter as we walked from the jets, with each of us embellishing our own little part of the event. The trip was a hoot and we were on a real high right up until the debrief began. Bearing in mind that we were in Eielson and the F-15s were back at Elmendorf, I was expecting Hannibal to take a quick telephone debrief with their leader, and then we would have a formation debrief in-house. If only.

The four of us walked into an enormous auditorium to find the F-15 formation up on a giant screen in front of us ready for a live debrief. We had a USAF ops clerk waiting for us, holding a microphone. Each time we had something to say, we had the microphone passed to us so that they could hear us in Elmendorf. It was a bit over the top, especially when Hannibal and Salsa (who were mischievous at best) started to signal for the microphone and waited for it to be passed down to them, just so they could say one single word in acknowledgement. It didn't help that we were sitting in the middle of a middle row in the auditorium, so it took a while to get the microphone to us in the first place. It was obviously rubbing the F-15 leader up the wrong way, but he didn't do himself any favours. Remember that the USAF in general, and F-15s in particular, had little or no sense of humour? After the Tailhook scandal hit the streets, the USAF thought it would be good banter to jokingly ban the use of words that might have a bit of ambiguity with sexual acts. The one they obviously thought was the funniest was 'head', so they substituted it for 'skull'. Therefore, when flying, you would skull 350 degrees rather than head 350. Ok, mildly funny once or twice at the beginning. The problem was that for these banter vacuums, it got so out of hand that anyone caught saying 'head' was picked up on it and almost reprimanded. So, what started as banter became a little childish, and then policy.

We just got sick of hearing them saying 'I was skulling 270' etc. and when we said 'heading' they would tut and shake their heads. Add to this the fact that their leader was pissed with us for not following the script, and you could see the thing getting a bit edgy. It appeared from the debrief that the F-16s had got through unmolested. And we had shot down three of the Eagles. Despite this, they tried to argue their way out of all of our kills. It just galled us and Hannibal doubled down on the mischief. He had given a one-word answer to a question about one of the engagements, and immediately passed the microphone back through the three of us to the clerk who then moved out of our row, back into the aisle. 'So, no further shots in that engagement?' asked the Eagle leader. After a short pause, Hannibal signalled for the microphone. The clerk edged into our row and passed it to Salsa, who passed it to me, and I passed it to Burn who passed it to Hannibal.

'Negative,' he said and then reversed the journey of the microphone back to the clerk. It was silly and childish, and I loved him all the more for it. We were sniggering like idiots as the F-15s got more and more annoyed.

If this kid didn't know where the cleaners was then, he would after this trip

It then got onto my little engagement, and I was asked if I got any shots off.

'Sidewinder shot at low-level, but the F-15 flared it off, so I converted into the stern and gunned him.'

'Yeah,' said one of the Eagle drivers, 'I took a visual AMRAAM so you were dead before the guns kill.' Then he sat back satisfied.

'Was this before or after the flares?' I asked.

'Erm ... there were no flares. I didn't deploy them.'

'OK. That's a Sidewinder kill on you then. Happy to accept we traded shots if you got an AMRAAM off so we are both dead if you want to go with that?' I asked. He was between a rock and a hard place. He either admitted to breaking a serious rule about using his flares, or he was dead. You could see the turmoil in him, but he chose the dead option. Bad choice as everyone knew he had used the flares anyway, so he might as well have taken the bollocking, but survived. I was guessing that his so-called visual

AMRAAM shot was bullshit, hence he jumped at the chance to get out of an embarrassing situation. I'm pretty sure they heard Salsa say, 'Fucking A!' as he passed the microphone back to the clerk. Anyway, we got to do the whole thing again in the afternoon on the way back to Elmendorf, with a very similar outcome, but a debrief which gave the F-15s another chance to pat themselves on the back.

Now, it may seem like this was going the same way as the previous year's det with the Eagles doing nothing to help build bridges. However, the next day, they compromised and said we would do a day or two of 1 vs 1s. I say compromise—I am pretty sure they expected to beat us, but this was our bag. The best dogfighting aeroplane in the world versus ... er, not that. Every mission was set up the same way. Two F-15s and two Hornets would form a 4-ship to transit to the play area and then we would split to opposite ends mixing one of each for a 1 vs 1. I walked into the briefing room with Smudge who was ex-Phantom and a 2,000-hour Hornet pilot. He was just awesome—laid back, but sharp as you like. We were met by our Eagle hosts. One of them was fresh out of the box and had that keen, but bewildered look on his face, like he was just happy to be there and couldn't believe his luck that he was flying fighters (a bit like me all the way through my Phantom tour!). His flight lead and overall lead for the trip was called Batman, but Boy Wonder might have suited him better because he looked about twelve years old. He had only just qualified as an air combat leader (ACL), but he had confidence oozing out of him.

He opened by asking how many hours we had on the Hornet. Smudge said about 2,000 and I said 400. This was a defining moment on the trip. Boy Wonder completely missed the fact that I was British. The accent, the RAF wings, and the fact that I had a bloody Union Jack on my arm went over his head. (Oh, and just in case there are any Royal Navy folks reading this, then yes, I do know it is only called the Union Jack when it is at sea. Nobody cares!)

'OK, Smudge. We need an air combat leader in each pair so if you lead Beaker, I'll show Tug the ropes.' Dear God, this kid had some front. Of course, I was an air combat leader and an ACTI as well, but hey-ho—let's see how the brief goes. Badly as it turned out. Boy Wonder patronised me from the start and it really got under my skin. As I said, he had just qualified as an ACL and decided he would use the trip to teach me a bit of air combat. To be honest, I would have laughed out loud and put him right to prevent further embarrassment when we got to the fights, but I held my tongue to see where it would go. Oh my! He even asked if I wanted to start with an offensive set to help build my confidence.

'Happy to go straight in if you are, Batman?'

'Well OK, Tug. But stop me in the air if you need a break, OK?'

'OK, mate. I think I'll be OK,' I said cheerily while mentally counting how many bullets I was going to launch up his jet pipes.

We launched as a four with Smudge and I closing up after take-off into close formation with the Eagles. OK, I was not a huge fan of any jet other than my own, but I have to say that the Eagle was a mightily impressive machine. It was enormous for a single-seat fighter and no kidding, the pilots looked like they were sitting up on a raised throne allowing them to look down on every other fighter out there. I would have loved a go in it. Just one mind you. No way it could prise me out of the best seat in the house. This trip was going to be retribution for last year (which was nothing to do with me, but Band of Brothers and all that) and also for the most patronising brief I had ever sat through. If this kid didn't know where the cleaners was then, he would after this trip because that was exactly where I was going to take him. We separated out to our end of the range and I went through some pre-combat checks which included going upside down to make sure there were no loose articles in the cockpit, and pulling a bit of G to ensure my anti-G kit was working. The last thing I needed was to black out on my first manoeuvre, or to be hit in the face by a stray pen or half a cheese sandwich that the last guy had left in there. Once I was out in battle formation, I called that I was ready, and he started us off.

'Outwards turn, go!' and we turned out through 30 degrees. We were working between cloud layers so no sun to use for advantage. I had no chance of losing sight at the turn in as his jet was monstrously big. After the inwards turn, he called 'tally' over the radio, but I kept quiet. 'One is tally!' he shouted again, but I just rocked my wings as we hurtled towards each other. This was the recognised signal that I had lost my radio. What he should have done was terminated the fight and my ruse would not have worked. He was young and newly qualified though, so tried to sort it out on the hoof. 'Two. Radio check,' he said as we merged and I screamed around behind his tail. He broke into me, but way too late and I creamed into his six and called 'Guns, guns, terminate.' It was all over in less than fifteen seconds from the merge. In fact, for him, it was all over for the rest of the trip, as he never recovered from the relentless pressure I put him under.

'Come 90 left onto 240. I am in battle port. Two is ready!' That call was designed to show him that I was in control. He was supposed to be the leader, but it was now me coordinating the formation and navigating us to the correct area.

'I thought you had a comms failure?' he said on the radio.

'Negative. All good here Batman. Two is ready.'

'OK. Er, outwards turn, go,' and we started again. He wasn't ready though and the next fight went badly for him. I ditched a load of speed pre-merge and turned just in front of him to snap into a ridiculous last-ditch nose pointing single-circle affair. Had he been smart, he would have just powered out of it vertically as there was no way I could have followed him up. I didn't have AMRAAM so no magic missile to do the hard work for me. I should have been stranded, but I knew he would have been shaken up by the first fight. It didn't help him that I randomly called 'Fox 2,' without pulling the trigger, as I was way inside min range. The poor sap broke hard into me to try and match my nose pointing, and to defeat an imaginary missile. I quickly called 'continue,' meaning the shot was no good for a kill and to keep the fight going. I had no idea what speed I had, but it wasn't very much. It didn't matter though as I was nearly behind him and he was bleeding energy like a stuck pig.

I was able to unload and get a few knots while keeping him defensive, and he was left with two choices. Either sit in the shit box with me and just bleed until I gunned him, or try to unload for speed and rate around the circle to get away from me. When I unloaded my jet, my nose came off him a bit and it tricked him into thinking he was rating away from me, so he unloaded to enhance that. All that did was give me the weapons separation I needed to shoot him with a Sidewinder.

'Fox 2, kill. Terminate. Come right onto 060. I am battle starboard. Two is ready!'

'One, terminate,' he bleated. It was time to turn the screw one last time. I turned it so much, the head sheared off.

'Tell you what, Batman. Do you want to go 2-shot kill?' This would mean we would need two valid shots before a kill could be called.

'Sure. Erm, rebrief to 2-shot kills each then.' And then—the coup de gras.

'Sorry mate. I meant do you want me to go 2-shot kill? Happy for you to stay at one shot if you like?'

'Copied. Yeah. Let's do that then.' He was completely beaten down. I could hear it in his monotone voice. The last fight, I played it properly. No deception at all. Just me and my wonder jet versus Boy Wonder and his 'all about me' jet. It was ugly. My Hornet performed flawlessly and showed off its moves, burning and turning itself inside out and annoying its much larger and more serious cousin in a complicated, but beautiful dance of death. I shot Batman the requisite twice, after playing with him for a little while, and it was all done.

To his credit, he was extremely professional leading me back through the cloud to Elmendorf, and our mixed 2-ship roared into the circuit for the break. I was welded onto his wing as we ran in, and then he turned into a frankly shockingly massive flat plate as he broke away from me downwind. Three seconds later, I followed him, went through the pre-landing checks, and turned finals. He did the classic F-15 showboat landing of airbrake out and hold the nosewheel off the floor for as long as he could, and I crumped my jet into the runway with no finesse at all. I had to admire his attitude—beaten up badly but still trying to style it out on landing. Maybe there was a bit of fighter pilot in him after all? Surely though, he would be humble and circumspect in the debrief? Alas, no. He still hadn't got the message that I wasn't a bog standard 400-hour Marine, and tried to teach me even more about air combat! OK, you are not on the runway now, mate, I thought. I let him have his head a little, but the turning point came when he asked me what speed I had in the second fight. Been here before on 121 squadron!

'Dunno,' I said.

'You don't know what your speed was?' he asked incredulously. 'I had 330 knots at this point,' he continued.

'Congratulations,' I said, 'you died with a great energy package on the jet. The reason I don't know how fast I was going was because it was irrelevant. I was too busy killing you at the time.'

'Huh?' I stood up.

'OK, look. Just have a seat, Batman.' Reluctantly, he sat down and I ran the debrief from there. I pointed out how he was thrown by the unusual, but still had the energy to defeat me if he had wanted to. His ego forced him to stay in a fight his jet wasn't built for, and he tried to beat me in my world. The fact that I didn't conform to the accepted conventions meant he was off his game from the start. Losing the first fight (albeit through a bit of deception) knocked him sideways and he was lost from there. He had never seen anyone throw random shit like that into a fight before. However, I took him through what his options should have been and how he should have recognised the situations he was in.

'How do you know all this stuff?' he asked after I had finished coaching him. I took him through who I actually was and what my experience was, particularly the bits about being an instructor and teaching a lot of ACM.

'Ah, OK,' he said and his shoulders slumped a bit. Poor kid, but maybe he had learnt a thing or two—not necessarily about air combat, but maybe about attitude and humility? At the end of the debrief, I shook his hand and thanked him for all the fun. We bumped into Smudge and Beaker afterwards.

'Man! Smudge was all over my ass!' squawked Beaker.

'Yeah?' said Batman. 'Well, I just got beaten up by Captain Fucking Combat here!' God knows what the guy going up against Fox was going to be like afterwards—probably suicidal.

Fucking Baller!

The Eagles didn't want to play 1 vs 1 anymore so it was back to the big missions the following week. I was absolutely hanging out of my ass with fatigue by the end of the first week. The sun shone between my curtains every night so sleep did not come easy. Thud had organised some white-water rafting for the weekend, but the last thing I needed was physical activity, so after a long lie in on the Saturday, I took one of the hire cars and drove alone and unafraid to Anchorage (city of my nightmares) to see the sights. I kept my eyes closed as I walked past a couple of the bars. I signed up for a boat tour out to see the glacier, and even though it was the end of July, the weather was still a crisp 10 degrees, so a bit nippy. It wasn't a long ride until we were right there alongside a wall of ice that stretched up the mountain like a lava flow. Once again, on my American adventure, I was gobsmacked at the natural wonders on show right in front of me. Almost on cue, the ice wall calved off a lump and it sploshed into the lake. A short while later, the wave hit the boat and we lurched and bobbed for a bit and waited for the next lump to drop. Once we had seen it happen a couple of times, and reflected on how the environment was changing, it was back to the shore and prepping for my next afterburner fuelled hooligan flight, with not a thought for what it was doing to the glaciers.

It really was a hooligan flight as well. 6 vs 6 against the F-15s with aeroplanes all over the shop. We managed to refuel our 6-ship from a C-130 tanker, then faced up again into the 6-ship wall of belt-fed AMRAAMS from the Eagles. I was breaking at 7G all over the joint as soon as my RWR was tickled. No idea who won or lost, but just glad not to have hit someone throughout the melee. I really wanted to hit someone the next day though, and it was Baller. He was leading our 4-ship against 4 F-15s and it was the early morning mission. I was number 3 with Solo on my wing and Hannibal was down as number 2. Solo was duty officer so was already in the squadron and as I made my way out to the car, there was just Baller standing by it and no sign of Hannibal. I said I would go and knock on Hannibal's door, but Baller said that he was already in work. Seemed a bit odd, so I went back in to check. I didn't know exactly which room he was in, so I gently knocked on the two doors it could have been. I didn't want to shout through the doors as it was God awful early and everyone else was kipping. No answer from either door so I figured Baller was right. He wasn't. Hannibal had overslept and was zonked out in bed. I might have been able to wake him had I known.

We got to the squadron buildings and met up with Solo, but no sign of Hannibal. Baller had a bit of a smarmy grin on his face and said, 'Well, if he doesn't make the brief, he can't fly the mission.' Bastard. He knew. I tried in vain to ring the Crack House, but it was time to brief and then we flew the trip as a 3-ship. Inside, I was both fuming and sick. This was the first time that I had seen a Marine actively screw over another Marine, and it made me ill. Furthermore, I felt I had let Hannibal down, as he had been a very good buddy to me. I put all of that down to 'Future Tug's problem', and got my head in the cockpit. The mission was to die bravely, which we achieved perfectly, and come back to die again in the debrief. Mission accomplished then. As I walked in from my jet, I passed Salsa walking for the next mission. Word had already got around that Hannibal had missed the trip.

'What happened, Tug?' I gave him the potted story and he just shook his head.

'Fucking Baller, man!' He shook his head again and headed out to his jet. As soon as the debrief was done, I rushed out to apologise to Hannibal. He was shocked and a little hurt. For a big, brusque, hard Marine, he was still human after all.

'Fucking Baller, man!' he said.

'Yeah,' I replied, 'fucking Baller.'

I scheduled myself a day off from flying the next day to catch up with Batman. After our air combat experience together, he had told me he was on alert for a couple of days during our second week. I was a bit of a QRA nerd so asked him if I could visit him in the shed and get a quick tour. As much as I loved QRA, it was a bit tedious, so visits like this helped to break up the monotony of the routine. Batman was delighted that I had asked. The F-15s at Elmendorf did QRA patrolling the border between Alaska and Russia. Two jets on permanent alert. Batman gave me a brilliant tour and was in his element when he sat me in the cockpit and took me through the controls. It wasn't a million miles away from the F-18, but I was acutely aware of how much aeroplane there was around me. It was bloody massive, and I wanted to have a go. It properly filled the alert shed and looked like it was wearing it, like some sort of undersized t-shirt. You could sense the immense power it had, not only in the engines, but in the weapons too. I thanked Batman for a great tour and headed back to the squadron.

Hannibal had quickly recovered from his shafting by Baller and was running the endgame of an elaborate spoof he had set up over a few days. We had a young Marine officer called Tub holding with us, before he began his flying training programme. I think he was the son of a general, so was fair game in Hannibal's twisted mind. He was spoofing the guy about bears in the training area, and what the 'bear state' was. He even went so far as to write fake orders regarding our response as the bear state increased. He tasked Tub to keep an eye on the state while we were on det. A sign was put up on the ops desk with the current bear state on it and Hannibal even got the clerk to tannoy any change in the state. Hannibal got Tub to brief up the state to him every day, but when it got to bear state red, the whole thing went into overdrive. The tannoy announced state red and Tub rushed to Hannibal with the orders to say that this was the worst level. The orders stated that all pilots had to carry 'bang sticks' with them in case they ejected and had to fight off the bears.

'Dear God!' shouted Hannibal. 'Tub! Only the group CO can authorise the issue of bang sticks. You need to go brief him up and then get to stores and draw them out. I'll stop the guys from launching until you get back with them. Hurry, man!'

'Yes, Sir!' shouted Tub and jumped to it. Hammer had a great sense of humour and saw the spoof straight away. He listened carefully and then signed the fake orders so that Tub could go and draw the bang sticks. Poor kid. About 30 minutes later, he slunk back into the ready room looking suitably embarrassed. The stores staff had laughed him out of the building.

'Fucking Hannibal, man!' was all he said.

My final trip in Alaska was supposed to be a standard 4 vs 4, and I scheduled myself to lead it. As I wrote the programme, I made sure I had Hannibal, Salsa and Solo in the formation (definitely not Baller), as I wasn't intending to walk into a face full of AMRAAMs. I wanted to explode in all directions and all altitudes to mix up the picture. It was a medium to high level mission, but the low-level area was available to us too. I had sorted my tactics and we walked into the brief to find that the F-15 leader had changed the plan without letting us know. He was doing a flight lead upgrade ride and announced that we would be MiG-29s escorting a SU-23 Frogfoot light bomber to a target, and it was their job to shoot it down. If they shot the Frogfoot they won, but if it got to the target, we won. My tactics were screwed then, so I would only have 5 minutes before walking for the jets to come up with a plan. He then introduced our Frogfoot crew which was a couple of civilian pilots who were flying a Falcon. I think they might have had jamming kit on board so were a training provider for the USAF.

By the way, I had no problem with him blindsiding us like that. It put us on the back foot straight away and I would have done the same thing myself to him. Good on him for trying to work an advantage from the start. Proper fighter pilot stuff, that. The problem for him was that he was dealing with me. When I get cornered like that, I can be a bit of a bastard. It didn't help that he had a superior attitude in the brief and it seemed to them a given that they would win. We had brought our own Marine Corps fighter controllers with us on this det, so I got them, the fake Russians, and my formation together to rebrief the new plan. Basically, we were going to cheat a bit, and then it would take some sharp work from the controllers as we flexed back into my rough bomb burst plan, albeit manipulated to sort the new scenario. If it sounds like a did a lot of cheating, then yes, I did. It was all part of being a fighter pilot and finding whatever edge you could.

I led us out to the play area as a 5-ship with our Frogfoot in the middle of us, and let down to low-level. This was going to use up a bit more gas, but was essential to our deception plan. I was working on just one fight for the whole trip whereas the Eagles had briefed up for two presentations. We were shit or bust on the first one so it made no difference to us. About 20 miles in front of the start point, we dropped off the Falcon who then set up a slow CAP perpendicular to the attack heading (yes—I said HEADING!) so that they would be masked from the F-15 radar. Having done that, I then dropped off Solo at the real start point down at low-level, to pretend to be the Frogfoot. I took Hannibal and Salsa up into the ether in close formation to mask the fact that there were only three of us. At the 'Fight's on!' call, we all faced hot and just hoped that the F-15s would miss the Falcon (which they did) and then split their forces and have two of them go after Solo (which they also did), while the other two obviously thought they could handle the four MiG-29s that were supposed to be up high, and area sweeping for the Frogfoot.

Hannibal and Salsa turned immediately cold as I speared hot at about 1.2 Mach to try and lure some AMRAAMS down range. I then turned hard cold to defeat those shots and as I passed Hannibal and Salsa (who had turned back hot in the meantime), I rolled inverted and pulled vertically downwards into what the Americans called a 'doppler pick'. Basically, the enemy radars should bite off on the hot targets while I disappeared from the scope and out of their altitude scan. Sometimes it worked and sometimes it didn't. Hannibal and Salsa bomb burst into random directions and then it was every man for himself with our GCI controllers working hard to coordinate four mad fighter pilots calling for 'Picture' every ten seconds and shouting 'Declare!' when we had a blip on the scope. A declaration of 'Hostile' from GCI gave us permission to shoot beyond visual range. At the start of the fight, it is easier to declare as everyone in front of you is most probably hostile. Once it turns into a furball though, it's anybody's guess who is who, so generally, you have to get eyes on somebody to confirm they are a bad guy. I have simplified things a bit there, as there are clever things like IFF and software in the radar, and data links to help you, but nothing beats your eyeballs.

The two Eagles that had gone off to shoot Solo got a shock when the 'Falcon' turned itself inside out to defeat the initial AMRAAM shots. By the time they had eyes on him, he had shot one in the face with a Sidewinder before becoming an AMRAAM pin cushion. I pitched up unseen towards an F-15 who saw me at the last minute and started flaring like it was bonfire night. He could flare all he wanted, but it wasn't going to stop the gun, and I pulled in hard behind him while rocking back on the weapons selector. My RWR went mental and I looked right to see another big slab of F-15 creaming into my six o'clock, so I ignored my prey and broke hard at 7.5G ditching all my speed with the airbrake out and forcing him to fly through whilst I almost stalled out of the sky. A boot full of left rudder, airbrake in and full left stick saw my Hornet swap ends and point its beautiful nose right at the Eagle and I loosed off a Sidewinder at him which he flared off. Hmmm—looked like I would need the services of Doctor Gun again, so I closed in and put the sight on, but just as I thought I would get the shot, I was called dead by our GCI. Rats!!! Either it was a delayed kill call from when he first got in behind me, or it was his wingman (my original bandit) re-entering the fight. The truth of it was somewhat different, but I would find that out later in the debrief.

I heard a kill call from Hannibal (that was on the first guy I almost killed) and a bit of a to-do from Salsa, and then it was all over. About this time, a very excited voice from the Falcon called that they were over the target and the exercise was terminated. The Hornets were out of gas, but the F-15s (which seemed to carry their own bloody petrol station under the wings) had enough for another split. Despite that, we heard their flight supervisor, who was the number 3 and checking out the leader, call for RTB (return to base) so we joined up as an 8-ship gorilla to fly back to Elmendorf. A few miles out, I separated us away from the Eagles for our own 4-ship break. I called us into echelon and watched in wonder at the Eagles hauling their enormous asses round the corner to go downwind. Everyone tucked in a bit tighter as we wanted our formation to look better than them, and we raged into the circuit like hooligans and flat-plated our wonder-ships to line up downwind and onto finals. That was my last trip in Alaska so it was great to finish on a high, leading my buddies onto the ground in our outrageously beautiful jets.

Sing us a song, Tug!

Big beaming smiles all round from us as I ran a quick formation debrief before going in with the F-15s. I made a point of thanking our controllers who had been just awesome and on-point with everything they said. Listening to the F-15s, it turned out that Hannibal had shot the wingman in my engagement so I guessed I had been killed by the guy I ended up fighting, and it was just a delayed kill call. There was a bit of awkwardness in the room around the Eagles, and their leader was not as cocky as he had been in the brief. In fact, he looked totally beaten down, so there was obviously a bit of drama that came out of their formation debrief. Top of the shop was that the Frogfoot hit the target, so he conceded defeat straight away. That was unusual for the F-15s to do, so I wondered what was up. They didn't even ask how he got through unmolested and just put it down to poor radar work on their part. I just winked at the Falcon crew who were grinning like Cheshire cats. If they weren't going to ask us directly what happened, I had no intention of telling them.

Eagle 1 admitted being caught out and ending up with a face-full of Solo and his rockets instead of the Falcon. They should have twigged when they saw his initial defensive manoeuvre, but just got the bit between their teeth because he was low and therefore must have been the bomber. And then it came to my engagement. As it happened, I was up against the flight supervisor, who recounted having me bang to rights and then seeing my jet disassemble itself from reality, and then getting in behind him.

'It was a great move,' he said, which puffed my chest out a bit.

'But you got the shot on me anyway?' I asked.

'No,' he said frostily and looked at the flight lead.

'Er, that was me coming in from the south,' he said. He had dispatched Solo and poked his nose north to join in the big punch up.

'I fired two visual AMRAAMs into your merge,' he continued quietly while looking at something that must have been very interesting on his flying boot.

'Ah, OK,' I said. So, he had launched two rabid air sharks into a merge that he had no declaration on. One of them definitely would have gobbled me up, but the other one would have looked for the next meal. That meal would have been his own flight supervisor.

'So, we would definitely have had a Blue on Blue in there and that is just unacceptable,' said the supervisor with a mix of steel and venom in his voice. Awkward had turned into downright uncomfortable at that point, and after thanking us for the trip, the supervisor said they had some things to discuss amongst themselves, in private. We hit the bar while they did their blood-letting and I bought the first round for my formation and our GCI controllers who had handled the melee brilliantly.

I spent the final day of the det on the ground, and at the end of it all we headed into the bar at one of the Eagle squadrons for a beer call. They had a very nicely fitted-out bar and we downed a few drinks with them. Batman had regained a bit of his swagger, which was nice to see, and we bantered about the 1 vs 1s. The guys from the last mission were there too, with the flight lead moping in his booze as he had right royally failed his upgrade ride. His supervisor chatted to me and wanted to know how the hell I had managed to fly him through, but the truth of it was it had been my glorious Hornet, and I think for once, he truly appreciated the downright shocking sting in its tail. I have said a lot of things about the elitist attitude of the Eagles. However, right there in the bar as we marvelled about each other's aircraft, and the skills we each brought to the table, we shared a bond based on our brothers and sisters in arms ethos. Yes, the F-15s were gobby, but by God, if we were going into day one of the air war, why wouldn't you want to sit behind an 8-ship wall of them while they fired off their AMRAAMs in the immensely disciplined way that they were famous for? They were unparalleled in that arena. Simply the best at what they did. As soon as it went to ratshit though, get them out of the way and let the more flexible Marine Corps Hornets sweep in and mop up. We enjoyed a very pleasant mutual backslapping affair that night in the bar. And then it came to the present exchange.

The F-15s, as usual, gave us a massive photo of an Eagle with all of their signatures around the outside. Chilli then stepped forward with a plaque and I swear the whole room held its breath. Thankfully, it was just a standard VMFA-134 plaque and once it was handed over and had been checked thoroughly for dog poo, we all breathed a sigh of relief.

'Sing us a song, Tug!' shouted Burn. The USAF looked a little concerned as I launched into the first one, but the Eagle CO calmly walked over and locked the door, nodded at me, and then visibly winced as the strains of 'I don't want to join the Air Force', headed into verses 2 and 3 which can only be described as 'fruity' at best. However, seemingly let off the leash for at least one night, the Eagles sang back to us and that was us for about an hour or so. Singing, drinking, and bonding before we headed back to the Crack House where we slagged them off from pillar to post for putting us in that shit hole. Pretty standard night really.

I slept most of the way back in the tanker and after two weeks of very little kip, I slept the sleep of the dead when I got back to Ocean Beach. I took a couple of weeks off to recharge and came back refreshed, straight into our weapons extravaganza. We had a lot of ordnance to get through, but we weren't the only ones. While I had been on leave, I had seen on the local news that one of the San Diego gun clubs had held its annual meet, out in the desert. It was a big affair attended by thousands of gun-toting citizens exercising their rights under the second amendment. They filmed a load of folks blatting off rounds into the desert aiming vaguely at some targets which were obliterated by automatic weapons of all shapes and sizes. One of the centrepiece events showed a guy towing a bloody anti-aircraft gun cage into position behind his pick-up truck. He climbed in the cage and loosed off hundreds of very big bullets down range. The gun lit up the night sky and the sound was nothing short of traumatic. People were howling with delight.

They wheeled out the 2,000 pounders

It was only when I got back to the squadron that I found out Gunny Peterson was one of the organisers of the event. When I found him, I told him I had seen his handiwork on the TV and he beamed with pride. He then asked me if I wanted to go out in the desert with him and his buddies to shoot some stuff.

'Not really my thing, Gunny. But thanks anyway.'

'You would love it Flaaht Lootenant Wilson,' he drawled.

'Guns don't really do it for me Gunny. I don't see the point in owning them as a private citizen.' I couldn't have sounded less Marine if I tried!

'There are only two things in this world that ah trust Flaaht Lootenant Wilson,' he said. 'The first is mah personal sidearm, and the second is the Great Lord Jeesuss Chraarst.' And there you had it. The world according to Gunny Peterson. He was deadly serious too. I didn't know what to say to that, so I just nodded and looked for the nearest exit. Thank God he was on our side.

In my next five trips, I dropped almost 30,000 pounds of exploding iron. There wasn't a grain of sand in R-2507 that hadn't been turned to glass with our fire and fury. What a ride! Every trip was one pass haul ass, and we explored every single option on the stores page regarding salvos, sticks and separation. We dropped some slick, and others retarded using the snake-eye fins which sprung out to slow the bomb down long enough for you to vacate the area and not frag yourself with your own portable mayhem when dropping at low-level. The pace as usual was relentless, but our Hornets lapped it up as we fought our way into the target area, dropped our bombs, and then fought our way out again. Fighter-bomber, bomber, and then pure fighter all in one trip. I even tried a few carrier landings using the lens, but quickly stopped that shit as it crumped my jet into the runway, compressing God knows how many of my vertebrae. I was also getting towards the end of my Hornet odyssey and wanted to enjoy every last second of my flying with the supermodel jet. Blower was about to start flying on the RAG so my countdown had started.

The countdown to the arrival of Baby Wilson mark two was also on, and once again I had set up a QRA style footing at home just in case she made an early appearance. Holly had been two weeks over baked so there was an expectation of that again. I had broached the subject of my mum and dad coming out to help, but Dad's health wouldn't allow another trip to California. However, Ron and Meg graciously stepped into the breach for us and we planned for them coming out, ostensibly to look after Holly while we coaxed number 2 out of her shelter. Anyway, we were still about a month away from that happening and I had a load more weapons to get through before then. Just when we thought we had rid the world of 500 and 1,000 pounders, they wheeled out the 2,000 pounders. My God, those things took some hauling. And the bang they made when we dropped them? They were seriously landscape changing. Although I was loving the explosive cabaret my jet was putting on, I did pine a bit for the air-to-air environment, so I programmed in a bit of 1 vs 1 vs 1 and some F-5 combat to spice things up a bit.

It was great to fly a clean jet again with no bombs or racks on board. It was almost like date night with my Hornet. We both dressed up and made an effort to recapture the magic of our romance for a trip or two before going back to the drudge of dropping bombs. Just enough to remind ourselves why we fell in love with each other in the first place. I was exhausted by the end of the month through having done Alaska and then surged with the bombing, and was just about to hit the sack one night when the news channels exploded with the story of Princess Diana's death. Most of the UK was sleeping as I watched wall-to-wall coverage of the unfolding event. It seemed to shake the world, but particularly in the USA where Diana was very popular. I have always been a royalist. I am proud to say I served in the Royal Air Force as opposed to the British Air Force. It seemed that all of the talk shows, and especially the talk radio stuff I tuned into while in the hot pits, wanted to turn the story into an anti-royal family exercise, and it made me very uncomfortable to hear uninformed idiots spouting what they believed to be gospel on a subject they could never understand. Even Total asked me why the Queen herself wasn't in tears over the whole thing.

'You are divorced, Total, right?' I asked.

'Yeah.'

'So, if your ex-wife died, would your mother shed a tear?'

'Nah. Probably dance on her grave, Tug.'

'There you go then.'

'OK. I can dig that!'

We finally got to the end of the bombs and were allowed to open the sweetie jar and take out all the missiles. I had shot an AIM-7 Sparrow from a Phantom, so scheduled myself in for a Sidewinder shot. There was a limited number of missiles so I had to share them out as equally as I could, because everyone wanted to shoot one. The set up for the Sidewinder shots was downright bizarre. Basically, you flew out to an arbitrary spot over the Pacific (I don't recall, but I am supposing there was an air-to-air range out there somewhere) and all the shooters gathered at one end of that bit of airspace. One lone, brave (stupid) Marine was at the other end with a rack of parachute flares. At the 'Fight's on' call, he deployed a flare which fell very slowly on its parachute, then high-tailed it out of there at 90 degrees, while we faced up with live weapons to try and get a tone on the flare. Once he was clear (ish) we were allowed to fire on the flare.

Mr Tug's 'I love me room'

I programmed Burn to lead the shooters with me as number 2, and Thud on the flares. Yeah, yeah. I know what you are thinking, but there was no malice on my part—honest. We flew with dummy Sidewinder rounds all the time, but to see the real thing on the wingtip rails as I walked to my jet was just awesome. There was a whole heap of checks with the Sidewinder, but to be honest, I did nearly all of them on every trip when I flew with the dummy rounds, so I was confident that I knew what I was doing. I opened the front of both LAUs to make sure the umbilicals were connected and then routed through the metal banana links. The banana link held the head of the umbilical so that when the missile launched, it separated from the umbilical. Failure to do so would rip the front of the LAU off as ably demonstrated by one of our other Marine Hornet squadrons about a year previously. I also checked the pip pin halfway down each LAU that ensured the missile wouldn't fall off the back of the launcher when we took off. Finally, I opened the back of the LAU to check the coolant bottle which cooled the seeker head so it was sensitive enough to detect a heat source.

Once the jet was started up, the ground crew shone an infra-red torch at the seeker head to make sure I got a growl, and the next thing I knew, we were lined up on the runway ready to go and wreak mayhem on Thud ... er, a parachute flare that deserved a damn good kicking. We transited quite a way out over the Pacific before Burn declared us clear to start, and waved goodbye to a sorry looking Thud as he separated from us. A few minutes later, Thud called that he had dropped a flare and Burn called that he had contact with it.

'Wait for me to clear!!!' bleated Thud which made me chuckle a bit. Once Thud had called himself clear, Burn calmly called 'Smoke 41. Fox 2.' And I watched in awe as his first AIM-9M flashed off the rail at 2.5 Mach, like a greyhound out of the traps, with its arse on fire. It did its zig-zaggy tail thing which is where it got the name Sidewinder, and then got its ass in gear and went straight to the flare and exploded. My turn. Thud repeated the process and I got a tone from my eager little death tube.

'Smoke 42. Fox 2!' I shouted, trying to be as cool as Burn, but absolutely blowing it in spades. I might have well have whooped over the radio—I was so uncool. Hell's bells, that rocket was fast. And the whoooosh from the motor as it bid me farewell was like opening a million bottles of fizzy pop all at once. I couldn't wait to do it again. I watched Burn's second shot and then I was in the hot seat once more. You might be thinking that it was all a bit samey by then? Bollocks, was it! I was even more excited for round two and thought I would try and watch it go off the rail the next time. Never saw it. It was so stinking fast, one moment it was there, and the next microsecond, it wasn't. So, Thud survived and we landed back on with the biggest smiles on our chops. The umbilicals were retrieved from the front of the LAUs and presented to us by the weapons technicians. Two more trophies for 'Mr Tug's I love me room'. After the excitement of that trip, it seemed like anything else was going to be a bit ordinary. It was back to the usual of lots of air combat, dive bombing with the practice bombs we had neglected while hoofing off the noisy stuff, and lots of radar intercepts. Every trip I flew seemed to be at least a 4-ship. It was just brilliant.

I picked up Ron and Meg from the airport in preparation for our new arrival. I was so grateful to them for coming out to help us. Holly adored them as if they were her grandparents and we could relax knowing that she would be in good hands. The reluctant Wilson was going to be induced so we had a confirmed date of September the 18th as her birth date—whether she liked it or not! I took Ron to see a Padres baseball game and it was just like when I had shared the moment at the Angels with my dad. Ron loved it. He had no idea what the hell was going on, but we revelled in the atmosphere, and in each other's company. He was a great man and I loved him. I was so lucky to have what in essence was a second father in my life.

I went into the squadron a couple of days before the main event. It seemed that the troops had 'discovered' a load of 500-pounders that we should already have dropped. They were obviously hidden under the carpet, or found in Gunny Peterson's garage or something, but they had to go bang somewhere regardless. They strapped eight of them to my jet and off I popped to do the deed. That all went as advertised, but my hop in the afternoon saw me recovering from the dive attack into a face-full of desert buzzard or some sort of giant monster bird. It hit the canopy with a loud bang and smeared its bits all across the left-hand side of the window. If it had missed me, it would probably have flown through my frag pattern and been barbequed and skewered, so shitty options all around, I guess?

I'd had plenty of birdstrikes before, so I pulled up calmly to a decent altitude and did a slow-speed handling check, before easing my way back to Miramar while declaring an in-flight emergency. It was no big deal, and after shutting down, all there seemed to be was a bloody smudge on the canopy and a bit further along the left-hand side of the fuselage. The jet had basically shrugged it off and just got on with it. The Hornet was a fantasy of finesse and gymnastics, but it was built in a bloody shipyard too, so could shake off all sorts of drama like that. I did some hooligan strafing the next day and then went back to Ocean Beach to prepare for the birth of our second daughter.

INTO MY HANDS!

Holly was more interested in going to the cake shop in OB for sprinkle doughnuts with Ron and Meg rather than wishing us bon chance, or wondering what her new sister was going to look like, so we drove off to the birthing centre ready for action. It was just an arbitrary single-storey building on an ordinary street, but inside it had all sorts of new-age stuff like birthing pools and swings and God knows what. The hippy midwives, who I had grown to absolutely love through the pre-natal classes, were about as relaxed as you could get, and they administered a pessary to induce the labour. I sat down in a very comfy chair and settled in to watch the show.

'OK, we'll see you back here in a couple of hours,' they said.

'Huh?'

'Go off and have a walk around somewhere, and when the labour starts, come back here.'

So, my day off, sitting in a comfy chair and randomly saying 'breathe' while all the action took place around me wasn't going to work out as I had planned. In fact, I was to take an extremely active part in the proceedings, but just didn't know how active at that point.

We drove to Balboa Park in San Diego, which is a beautiful area full of gardens and museums, and shuffled about as the pains grew inside my wife. I didn't dare suggest we go into the Air and Space Museum to look at the Phantom they had strung from the ceiling, but it was a close-run thing. After a little while, early labour started and I drove us back to Shangri-La. This was it. In a few hours, we would meet our newborn—I couldn't wait. Now, as this is supposed to be an aviation memoir, I will spare you most of the gory details of the magic of childbirth, but there are a couple of things worth getting out in the open. The lack of pain relief was certainly an issue. At one point, my wife was squeezing my hand so hard that she drew blood in my palm with her nails. It all came to a head when she looked me squarely in the eyes and hissed:

'If you don't get me some pain relief now Tug, I am going to fucking kill you!' As I said—the magic of childbirth. I looked up at the head hippy, Tabatha, and pleaded with my eyes as the blood ran down my wrist.

'I have just the thing,' she said gently, and I breathed a huge sigh of relief as she went off to get some seriously strong narcotics, or so I thought.

No such luck. She came back with a bottle of lavender oil and dabbed it on her fingers before rubbing it into my wife's temples.

'Feel the power of the lavender,' she said, 'your pain is your power.' My wife fixed me with a steely glare, and I knew right there that I was a dead man.

Shortly afterwards, came my starring role. It seemed that the head was fully out and Tabatha said, 'OK, Dad. It's time to come and help your daughter into the world.'

Not for the first time that day I said, 'Huh?'

'Your daughter is about to be born, so come down here.'

I am pretty sure all of that was their job, but down to the business end I went. They told me to put my hands under her head and wait for the next push. They then stood back, leaving me looking like the most nervous catcher in the slips. Where the hell was the baseball glove when I needed it? Another push saw the first of her shoulders break free, and very quickly afterwards, she flew out into my hands. INTO MY HANDS! My daughter was in my hands. Not the midwife's, but mine. I have tears in my eyes as I write this. It was the most awe-inspiring moment of my life. Shooting a Sidewinder had absolutely nothing on this. My daughter was less than 10 seconds old, and I was the one holding her! Life does not give you a better or more beautiful experience than that.

There must have been something in my eye at the time, as tears started streaming down my cheeks. Tabatha and the team eased in and started doing midwife stuff as I held the kid with no name, in a state of utter shock and euphoria. What a moment. Next thing was, I had cut the cord and she was wrapped up in blankets and it was all over.

'What about a name?' asked one of the midwives.

'Laurel,' said my wife, which was one of the names we had bandied about. So, there she was. Laurel Mary Wilson. Daughter number two. We were left alone for a bit to rest and reflect, and after about 20 minutes or so, I said, 'You know we are being posted back to Leeming? Well, Laurel is a great name for California, but not so much for North Yorkshire. How about Laura?'

'Yeah. Laura sounds good,' said my wife, on the brink of collapse. So, after only an hour of life, we changed her name on the paperwork to Laura. She would have got so much shit from other kids in North Yorkshire with a name like Laurel. You dodged a bullet there, kid—thanks to your dad. You are welcome, by the way. There was a bit of stitching and other medical stuff to be done, and then they were preparing to chuck us out! When Holly was born, my wife had three days in hospital to recover, but the hippies wanted us out pronto. Before leaving though, they had to ensure that my wife had eaten something and could breastfeed Laura. I headed off to Starbucks around the corner in search of food, but before leaving, I changed my shirt. The one I had arrived in was covered in blood and Laura-goo, so I took out my special Dad t-shirt and put it on. A few weeks earlier, my wife had bought me a white t-shirt and some fabric paint. On the front in big letters, it said 'Dad' and had Holly's hand prints under it. On the back were Holly's footprints. It caused quite a stir in Starbucks.

As I was waiting for the drinks, a woman said, 'Hey! Great shirt.'

'Thanks,' I said, 'my eldest daughter made it.'

'Cool. How many kids you got?' Californians—they just want to talk.

'Two. My eldest is three and a half.'

'Alright! And the youngest?'

I made a big deal of looking at my watch. 'Oh. She is just three hours old.'

'OH WOW!' and the whole of Starbucks burst into applause. Random guys came up to me, patting me on the back and wishing me good luck. I collected the drinks and food.

'That'll be $18.75.' So, the goodwill I was experiencing didn't extend to Starbucks HQ.

The shock of being turfed out into the night with Laura only 4 hours old hit us as I strapped her seat into the car. Dear God, she was tiny, and the seat drowned her. Ron and Meg were beaming as we brought her into the house, but Holly was fast asleep in bed. Feeding Laura through the night proved to be a little traumatic, as she was throwing up the milk and a load of mucus with it, as well as choking a bit. We were like zombies the next morning, so thank goodness we had all the help we needed from Ron and Meg. Holly was less than impressed that there was another golden child in the house, so we had wasted all that money on 'Big Sister' storybooks and badges. She was even less impressed each time Laura tried out her pipes and cried for food. We were a little concerned about the mucus so Ron called Annie to get some advice. Annie was a registered nurse, but was also a qualified and practicing midwife—handy, hey? She told me it sounded like her stomach had not been cleared out and then, over the phone, instructed me on what to do. While Ron held the telephone to my ear, I took hold of Laura and used the rubber pipette that had come in our home pack from the birthing centre, to effectively suck all of the birthing crap out of Laura's guts. I was petrified of hurting or damaging Laura, but Annie calmly talked me through it and it did the trick. No more choking or mucus (give me a complicated CAS mission any day of the week rather than do that again). I couldn't thank Annie enough for what I saw as her saving Laura's life. It wouldn't be the last time Annie would save Laura's life.

Pretty sure Tennyson didn't fly the Hornet

After two weeks off, it was time for me to return to VMFA-134 for my final three-month fling with my beautiful dream jet. I had got Ron and Meg off back to the UK and Holly had now accepted that the puke and poo machine was probably going to be around for a while, so she had better just deal with it. I had a basic intercept trip to get back into the swing and then slap bang into a 1 vs 1 combat frenzy. It was nice to see I hadn't lost my touch and neither had my Hornet in our two-week trial separation. In fact, I had never felt so at ease in a cockpit before. Typical. I get comfortable with a jet just before I had to leave it behind forever. It's a good job I was comfortable, because the end of October saw me involved in a huge bloody gorilla of a trip, where four of us plus four F-5s went up against a mixed 8-ship of F-15s and F-16s. Jesus, they were throwing the whole inventory at that one. The 15s and 16s tanked from a KC-135 and we tanked from a C-130 and we set it all up again afterwards. There were so many aeroplanes and so little sky, I had metal flashing past my nose constantly. God only knows what happened on that trip (and he wasn't going to tell us) as we weren't carrying any pods or anything like that.

I remember running away bravely at low-level and then turning back hot to poke my nose towards the carnage. I got an instant contact on my radar, but the aspect vector was enormous with a speed readout of about Mach 2. 'Must be a jamming pod,' I thought as the target raced down my scope way too fast to be anything real. I was then called dead and mere moments later, an F-15 screamed past me like a missile, doing nearly Mach 2.

'Oh, it was real then,' I thought as I slunk away from the fight in resignation. Another corpse on the golden altar of the F-15. Still, a massive hoot though. I was wringing the neck of my Hornet on every trip, trying to make the most of every last minute I had left. I couldn't be bothered to bash the circuit though so it was one landing on every trip like a proper fighter pilot. I was trying to cram in as many sporting events as I could too. American football tickets were rare as rocking horse shit, but one of the Aussie expats had scored a couple and asked me if I wanted to go. I jumped at the chance and we headed out to the stadium to watch the Kansas City Chiefs take on our hometown San Diego Chargers. The seats were right on the top row in the nosebleeds, and it was difficult to follow the action as twenty-two ant-sized bruisers bashed into each other for the best part of 3 hours. What a spectacle though. The Americans do sport in a big way and the colours, the fans, and the whole atmosphere was amazing.

Better still, I was able to buy a mini-season ticket for six basketball games at the Clippers in LA. LA's famous team, the Lakers, played across town from the Clippers who were relatively shit. No wonder I could get tickets. However, the opponents list for the six games read like a roll call for the biggest names in the NBA. The Houston Rockets had Hakeem Olajuwon, Clyde Drexler and Charles Barkley. The Lakers had Shaquille O'Neal and Kobe Bryant. The Spurs from San Antonio had the twin towers of Tim Duncan and David Robinson, but best of all, the Bulls were coming to town. For that Bulls game, I asked Harry O, who was fresh out of TOPGUN, to come along as a bit of a thank you for the amazing weekend he had given me in Chicago and Indianapolis. We cheered ourselves hoarse as Jordan dropped 49 points on the Clippers. I swear to God that even the Clippers fans were shouting '50! 50!' such was his popularity.

With Harry O back from TOPGUN, I was 'demoted' back to gash shag ops scheduler guy, which suited me just fine. My moment in the spotlight was over and I was looking to wind down and start preparations for returning home to the UK. My Hornet wasn't done with me yet though. It was like she wanted to throw as many dance moves my way that she could, to show me what I would be missing. Believe me, I didn't need reminding. Flying was never going to be as good as this again. The F-18 coupled with VMFA-134 was going to be the pinnacle of my career and it was going to kill me to leave it behind. However, as Tennyson once said, 'Tis better to have loved and lost, than never to have loved at all.' Pretty sure Tennyson didn't fly the Hornet, but he knew what he was talking about there. It seemed like word had got around that Mr Tug was leaving the States, as every fighter under the sun pitched up and wanted to fight us. There was always a 4-ship of some exotic jet to go up against, and I filled my boots with G, pirouettes, and totally mad moves that were detached from reality. I was at one with my aeroplane, and loving every second of it. Yet, lurking there in the background was the inevitable march of time towards my end date, when the Hornet would just shrug me off and move onto its next beau.

I would miss the Marines as well, especially the reservists. 134 had been a ragtag of characters who did things a little off the wall, but with an underlying pride that transcended their part-time status. It was the perfect fit for me and took my joy of flying and fighting to a new level. I loved the fact that we were flying the oldest Hornets out there, but we could still give anyone a bloody nose. And that whole attitude of 'Come on have a go if you think you're hard enough!' bolstered the pure (unpromotable) fighter pilot inside of me. Yes, I had turned a bit feral and played things a bit fast and loose. I wasn't getting picked up for squadron leader rank, so didn't have to grow up. That was, by far and away, the time of my life from an aviation point of view.

MAG-46 decided to hold an all-ranks dining-in night at the Miramar O-Club, and there was going to be in the region of 120 attendees, so pretty big for a dinner night. I had not been to a stag night before with the Marines, and was warned to bring lots of $1 bills as the tradition was to fine members for the slightest indiscretions of behaviour or dress code. I made up a red and yellow bow tie and sewed the squadron badge onto my cummerbund to show the colours. I also put on my 'seely shirt' under my mess jacket. We had 'seely shirts' made in Cyprus and they consisted of a standard white dress shirt front with wing collar and cuffs. However, the back and sides were made from any old crap patterned material the tailor had left over. Mine was a gruesome mix of floral and paisley patterns that looked like it had been given to Holly in the crayon factory. I took a room in the O-Club as I thought it would be a boozy night. As soon as I arrived in the bar for pre-drinks, Gunny Tinker collared me.

'Looking forward to hearing you sing tonight, Sir,' he said.

'Not planning on singing tonight, Gunny. It's way too formal for that,' I replied.

'We'll see, Sir,' and off he walked.

I've had trouble passing water

The dining room was huge, with a long top table and seven or so long tables coming down off it in rows. It was all laid out in rank order, so I was on a table with a few captains and the most senior of NCOs and warrant officers. I didn't know any of them as MAG-46 was so big, but they all wanted to check out the odd guy and my bow tie was a big talking point. Hammer was the president and banged the gavel for silence. He then called out a few names and charged them with dress code violations and fined them. They had to get up and put a dollar in the pot which was at the end of one of the tables. They then started dobbing each other in for being late, or having the wrong dress buttons on their uniforms, or for wearing pre-folded bow ties. There was a constant stream of people getting up and putting their dollar bills in the box. I loved military traditions and was enthralled by this.

The food came and went and then it was time for more tradition. A bell was rung and one of the Marines stood up and called out the name of a battle to honour the dead Marines. We stood and toasted. Then the bell rang again and a different Marine called out another battle etc. etc. They included the Battle of Britain, as they had a Brit among them, and then we toasted those who had fought in Vietnam. As we stood to toast, I saw that two of the NCOs sitting opposite me stayed seated and silent. After that formality was over, I leaned across the table and said, 'I hope you don't mind me asking S'arnt-Major, but why didn't you toast the memory of Vietnam?'

'Sir,' he replied, 'you don't toast if you were there.'
'You were in Vietnam?'
'Yes, Sir,' he replied with a proud look in his eye.
'Holy cow!' I then spoke to him and his buddies for the next 20 minutes or so about Vietnam before Hammer banged the gavel again and the room went silent.

'My fellow Marines! It appears that we have someone among us who has not contributed to the pot. Flight Lieutenant Wilson—would you care to add your dollars to the drinking fund?' I stood up as everyone cheered and then waited for them to quiet down.

'What's the charge, Sir?' I asked.

'You are British. That's crime enough,' he bantered. More cheers. I put on a fake outraged face and walked to the pot making a great show of putting my cash in. When I got back to my seat, there was silence. I sat down and then almost immediately stood up again.

'Mr President!' I shouted, 'I wish to level a charge.'

'On who, Flight Lieutenant Wilson?' he asked.

'Well, Sir. On everyone here, but mostly on you.' There were howls and cheers at this. Someone had the balls to threaten the president?

'OK. Take your shot,' said Hammer with a glint in his eye. I picked up the orders which were on each table and read out the bit that said Marines would be fined for abusing the Queen's English.

'Sir, I put it to you that everyone here has abused the Queen's English with their accents and American words. I am the only one here who truly speaks the Queen's English, yet you have not fined anyone tonight for that crime. Therefore, I find you are ultimately responsible, Sir.' Lots of cheers and shouts of support. Hammer broke into a big grin.

'Nice try, Flight Lieutenant Wilson, but as President, I can do pretty much what I want, so how about you just put $5 in the box and we'll say no more about it.'

'It was worth a try, Sir,' I said and went to get my money out. Gunny Tinker then leapt to his feet.

'Mr President!' he shouted, 'I have a better idea for fining Flight Lieutenant Wilson!'

'And what would that be, Gunny?'

'Get him to sing us a song.' The bastard was grinning from ear to ear.

'SONG! SONG! SONG!' chanted the crowd.

'Very well. Flight Lieutenant Wilson? Sing us a song.'

Most of the songs I knew were fairly rude so I quickly wracked my brains and came up with a risqué one I thought I could get away with. Before singing, I removed my jacket and another cheer went up as my 'seely shirt' was revealed.

'OK, Sir. There is a song called "The question and the reply." I will sing the question, and maybe Gunny Tinker can sing the reply back to me?' I then sang:

Was it you who did the pushin'?
Left the stains upon the cushion?
Footprints on the dashboard upside down (oh upside down)
Was it you, you sly Woodpecker?
Got inside my girl Rebecca?
If it was you better leave this town.

It got everyone laughing and then I said, 'And the reply, Gunny?' They went wild ribbing him. 'How about I sing it for you, and you pay my fine for me?' he was beaming, so I sang for him …

Oh, it was I who did the pushin'
Left the stains upon the cushion
Footprints on the dashboard upside down (oh upside down)
Ever since I had your daughter
I've had trouble passing water
Guess that makes us even all around

Gunny got out of his seat, came over and shook my hand and paid my fine while the applause rang out. It was a brilliant night. The Vietnam vets wanted to buy my drinks for me and just before the formal part of the dinner was over, Hammer banged his gavel and announced that he fancied hearing another song so I had to stand up and belt out another. This time I chanced something a bit ruder and just got away with it, but thankfully that was the end of the singing and we all repaired to the bar. I wasn't allowed to pay for another drink that night and eventually retired hurt to bed. Another fantastic experience with my brothers and sisters in arms. Semper Fi.

Back at work, I was revelling in a load of air combat trips and then we had to go and spoil it all by finding some more bombs to drop. Chilli and I headed out to R-2507 with four live 500-pounders each and orbited around the dummy airfield trying a mix of different delivery methods with each bomb. I knew this would be my last proper bombing trip so I made the most of it, dropping only one bomb each time and then watching the kerfuffle erupt as they hit the ground. OK, I'll say it … I was going to miss the bombing. Not the practice bombs, mind you. You could shove them, but these flashy-bang things were amazing and a lot of fun to drop. At the end of the debrief, I jokingly said to Chilli that one good thing about going home was that I would never have to see another bloody bomb. That would come back to haunt me.

Don't fuck with me, son

My final adventure with my favourite jet was going to be at Nellis in Vegas again. The weapons school had asked us to fly in and support the Op week of their latest course. They had some German F-4Fs, which had just been equipped with AMRAAM, opposing them, and along with the resident F-16 aggressors, we would help to provide some extra firepower, along with a few jets from the Dallas Cowboys. I had just passed 500 hours in the F-18 having flown my arse off in the year I had been on 134. I felt that wasn't a bad total to go home with, especially considering that I had been on the ground for about six months of my tour for one reason or another. We flew into Nellis on 1 December into crystal clear air. It was chilly, but the sun beat down on the Las Vegas strip illuminating it like some ancient temple to the God of Decadence. We got settled into our spaces at the weapons school, and I went to see their scheduler so I could write our programme for the next day. We needed to run an early shift as they were maximising the daylight hours to cram as much in as they could. Things were changing at Nellis. 'The Box' or Area 51, was no longer sacrosanct so long as you flew an F-15. The resident F-15s had been given permission to overfly it without penalty. The rest of us plebs still had to avoid it like the plague which made it a bit false, but there we are. It wasn't like the Eagles to give themselves an advantage now, was it? The other major change was that Tonopah was now open and available.

Tonopah was a semi-secret airfield to the north-west of Area 51, and housed the F-117 Nighthawk Stealth Fighter, way before anyone even knew it existed. Therefore, it was a big avoid for any other aeroplane, just like Area 51. For this exercise, the weapons school wanted us and the Cowboys to deploy two Hornets each to do QRA out of there for the big exercise. It was supposed to be a big surprise for the candidates on the weapons course as they would not expect a couple of fighters to suddenly pitch up out of nowhere. This was too good an opportunity to miss, but I figured that a Brit going to Tonopah might be verboten, so I checked with the USAF major running the exercise. He assured me that Tonopah was open to all (it wasn't), and that I would be OK to go there (I wasn't). So, I scheduled myself for the oh-dark hundred push with Salsa leading our pair. I thought it would be a step too far for me to lead, and for Tonopah Tower to hear a British voice calling for recovery on the radio. Salsa was as pumped as I was to go there so all good. Chilli and Fox would be on the other early push about 45 minutes after us. I was very excited about it all as we jumped into the vehicles to head to the hotel.

The USAF had put us up in a Super 8 motel, which was not the nicest of places they could have chosen. However, it was only a week so no drama. Actually, there was lots of drama as we arrived. The motel was situated in an underpass of the I-15 motorway, opposite a strip club. As we pitched up, there were tons of police vehicles with flashing lights, surrounding the club. It turned out that there had just been a drive-by shooting about an hour before. As much as I loved adventure, this was probably a step too far for me. I checked into my room and wedged the chair under the door handle, as that was bound to stop a bunch of gangsters armed with automatic weapons. Where the hell was Gunny Peterson when I needed him? The next morning, it was still dark (or as dark as Vegas can get with all the flashing neon) as we got to Nellis, and all hell broke loose when I turned up for the brief. Once the directing staff heard that a foreigner was going into Tonopah, there was much mumbling and they Joe'd the major who I had spoken to the previous day to tell me I couldn't go. I was OK with it—it was a long shot anyway. However, when I told him we would only have one jet on alert for the first push, he insisted we supply two or the whole exercise would be a bust. Not sure that was strictly true as the Cowboys were putting two jets in there, but when I told him we couldn't get anyone else in time he got a bit chippy.

'Well, Sir. If you remember, you assured me last night it would all be OK. I would have scheduled somebody else if I had known otherwise.' He had nowhere to go with that so scooted off and Salsa prepped to go off on his own. The next thing I knew, Chilli and I were summonsed to an office where the general in charge of everything had us stand to attention while he briefed us on what was going to happen.

'When you arrive at Tonopah, every door will be closed to you. You will be met at your aeroplane by an armed guard who will escort you everywhere. You are not to leave the ops building at all during your stay. At the appropriate time, you will be escorted back to your aeroplane. You will start up and take-off and nothing else. Do you understand?'

Chilli was smiling so much I thought I would lighten the mood (bad move).

'So, no cameras, General?' I quipped.

'Don't fuck with me, son,' he deadpanned back.

'Yes, Sir.' So, Salsa and I walked together out onto the vast Nellis pan which was covered in fast jets.

'Can you believe it, Tug? Tonopah!' he said, like an excited schoolboy. Even with all of his experience (Phantom, Hornet, Gulf War), he could still find something to get giddy over. The sun was coming up as we climbed into our F-18s—the most exotic machine on the pan—and we blasted off in a pairs take-off into the icy cold blue of the Nevada desert. I eased out into fighting wing and got my head out of the window. I had flown in and out of Nellis a lot in the last three years, but it was still breathtaking to see the casinos and resorts jutting out of the nothingness, and then stopping abruptly at the edge of town, to give way to long straight empty roads poking out into the desert.

'Man! Look at those craters, Tug!' called Salsa over the back radio. Below us were huge circles all over the desert. We were flying over the Yucca Flats where the US had conducted lots of underground nuclear bomb tests in the '50s and '60s. People used to go to Vegas on atomic bomb breaks to put on their sunglasses and watch a nuclear explosion! As stunning as it was, I knew that this area of the Nellis ranges was heavily restricted and I definitely shouldn't have been flying over it. General Angry was not going to be pleased, and I had visions of us being carted away by the CIA with a bag over my head; the waterboarding; the brutal internal examination etc. Tonopah came in sight and Salsa called us over to the Tower frequency.

'Silverbow Tower, Smoke 11 and 12 inbound. Two F-18s for the join.'

'Smoke 11, you are cleared to join, runway 32, pressure 29 decimal 62, winds light.'

I closed in on Salsa's wing and we broke beautifully into the circuit. The Hornet looked absolutely stunning, but it certainly wasn't the most exotic thing that had flown out of that base, that's for sure. I plonked it down behind Salsa and we slowed down to exit the runway up at the far end. The airfield elevation was five and a half thousand feet, so that looked a bit odd seeing that on the altimeter on landing. I had been used to landing for the whole of my RAF career with an altimeter pressure setting called QFE. This gave you an accurate height above the ground in localised spots like an airfield. The last three years, I had landed using QNH on the altimeter which gave you your altitude above sea level. Therefore, you had to add the airfield elevation above sea level to your circuit height and landing. Yeah—I know. Complicated or what? Tonopah was easily the highest airfield I had flown into.

The taxiway was lined with aircraft shelters which I knew used to house the F-117s. Every shelter was buttoned up tight so I couldn't see inside them. Someone must have told them that Mr Tug was in town and my nose was kept out of whatever was in them now. Probably ET's bicycle or something. As I arrived on the chocks in dispersal, there was a man in combat uniform with a pistol strapped to his thigh, waiting by the side of my jet. I shut down and when I got to the bottom of the steps and took my helmet off, he said, 'Sir. I am to escort you during your stay here. I will not leave your side. You are only permitted to go into the operations building and back to your aircraft. If you do not comply, I am authorised to use deadly force.'

'Er ... OK.' Welcome to Tonopah. My shadow then escorted me inside, where the Cowboys were already waiting and chuckling about the absurdity of the situation. I have to say that he was true to his word. He didn't leave my side for the whole hour I was on the ground, even when I went to the toilet. Now, I can't do a wee when somebody is watching me, but there was no way he was going to leave me alone, even at the urinal. I flexed every possible internal muscle that I had to try and squeeze the piss out of my reluctant bladder, and finally relaxed as it flowed out.

On the way back to the little crew room, I passed a small control room which had a kindly looking old guy in civilian clothes in it. I checked with Sergeant Velcro that I was allowed in there and he nodded, so I went in for a chat. The room was bit like a small air traffic control room and was obviously the hub of ops. I noticed most of the stuff on the walls was covered over with temporary blankets.

'Hi there,' I said.

'Hey! You must be the Brit?' he said all nice and friendly. 'You've caused quite a stir this morning.'

'Yeah, sorry about that. I will be out of your hair soon.'

'Yes. We know you will.' Ah—not so friendly then.

'I guess you've seen some pretty amazing stuff fly out of here over the years?'

'Nope. I've seen nothing of the sort,' he said, followed by a long pause of silence while he looked me directly in the eye.

'Ah, OK. Well, nice chatting to you,' I said awkwardly and wandered out. The Cowboys were just walking for the first QRA launch, so Salsa and I would be going about 20 minutes after that. I got him to one side and whispered about the Yucca Flats being out of bounds for me. He just shrugged that Marine shrug and smiled. He was such a cool guy; he didn't give a damn.

Woah!

Two more Hornets broke into the circuit as we taxied out. It was Chilli and Fox pre-positioning for the next launch. We got airborne and checked in to hear the German Phantoms swapping AMRAAM shots with the F-15s. We raged across the desert at low-level underneath it all and pitched up vertically into a pair of Eagles, shooting them down with Sidewinders, before we got absolutely monstered by another pair about ten miles behind them. I must have looked like a pin cushion with all the bloody missiles sticking out of me. I was proper dead. We exited the fight and returned to Nellis via the complicated recovery procedure which saw us having to pass through various "gates" at set altitudes, until we could see the airfield and continue visually. McCarran airport, Las Vegas, was close by, so everything was done procedurally. To be honest, this was a good thing, as if you left it up to 100 fast jet pilots who were airborne, to sort it out for themselves, it would have been nothing short of bloody carnage.

The mass debrief was interesting. Firstly, because the F-15s had been caught out by the fact that there were QRA jets launching out of Tonopah. They hadn't been briefed beforehand about it, so the surprise factor had worked and provided a valuable learning point about expectation and dealing with the unknown. The most interesting bit though was the interaction with the German Phantoms who were on the Red Air side. A big part of the debrief was validating any shot taken. It seemed that every long-range AMRAAM shot the Germans took was discounted by the F-15s who were leading Blue Air as being woefully out of range. The Luftwaffe boss asked why their shots were being rubbished, and a colonel from the Eagles told him condescendingly that the ranges they were using were just ridiculous. There was a bit of high-brow superior sniggering coming from the Eagles.

'But these are the ranges the US military gave us in our manuals when we bought the AMRAAM from you,' said the Phantom boss. 'Are you saying that the manuals are wrong and the weapon is not as capable as you said?' Ouch! The whole place went quiet and the F-15 colonel blushed and blustered, until the general in charge of the exercise stood up and tried to smooth it all over. The sniggering was all on the German side then and, miraculously, their shots began to count.

That afternoon, I was on a trip that is described in my logbook as 'many vs many'. There must have been over a hundred fast jets up in the Nellis ranges, so how the hell we coped with it all I will never know. I didn't care. I had been to a secret base and taken a piss with an armed man standing right behind me. Man, there was nothing I couldn't do. Good job we were carrying pods because it was an absolute shit show. The F-15s shot down a couple of their own folks and we ended up raging in on the deck and just pitching up into a sea of military hardware. It was a case of clear your nose, bite your lip, and just get in there. I was barely hanging on as I pressed into guns range on an Eagle which promptly buggered off into the box. I just couldn't get close enough soon enough, and had to break off the attack before I violated that hallowed airspace. They sucked up me going into Tonopah, but there was no way I would get away with blasting over the airfield at Groom Lake.

When the exercise was played back on the big screen afterwards, everyone booed the Eagle driver as he entered the box and then everyone shouted 'Whoa!' as I just skirted the border and got away with it. What a hoot! The next event wasn't such a hoot. Chilli and I were conducting a low-level patrol along the northern edge of the box when we got monstered by a package of F-15s. After a few defensive manoeuvres, we got split and then the flashing attention getters came on with an associated OIL caption on the warning panel. I pulled the throttle back to idle and cleared out of the fight, rocking my wings to show that I was not a live player. I went through the drills and it necessitated me shutting the engine down. That wasn't the first time my Hornet had done that to me, but it was a very rare occurrence. Maybe she knew I was about to end our affair and slink off into the night back to the UK, so this was her final slap in my face? My route back to Nellis was going to be longer than usual as I couldn't go straight line as that would have taken me through the box. I could see that Groom Lake was the nearest strip of concrete, and there it was, right outside the window. Cue Mr Tug's clever plan. Declare an in-flight emergency; they will vector me to Groom Lake; I will then have been into two secret bases in as many days. Tonopah was cool, but this was the big one!

I declared my in-flight emergency and was immediately vectored due east to avoid the box.

'I need the nearest airfield,' I said.

'Copied. Nellis is your nearest.' So much for that plan. The US was willing to bury an F-18 in the Nevada desert rather than let a Brit see the spaceships in Area 51. I landed safely into the cable on runway 03 at Nellis, and all of Area 51's secrets remained safely out of my grasp. Safe all round then. I had one more 'many vs many' hops and that was the end of my final det with Ms Hornet. We flew back into Miramar later that day and put the jets to bed. I only had two more weeks of flying left and that would take us to Christmas. I had planned for us to fly back to the UK at the end of January '98 so we would have a whole month to sort ourselves out. And boy, would we need it.

Next is never going to be any good

We had registered Laura's birth in San Diego, and also with the British embassy. She would need an American passport of her own in order to leave the country. That meant she needed an official photo for the passport. What a waste of money! We had to take her to an official government office to have it taken, but she still looked like a blurred blob on her passport (sorry Lu—but it's true!). We also had to arrange two car sales, and a clean of the house, as we had negotiated with the agent that we would just pass it on to Blower when we left. In essence, we were just reversing what we had done three years earlier on our way out to California. I was extra lucky in that Alf was at Leeming on XI Squadron and arranged to do a march-in and accept our married quarter for us. Three years on and he was still sorting me out and getting me squared away. Great guy.

The next muster weekend, I took Blower along to meet the guys on the squadron. There was a bit of a ceremony where I presented a framed RAF badge to Chilli and the squadron with my details and dates on it. I gave a little speech and have to be honest and say I was somewhat emotional as I told them that the time I had spent on 134 had been the best flying of my life. Chilli then said a few words and I was presented with two things that I have treasured ever since. Firstly, Harry O gave me a framed photo of us standing on the Bull's head in Chicago. What an amazing memory. Then Chilli stepped up with a big smile on his chops.

'You know, Tug told me recently that he was happy he would never have to see another bomb again. Just so you don't forget about us Tug, we got you this.' He brought out a blue 26-pound practice bomb that had engraved plates on the fins with my name on one and the American flag on another. On the side of the bomb, in big sparkly letters was the word 'BOOM!' I was utterly speechless and even had a tear or two in my eyes. I also got presented with a huge framed print of a brown Hornet and all the guys had signed their names on it and left a bit of banter in their messages.

That night, there was a farewell at a local restaurant with wives, where again Chilli said some nice words about me, and I responded by telling them he was the coolest mellowest boss I had ever served, and how much I would miss the squadron, the Hornet, and most of all, the Marine Corps. Afterwards, I had to submit a written report to the embassy about my time on exchange, and filed an honest account of what had happened to me. Apparently, this was absolutely the wrong thing to do. I was supposed to write that everything was great etc. etc, but I didn't get the brief. I wrote that my time under Killer on 121 and the whole of my time on 134 was awesome. I also wrote that the RAG was painfully slow and that the six months under Nutmeg were little short of disastrous, and detailed the ridiculous nature of the security clearance. The brief I didn't get would also have told me to send my report to the embassy only, but I copied in Chilli and Hammer as I wanted to show them how good VMFA-134 was. Apparently, my report winged its way around Miramar, gathering a bit of pace and notoriety. What were they going to do? Not promote me to squadron leader? They already had that covered. It sounds like I was trying to get back at Nutmeg, but the truth was that I was just a bit stupid and didn't think about what the repercussions would be. 'Don't ask for a report if you don't want to know what really happened' is what I thought. Ah—I see now why I wasn't promoted!

The week before Christmas was my last week on the F-18. I flew five times and tried to pack in as much as I could. Intercepts, air combat, hot pits, leading, flying in close formation, supersonic, painting Miramar with the air-to-ground radar, circuits ... scratch that—one landing only per trip. The weather in Southern California was beautiful and clear that week and it was killing me that it was my last look at it. Every landing brought me one step closer to the end. And then, on 23 December 1997, it finally arrived. My last trip in the rocket ship. A 2 vs 2 air combat hooley that I led, ripping the wings off and dancing around the sky, pulling impossible moves and losing myself in the sheer joy of it all.

One hour and ten minutes of my life to take my total to just over 521 hours. One hour and ten minutes to say goodbye to the sexiest contortionist of an aeroplane you could ever meet. One hour and ten minutes that I would give my eye teeth to do over and over and over again in a never-ending loop of aviation ecstasy. But there it is. The final line in my logbook that says F/A 18 Hornet 162442. Chilli's signature under that line—a final full stop on my F-18 Marine Corps Hornet fantasy. A moment of sorrow and then—what's next? Who cares! Next was never going to be any good after that. Next was the grind. Next was a jet I had little or no love for. Next was vastly over-rated.

The luckiest man in the world

A month to get sorted meant a lot more time at home, and getting more acquainted with Laura. I had got into a routine of doing her evening feeds while sitting on a rocking chair, watching the NBA on TV, and then turning the volume off so I could sing and rock her to sleep. I sang lullabies—just in case some of you were thinking I pulled out the rude bar songs. Chilli's Christmas card arrived in the post. It had a picture of a Hornet on the front and said 'Peace on Earth ... through Close Air Support!' which made me chuckle. In order to cling to the California lifestyle as long as possible, we spent Christmas Eve through to the 27th in the Disneyland Hotel up in Anaheim, and gorged ourselves on an American Christmas Disney overload. It was magical—of course it was. A month later, after almost crying while selling my Mustang, we were packed up and on a flight to DC for a couple of nights before flying out of Dulles on the RAF VC-10 that had deposited us there a lifetime of experiences ago. Laura was four months old and decided to cry all the way over on the flight. Yes, we were that annoying family with the bleating baby. She would only quiet down if I held her and walked up and down the aeroplane. So, that's what I did for hours on end. I practically walked across the country to DC.

I had a couple of interviews at the embassy where my end of tour report came up. I got a semi-bollocking, but apparently got away with it as everything I had said was true—especially the bit about the security clearance faff. I went around all the admin staff to thank them for three years of brilliant support and help, and then headed back to the Embassy Suites Hotel for a couple of nights to prepare for our eventual repatriation. I had booked a big limo to take us out to Dulles and charged it back to the embassy. This was going to be my last chance to live the high life, and seeing as I was going to be remaining on flight lieutenant wages, I figured the RAF could afford it. We had a massive amount of baggage and baby stuff so a normal cab wouldn't have cut it (how does that sound for an excuse? Weak?). Laura slept all the way back to Brize Norton, thank God, and we touched down on a cold blustery day where our California sun tans instantly faded back to pasty white—like we had never been there. But we had, hadn't we?

Ending the book there would be a bit abrupt, so I had better do some of that reflection stuff, I guess? Where the hell had three years of our lives gone? Life passes quickly when you are having the time of it. We had packed so much into that small fraction of time that I can barely believe what we did. As a family, we had been to San Francisco, Yosemite, the Grand Canyon, Vegas, Hawaii (twice!), not to mention actually living in San Diego. San Diego! On the government's dollar, I had been all over from Alaska to Key West and many points in between. All the famous places and those great experiences crammed into such a short space of time—like the most intense holiday you could ever plan. Yet, we felt we were just living a normal life. How incredibly lucky we were.

And me, the luckiest man in the world, got to experience three life-affirming things while I was there. Firstly, the friendship I shared with Muck and Indy. Two more different people, you could not meet. Indy was the nicest aviator I have ever come across. High quality, extremely capable and professional, but compassionate and unselfish with it—an almost impossible combination in a fast-jet aviator, but he managed to pull it off with an ease that beggared belief. He was a much better man than I could ever aspire to be. And Muck. Ah, yes Muck. A force of nature, that nature didn't even know existed, and if it did, it would be ashamed of itself. Socially explosive, extremely funny, and frustratingly odd at times, he was nonetheless an absolutely gifted and hard-working fighter pilot. I loved them both.

Secondly, this tour gave me the US Marine Corps. My brothers and sisters in arms. Completely brilliant and massively frustrating in equal measure. Fiercely loyal and patriotic to their core. American patriotism can sometimes seem to be surface deep—a show for the audience. That is not the case with the Marines. To them, loyalty to their country, their flag, the Corps, and most importantly, their fellow Marines, is not everything—it is the ONLY thing. And for that, I will love them forever. Yes, I brushed up against a couple of them, but I met so many high-quality individuals as well. Killer led his squadron with a confidence and ease that I could not fathom, seeing how some of the WSOs had been treated on the RAG. Hoover showed me that there was room in the Corps for the most basic and raw of human emotions. I will never forget the tears on his cheek as he remembered his fallen comrades in that museum at Pensacola, and his altogether friendly demeanour, plastering that welcoming smile on his face everywhere else I saw him.

Semper Fi until I die? You are damn right!

Handy and Rabies trying their best to get better with each trip, and having to put up with my direct debriefs. Hopefully I helped them in some way and they went on to be much better aviators than me. And if not, at least I gave them the most fun they had ever had in an aeroplane when we fought those beautiful Phantoms in Death Valley. And not forgetting poor Bluto. The WSO I flew with the most. Despite struggling from time-to-time, he powered through with a smile on his face and a determination to be the best he could be. And then I saw him in his natural habitat as a FAC(A), controlling multiple formations as if he was sorting out his desk drawers. Mightily impressive, and way beyond my capability. Taken too soon alongside Puke, and no consolation that they died an aviator's death.

And then, holy hell! The reserves of 134. Chilli, the most mellow boss in the world. Unfazed by anything and just happy to let life ride. Harry O who was my true brother in arms for a year and who gave me the best weekend ever in a jet. Fox, the world's greatest fighter pilot (fact). He was where we were all aiming to be. Knowledgeable, dedicated, ultra-professional, and just a whole lot better in the air than anyone of us could dream of being. And finally, Hannibal and Salsa. Partners in crime, and my banter opponents. Talk about making flying and fighting a joy and a laugh. Even at the more advanced stages of their flying careers, they still had the drive to make it fun. VMFA-134 was more than a squadron to me. It was my spiritual home and I was ruined forever after it. Nothing else would compare. Final thing with the Marines. All of them signed up to the belief that nobody was more important than the Marine on the ground in contact, facing the enemy head on. Fighter pilot ego is all well and good, and is even necessary to be able to succeed, but no way does it trump that most basic of Marine Corps beliefs. Semper Fi until I die? You are damn right!

Last, but not least, this tour gave me the beautiful F-18 Hornet. Dear God, what more can I say about it that I haven't already written? The answer to that is nothing. Anything I haven't told you, then I am going to be selfish and keep it to myself. Some memories should only belong to the lovers themselves. All I can say is that my heart broke at the end of that last trip in the Hornet. I felt the same way as I did when I had my last trip on the Phantom. Pure and simple—upset and resignation that something special was over, forever. We should always look to what is next rather than dwell on what has passed. Not a hope in hell of that happening. My next jet was going to be the Tornado F3. Pretty much like flying a fridge-freezer having been in a Ferrari for the last three years. Oh well. Open mind and all that? I wonder how that will pan out?

(It was at this point that I tried to pitch book number four to the publisher!)